THE · ALL · SEEING EYE

Being a Monthly Magazine
which is published in Los
Angeles on the Fifteen-
th day of every month
edited by
Manly P. Hall
and
devoted to the Search for the
Fundamental Verities Existing in the Educational
Systems · Religions
and Philosophies
of All Ages

M · A · Y
MCMXXVII

The ALL-SEEING EYE

DEVOTED TO THE SEARCH FOR THE
FUNDAMENTAL VERITIES EXIST-
ING IN THE EDUCATIONAL
SYSTEMS, RELIGIONS,
AND PHILOSOPHIES
OF ALL AGES

Vol. IV   MAY, 1927   No. 1

PUBLISHED EVERY MONTH BY
THE HALL PUBLISHING COMPANY
301 TRINITY AUDITORIUM BUILDING,
NINTH AT GRAND AVENUE, LOS ANGELES, CALIFORNIA

MANLY P. HALL . . . . *Editor*
HARRY S. GERHART . . . . *Managing Editor*
MAUD F. GALIGHER . . . . *Associate Editor*
HOWARD W. WOOKEY . . . . *Art Director*

CONTENTS

PER COPY, 25c—SIX MONTHS $1.00—ONE YEAR $2.00
FOREIGN, SIX MONTHS $1.15—ONE YEAR $2.25

Application has been made for Entry as Second-Class Matter.

Do You Know?

That Franz Schubert, the great composer, received less than two dollars apiece for some of his greatest compositions?

That Tibetan antiquities have been discovered about one hundred feet under the ground during recent excavations near Mexico City?

That Plato, whose real name was Aristocles and one of the three greatest minds of the ancient world, was sold as a slave by the King of Sicily?

That according to recent discoveries made by Sunkar Bisey, Hindu scientist, the East Indians constructed wet and dry cell electric batteries over 5000 years ago?

That there is a gentlemen's agreement among the religious powers that be, to the effect that no effort shall be made to assign dates to incidents of Biblical history?

That Mt. Hercules on the Island of New Guinea, and not Mt. Everest, is the tallest mountain in the world? Mt. Hercules is 32,768 feet high, Mt. Everest is a little over 29,000 feet in height.

That Shakespeare, the man who is supposed to have penned those immortal lines, "The quality of mercy is not strained" while himself well-to-do, and therefore not in need, sued a fellow townsman who was in financial straits for two shillings (48c) and made the town pay for the wine with which he treated his friends?

That any fifty objects are capable of being arranged in 1,273,726,838,815,-420,339,851,343,083,767,005,515,293,749,454,795,473,408,000,000,000,000 combinations? Using this as a base, work out the number of combinations that the billion and a half or more inhabitants of the earth can assume. Then say that there is no variety and that life is monotonous.

The EDITOR'S BRIEFS

On Education

"Education is emancipation from herd opinion," writes Everett Dean Martin, who then adds that it is "self-mastery, capacity for self-criticism, suspended judgment, and urbanity."

We are profoundly impressed with the importance of the first six words: "Education is emancipation from herd opinion." Can there be a more dangerous form of "herd opinion" than that which results from the gathering together of hundreds of young minds from every walk of life into one room and there teaching them all the same thing in the same way?

Does the cramming of a mind with a heterogeneous congeries of unassimilated facts produce a thinker or a mental dyspeptic? It is not what a man *knows* that makes him wise; it is what he knows *about what he knows* that makes him wise!

The mere dissemination of facts unaccompanied by their application to the problem of daily existence is comparatively useless to the average individual. Therefore education should properly include the study of applications.

The student should incessantly ask himself: "What does this thing I am learning mean to me now? How may I use this knowledge to attain the greatest good to the greatest number? How will it assist me to more successfully solve the problems of my own life and those lives which will in the future be influenced by my attitudes and my knowledge?"

The word "education" is derived from the Latin *educo,* which literally means "to draw forth" or "to bring out." Thus, the primary purpose of education is to draw forth from the student that knowledge and understanding which is latent within the subjective nature of every human being. He is best educated who can most fully express his own innermost urges and convictions.

It is curious that modern educational institutions are too prone to interpret *educo* to mean "cram in"—fill the young mind with the thoughts of others, and declare him an abnormality and a menace if he dares to interpret any subject at variance with the rules laid down on page 152 of the little green book by an eminent authority!

Instead of using academic education as a means to the attainment of self-expression, we accept the means as the end by permitting the thoughts of others to fill our minds and crowd out our own individuality.

We may diagrammatically divide the individual into an "outside" man and an "inside" man, and we best accomplish the real purpose of education when we succeed in bringing the "inside" "outside."

A critical examination of educational methods discloses that the only mental faculty really developed to a superlative degree is memory. Too often it is memory—and not thought—that insures graduation from our modern schools. Sometimes when even memory fails, legerdemain may be resorted to!

[3]

Any well-trained parrot (often to the mortification of its owner) can recite mere words that have been continuously repeated in its presence, and as a reward for this accomplishment we change the water in its cage occasionally. When a human being has successfully mimicked his instructors for twelve or fourteen years, we reward his cleverness with a sheepskin bearing the signature of the individuals who have done his heavy thinking for him.

We do not speak disparagingly of education because we fail to realize its invaluable contribution to society and the well-being of humanity; but rather because we believe that it can accomplish even greater good if it will devote more time to the building of individuals and less to the production of stereotyped men and women.

The major part of the time spent by the child in school is devoted to a study of the accomplishments of others. But the awe and respect generated by such study is far more likely to produce followers than leaders.

The youthful mind discovers somewhere among the hosts of the famous or infamous in history some favorite hero or heroine. He then erects an altar to his newly-found god and hero-worship ensues.

Apropos of this is the story of the man who was told that he looked like Theodore Roosevelt. Obsessed by the idea, he thereupon studied the life and characteristics of this great American. He gradually came to idolize all the accomplishments and attributes of the immortal Teddy; he began to wear Rooseveltian clothes, to smoke Rooseveltian cigars, and even to smile the unforgettable Rooseveltian smile; in fact he did everything that Roosevelt did except to amount to something!

The moral is simply this: When we follow in the footsteps of others, we do ourselves a terrible injustice. There is an individuality within each of us—capable of infinite achievement—that must express itself in its own peculiar way. So long as we copy others, so long as we are servants to the discoveries, the theories, and the reflections of others, the individual greatness within each one of us is denied suitable expression.

The lives of the great and the true who have gone before are noble examples from which we may gain much of inspiration and knowledge. In its final analysis, however, each must live his own life, and when we permit ourselves to substitute the achievements of others for individual achievement, we lose the greatest opportunity in life—the opportunity to be ourselves.

Those whose names are preserved on the pages of history, who have accomplished the most for the good of the world, in nearly every case have broken away from precedent and blazed new trails of their own. Today we are sadly in need of pioneers who are not afraid to sail their ships into uncharted seas—explorers who dare to contradict with views of their own the pedagogues of art and science.

Is it possible to imagine a more pathetic miscarriage of education than that evidenced by the youthful scholar who, when asked why he knew a certain thing, glibly replied: "It must be true; Dr. Jones just told me so"? That mind is absolutely inactive that knows things to be true because another has affirmed it! That which the mind has not demonstrated for itself by logic and reason is valueless as an element in higher education.

We may believe we have acquired a smattering of history, geography or arithmetic with a minimum of cerebral activity. But this is only because we do not possess the faintest conception of the actual meaning of these subjects. History is the key to the unfoldment of the human mind; geography is the key to the unfoldment of nations, languages, religions, and philosophies; and mathematics is the key to the unfoldment of the universe and the human soul. But the analogies upon which an understanding of these subjects depends can only be worked out by a highly evolved mind. These analogies constitute the point where the thinking power enters the picture; they are also the point where the average man and woman—educated according to modern standards—fade out of the picture.

Special emphasis should be laid by educational institutions upon the innate superiority of those types of mind which dare to differ. If education will devote itself to equipping the individual to think for himself, we will have a far more impressive number of creative thinkers to solve the ever-complicating problems of modern civilization.

Do those people who are seeking to prevent the teaching of evolution in the public schools realize that dogmatic methods of education will accomplish for education what the Inquisition accomplished for theology?

Modern education is too often a case of the blind leading the blind. The teacher, trained according to a certain textbook, is mentally unfit to instruct beyond the narrow limitations of a few printed pages.

In Greece a different practice prevailed. There the teacher must prove his point and the student could question the accuracy of any statement at any time. We ask you what would happen were every modern teacher forced to prove the things he teaches? And yet can any person conscientiously ask another to understand or to admit as true a statement which he cannot prove himself?

Democracy is the most difficult form of government of which we have any record, for its successful operation implies that the people of a country shall be *educated*. It implies that their wisdom shall be sufficient not only to make laws for themselves but laws for each other. A democracy whose individual units are not equipped to delegate their own destiny is bound to fail in its purpose.

Diogenes said: "The foundation of every state is in the education of its youth." True education implies, first and foremost, self-knowledge. It means that when the youth has laid aside his books and, taking up the tools of labor, becomes a part of the vast organism of human society, he shall become not only a center of intelligence capable of protecting himself from the pitfalls of indecision but also qualified to establish—or participate in the establishment—of that most fundamental structure of society, the home.

True education therefore has a threefold mission: (1) It must equip the youth to maintain himself in the commercial plan so that he may always be an independent and self-supporting unit. (2) It must prepare him for the gigantic cosmic responsibility of establishing the next generation by a thorough understanding of those relationships, ignorance concerning which is the fundamental cause of the world's social evil. (3) It must equip him to make a mental, ethical or physical contribution to the world which has borne him and given him the opportunity to express himself, for no life is complete unless it accomplishes at least one thing that has not been accomplished before.

What we need today is not an education which enables the individual to become a mere cog in the pounding commercial machine grinding out the lives and souls of men. What we need today is that form of education which will enable the individual to smash the machine that is smashing him. The machine is not intelligent and controls non-intelligent creatures. There is but one power capable of destroying the false structure of modern ethics, and that power is the human mind.

The salvation of the world therefore depends upon thought, and education is the medium by which the potentialities of mind may be developed. Great is the responsibility upon the shoulders of educators, but their opportunity is as great as their responsibility!! Lord Brougham once said: "Education makes people easy to lead but difficult to drive; easy to govern but impossible to enslave."

Opinions

"I do not believe what has been served me to believe. I am a doubter, a questioner, a skeptic. When it can be proved to me that there is immortality, that there is resurrection beyond the gates of death, then will I believe. Until then, no."—*Luther Burbank.*

* * *

"Each life we live simply adds to our total experience. Everything put on earth is put here for some good—to get experience which will be stored up for future use. There is not one bit of man—one thought, one experience, one drop—that does not go on. Life is eternal—so there can't be any death."
—*Henry Ford.*

* * *

"To me the universe is simply a marvelous mechanism and the most complex forms of human life, as human beings, are nothing else but automatic engines, controlled by external influence. * * * Indeed, we are nothing but waves in space and time which when dissolved exist no more."—*Nikola Telsa.* (*From an Eastern newspaper.*)

Alexander The Great's Letter to Aristotle

Alexander to Aristotle, health.

You were wrong in publishing those branches of science hitherto not to be acquired except from oral instruction. In what shall I excel others, if the more profound knowledge I gained from you be communicated to all? For my part I had rather surpass the majority of mankind in the sublimer branches of learning than in extent of power and dominion. Farewell.

The letter was preserved by Plutarch. (See *The Life and Actions of Alexander the Great* by Rev. Williams, London, 1829.)

HILOSOPHY
SCIENCE & RELIGION

The Great Pyramid

By MANLY P. HALL

Supreme among the wonders of antiquity and unequalled by the achievements of subsequent architects and builders, the Great Pyramid of Gizeh bears mute witness to an unknown civilization that, having endured its predestined span, passed into the dim oblivion of prehistoric times.

Who were the illumined mathematicians who planned its parts and dimensions; the master craftsmen who supervised its construction; the cunning workmen who trued its stones?

Eloquent in its silence, inspirational in its majesty, divine in its simplicity, the Great Pyramid is indeed "a sermon in stone!" Its awesomeness beggars description, its magnitude overwhelms the puny sensibilities of man, and among the shifting sands of time it stands as a fitting emblem of eternity itself!

The Great Pyramid is the unsolved riddle of the ages. Years have been devoted by eminent scholars to the study of its many marvels. But no matter how profound these intellects have been, the Pyramid has proved itself to be still more profound. One learned Egyptologist, after devoting the best years of his life to its study, declared that a complete understanding of the Pyramid's true purpose would require a perfect knowledge of not only every art and science now known to mankind but also many others of which present humanity is unaware.

Ou race has turned to the goal of objective attainment. It is conquering the visible, tangible universe which surrounds it and of which it is a part. It is flying through the air and sailing under the sea. It is exploding electrons and projecting magnificent units of electrical energy through the invisible vistas of space. It is manufacturing guns that will hurl tons of metal seventy to eighty miles. It is reaching out into the unknown elements of Nature in search of destructive forces which, if discovered, will jeopardize the destiny of the planet itself. Yet with all this knowledge man is hopelessly ignorant of himself. He is ignorant of the cause which brought him into being, the reason why he is a manifesting creature, and the ultimate towards which he is being swept with irresistible force.

Whereas we explore the visible, antiquity explored the invisible. Whereas we construct machines to do our labor, they called upon the elements and with that power possessed by primitive peoples controlled the air, the earth, the fire, and the water, and made servants out of the winds. What is more, they accomplished all this without following that circuitous route by which modern civilization seeks to attain the same end.

We declare the Great Pyramid of Gizeh to be the imperishable monument of ancient achievement—a divine legacy from an unknown past, constructed at the cost of infinite labor and infinite patience that all posterity may know the will of the gods and the path of attainment. In its measure-

The Initiation in the King's Chamber

ments man may read, as in a book, that secret doctrine which the first civilizations of antiquity bequeathed to their heirs, successors, and assigns.

In view of the numerous eminent authorities who have written concerning the physical dimensions and composition of the Great Pyramid, it does not seem advisable to spend much time on ground already so thoroughly covered. We will therefore merely touch on a few high lights of its construction and then pass on to a consideration of its philosophical significance.

While not the tallest of structures, the Great Pyramid is undoubtedly the largest building in the world. It has a ground area of a trifle less than 13 acres, covers nearly three times as much space as the Vatican at Rome, and is over 150 feet higher than St. Paul's Cathedral. The base line of each of its sides is over 750 feet in length and its vertical height is about 482 feet. The weight of the Great Pyramid is estimated to be somewhere in the neighborhood of 5,273,834 tons, while the weight of the earth is estimated at 5,273,000,000,000,000,000,000 Pyramid tons. It is noteworthy that the first four figures in each calculation are the same.

The age of the Great Pyramid has been the subject of much speculation and dispute. Up to recent years it would have been stark heresy to declare a building to be more than 7,000 years old at the utmost because science—controlled by theology—dared not disagree with the orthodox findings of bigoted theological historians. But as that day has passed and estimates now place the age of the earth at over 300,000,000 years, it is possible to approach much closer to the probable facts than it was in the last century. The prevalent idea that the Great Pyramid was built a few thousand years B. C. is controverted by all the evidence at hand. Distinct marks of erosion are now to be seen high up on the sides of the Great Pyramid which *ipso facto* proves that at some time in the infinite past the waves of a great sea nearly 300 feet in depth broke against its ancient walls. There is no record of any such flood in historic times. Even Biblical historians are prone to admit that the Great Pyramid was erected before the Flood and that it was the Deluge of Noah that left the erosion marks upon its walls.

The Great Pyramid is at least 25,000 years old; it is much more likely to be from 60,000 to 100,000 years old. It stood long before the Egyptians established their post-Atlantean empire. It was the House of God. One scientist, after estimating with great care the intricacies of its construction, bowed his head and said: "None but God Himself could have built it. It was not the work of man."

We affirm that man, however, did build it, but we declare it was not the man that modern science advances as representative of the human race 100,000 years ago. It was no Pithecanthropus or Piltdown man, no Neanderthal or Cro-Magnon with brain capacity but little in advance of the anthropoid, who trued its stones or calculated its relationship to the motion of the heavenly bodies! No Stone-Hatchet man worked out its mathematical equations, no cave-dweller mixed its indestructible mortar! Its achievements were the achievements of a race of supermen excelling in pursuits of which modern civilization is comparatively ignorant.

Is it possible that somewhere in the dim past this earth was peopled by a mighty race as resplendent in scientific achievement as it was profound in philosophic precept? A myopic science will most likely answer "Absurd! Impossible!" Yet the fact remains that the builders of the Great Pyramid were well acquainted with both the mysteries of universal dynamics and the nature of the human soul.

All the wisdom possessed by the ancients seems to have been epitomized in the structure of the Great Pyramid, and he who solves its riddle must necessarily be as wise as he who contrived it!

The Great Pyramid is the perfect emblem of Divinity, the absolute symbol of humanity, the complete type of Nature, and the image of time, eternity, and existence. In one simple geometrical figure, constructed according to an eternal principle, is set forth the secret of all things—all processes, all laws, and all truth.

Using the Pyramid measurements as a basis, Mr. William Petrie computed the distance of the sun from the earth as 91,840,000 miles, which was about three and one-half million miles less than the accepted mean distance. Several years later the distance was recalculated by an international gathering of astronomers, who estimated the true mean distance to be 91,500,000 miles. In all probability, the Great Pyramid measurement is more accurate than even these later findings. It is therefore evident that the men who built the Great Pyramid were not only astronomers but that their skill in computing celestial distances was at least equal to our own.

While it is undoubtedly true that many of the pyramids were used as tombs, it is quite certain that the Great Pyramid of Gizeh was never intended as a sepulchral vault. No mummified body was every found on it and the sarcophagus in the King's Chamber is suspected of having been constructed for any one of a dozen purposes ranging from a baptismal font to a grain bin. Leaving the materialist to flounder in the midst of incalculable sums and endless contradictions, let us examine the form and composition of the Great Pyramid in the light of the Egyptian esotericism—the secret doctrine of the priests.

The Great Pyramid stands with its four faces to the four cardinal angles. The entrance part way up the side is in the north and so cleverly concealed that it is practically invisible from below. The entrance consists of a square surmounted by a triangle, thus signifying that the earth is surmounted by spirit. The entrance is hidden to signify that the way of light is difficult to find, and narrow is the gate that leads to eternal life and none may enter except he bow his head to the inevitable. The square base of the Pyramid in the Mysteries signifies its sure foundation upon the earth, for Nature is the base upon which must be raised the Divine House—the structure of wisdom must have a solid foundation in the laws of Nature. As the word *pyramid* signifies light and fire, it is a material edifice built in the symbolic form of a flame, with its point upward. This point may be considered as an indicator that wisdom is above and ignorance is below. The square base further represents the four elements, and the sides of the four spirits which guard the angles of the world.

Among the ancient Egyptians the triangle, or pyramid, was symbolic of immortality, for it was a point rising out of a square, thus signifying the resurrection of spirit out of matter—the 1 out of the 4. The 5 points are the number of the priest and also the secret Pythagorean emblem of man. The 5 is the Initiator—the Dragon-Slayer—He who attains to Self by the destruction of the Not-Self.

In substantiation of our belief that the Great Pyramid was the Sacred House of the Mysteries, we quote from that eminent authority on Masonic symbolism, Albert Churchward: "We contend that the Great Pyramid of Gizeh was built in Egypt as a monument and lasting memorial of this early religion, on true scientific laws, by divine inspiration and knowledge of the laws of the universe. Indeed, we may look on the Great Pyramid as the first true Masonic temple in the world, surpassing all others that have ever been built."

This thought opens up a great field of speculation. Was the Great Pyramid the true House of SOL-OM-ON? Was the architect of that House the immortal Hiram Abiff, whose name means "Our Father CHiram," or the creative fire? Were the stones for the Great Pyramid cut by bronze saws, with teeth made of diamonds, or were they cut by means of cosmic fire or the *schamir* with which Moses cut the jewels for the breastplate of the High Priest? What was the *schamir,* the sacred stone, which disintegrated anything it touched? Was it the Great Magical Agent of the universe focussed upon a point prepared according to the secrets of the Mysteries? We favor the idea that the Great Pyramid was the real Solomon's Temple. We know the allegory has been sadly distorted and, while to the modern Mason it may seem incredible that the Great Pyramid could be the birthplace of his Craft, we would ask him to answer two questions: What building greater than the Pyramid has any architect designed or any craftsman executed upon the face of the earth? For the administration of the three degrees of Blue Lodge Masonry what structure more fitting than the Great Pyramid could be found, with its three appropriate chambers and a sarcophagus ready at hand in the King's Chamber for the giving of the Master Mason's degree?

Egypt has always been regarded as the land of mystery. She surpassed all other nations in her knowledge of architectonics, chemistry, and astronomy. She is looked upon as being the cradle of science and philosophy and while we know comparatively little concerning the exact nature of Egyptian culture, we are continually confronted by evidence of its superiority. In fact we know a great deal less about Egypt than we care to admit, and being fundamentally materialists, most Egyptologists have given little consideration to the religious equation—the supreme element in the history and civilization of all ancient nations.

In spite of all evidence to the contrary, we shall yet discover that the Rosetta Stone is not the key to the Egyptian hieroglyphics. We shall yet realize that the true meaning of the Egyptian ideographs has never been revealed. We are totally ignorant of the knowledge possessed by the better minds of the ancient Egyptian world for a very simple reason: The Egyptians, like all other enlightened races, divided their knowledge into two parts —*exoteric* and *esoteric.* The exoteric was that portion of learning revealed to the many and the esoteric that part reserved for the illumined few and never reduced to writing save in the form of hieroglyphics and symbols which were meaningless without that key which was the treasured possession of the initiated priestcraft.

The Egyptian culture with which we are conversant is only the exoteric part revealed to the uneducated multitudes of the ancient empire. That finer culture—the real wisdom of the Egyptians—was preserved for the elect, and our world is far too gross and materialistic to comprehend the subtleties of Egyptian escotericism. Therefore we grope blindly amidst images and emblems which, finding no meaning for them, we pronounce meaningless!

According to the secret teachings, the Great Pyramid was the tomb of Osiris, the black god of the Nile. Osiris represents a certain phase of solar energy and therefore his house, or tomb, is emblematic of the universe within which he is entombed and upon the cross of which he is crucified. Thus the Great Pyramid is not a lighthouse, an observatory or a tomb, but a temple. Marsham Adams calls it "the House of the Hidden Places" and such indeed it was, for it represented the inner sanctuary of Egyptian wisdom—or perhaps it would be more accurate to say, pre-Egyptian wisdom. Hermes was the Egyptian god of wisdom and letters, the Divine Illuminator, worshipped through the planet Mercury, and ancient references to the effect that the Pyramid was the House of Hermes emphasize anew the fact that it was in reality the Supreme Temple of the Invisible and Supreme Deity. In all probability, the Great Pyramid was the first temple of the Mysteries—the first structure erected as a repository for those secret truths which are the certain foundation of all modern arts and sciences.

The Great Pyramid, says the secret book, is the perfect emblem of the Microcosm or man, and the Microcosm is the inversion of the Macrocosm. The Macrocosm is the universe without, consisting of unnumbered stars and planets encircled by the mighty egg of cosmic space. All that is in the Macrocosm is to be found in miniature in the Microcosm. As man is "the image of God," so the Great Pyramid is the image of the universe. And—what is more—it is scientifically correct as an image of the universe.

Many authors have treated of the physical marvels of the Great Pyramid, but the modern world is still so ignorant of ancient superphysics that it fails to grasp the subtle import of primitive symbolism and primitive religion. We know that such structures as the Great Pyramid, the Cretan Labyrinth, and the Delphian Oracle were erected to conceal and yet perpetuate certain definite scientific and philosophic theorems.

The policy of the ancient world was concealment. Knowledge was never revealed except through parables and allegories; facts were never directly expressed—they were hinted at. Planets were personified as gods and goddesses; the sun was a shining-faced man with flowing golden locks; the earth was the Great Mother, her true nature concealed under veils and robes that only the illumined might remove; the elements were personified; the universe was an egg; force was a dragon; wisdom was a serpent; evil was a grotesque image —part crocodile, part hog; the Absolute was a globe; the threefold creative power was a triangle, and the fourfold universe of material substance was a square; or, again, spirit was a point, manifestation was a line, intelligence was a surface, and substance was a solid. Thus it is evident that symbolism was the universal language of the ancients. We may laugh at their curious myths and accuse them of idolatry and ignorance, but we are the ones that are ignorant and superficial when we assume that the great minds of antiquity —the founders of the arts and sciences and the patrons of learning—were ignorant of the true state and nature of Divinity and humanity.

Somewhere in the dim forgotten ages primitive man—still responsive to the subtle influences of Nature and still without the separating power of individual thought—carved in stone or preserved as tradition and legend a certain rudimentary knowledge. He may have secured this knowledge by a process of natural receptivity or from some previous race that inhabited this earth before the coming of present humanity. After the lapse of ages, this unknown people became the fabled gods who walked the earth and talked with man in the first days of his existence. Many of the Platonists believed that existence was eternal; that the universe had never been constructed and would never be dissolved; that the worlds had always been; and that over the face of them swept periodic waves of force and power. While modern science refutes the theory and produces evidence that universes come into being and go out of existence, still the world is very old and humanity is very young. No one knows who our progenitors were. It may be true that man rose up from the muck and mire of the prehistoric fens—that first he appeared as mosses and lichens, leaving no record on the molten surfaces of the Azoic rocks. But the true origin of life is spiritual—not physical—and it is also quite certain that side by side with the growing forms of men and beasts there has advanced a mysterious and secret culture, whose outward expression we recognize as religion, philosophy, science, and ethics, and in its innermost sense as knowledge, wisdom, and understanding.

Man has never been without knowledge of his origin and the purpose of his existence. Those divine powers who regulate the destiny of creation—whose manifest works bear witness to their reality but whose form no man has seen—have always had their covenant with men; they have always been represented among humanity by certain sages and prophets. The temples were the houses of these gods, dedicated to their worship, protected from all desecration, and cleansed of all evil, that to these sanctified areas in the midst of a world of sin and strife the gods might come and there deliver to the leaders of tribes, nations, and races those laws and mandates necessary to human survival.

While the world has made rapid progress in scientific lines, it can claim but little religious growth in thousands of years. We are still unstrung by the battles of sectarianism; we are still pushed and pulled by contending theological factions, and as the supreme proof of our spiritual ignorance we still have a number of contradictory schools of religious thought. In other words, our little backyard world harbors scores of little backyard creeds. It therefore has no true religion, for it is quite evident that Divinity is a Unity and therefore can only be worshipped in unity and not in diversity.

While it is undoubtedly necessary that there be numerous forms of religion adapted to racial limitations, national attitudes, and geographical environments, still it is equally true that those religions must comprehend their own fundamental unity and realize that their differences are not in essentiality but in triviality.

While the ignorant masses worshipped at the altars of this god or that god, the wise men of antiquity were not fettered by religious prejudice, but recognized in these hosts of divinities the personified emanations and attributes of One Supreme Father. Accordingly, the Greeks went forth in search of wisdom and their quest led them into the temples of every faith and doctrine of the world.

Did the religion of the Greek philosopher limit him to Zeus, Rhea, Hermes, or the numerous other deities whose marble images sat in the magnificent temples rising on the brow of the Acropolis? Assuredly not!

The Greek initiates were received into the Mysteries of Egypt, Persia, Chaldea, Babylonia, Phœnicia, and India. Returning home again, they were not considered as heretics—false to their own gods—but as illumined and venerable sages almost worthy of worship. The Greeks esteemed the excellence of Brahmin thought, and likewise the Brahmins knew that the Chaldeans and Phœnicians were not unlearned in natural lore. They exchanged freely with each other the knowledge they possessed, for Brahma was but the name of a Nameless Principle, and if the Greeks wished to call their deity Uranus, Chronos or Zeus, what mattered it? It was the Principle—not the name— that was worshipped; it was the wisdom—not the terminology—that was worthy of study. So among the initiates of antiquity there prevailed a great broadness and depth woefully lacking in the "worldly wise men" of today.

In certain sanctified localities were erected temples, not to this cult or to that creed, but to the World Mystery Religion—the one faith of mankind, the all-inclusive doctrine that sometime again must be recognized as the dominating religious institution of the world. From the East, the West, the North, and the South came the learned of all nations seeing acceptance into these Sacred Houses which stood as gateways between the mysteries of visible Nature and the mysteries of the causal universe.

The Great Pyramid was such a sacred edifice, dedicated to the God Hermes—the personification of Universal Wisdom. To gain admission there a man need not be of Egyptian blood, nor of any particular race or creed. There were but two requisites: he must be *clean in heart, mind, and body;* and he must *desire wisdom with a desire stronger than that for life itself.*

So from every part of the ancient world seekers after truth came to the House of the Hidden Places to learn of God, to learn of Nature, and to discover that arcane doctrine which may be revealed only to those who have passed successfully the tests and temptations constituting the initiation rituals of the Mysteries.

We have said that the Great Pyramid is the symbol of the world. It is also the symbol of material existence, for physical life is a series of incidents taking place in certain environments and largely influenced by the environments in which they occur.

Thus it is evident that the various chambers and parts of the Great Pyramid signify esoterically the divisions and avenues of life. As the Cretan Labyrinth contained within it the Minotaur or Bull-Man, whose name in the secret language of the Mysteries means "the beast mind" and which devoured each year the quota of youths and maidens exacted by it as tribute, so earthly life is a winding labyrinth of mystic passageways and chambers, within which dwells the Minotauric beasts—temptation, sorrow, suffering, and death.

Recall the story of Dante's descent into the Inferno or the wanderings of Æneas through the underworld under the guidance of the Cumaean sibyl. Hades—the underworld of the Greeks and Egyptians—is not, as generally supposed, the sphere of the dead. In reality Hades is the material physical world in which we live our material physical lives. Though we believe ourselves to be alive, we but dwell in the underworld of the Greeks, for its tortuous subterranean passageways symbolize that span of earthly existence stretching from the cradle to the grave.

According to the ancients, there are two gates—two mighty doors—one leading into the House of Life and the other leading out. Man enters at the Gate of Cancer—the ancient symbol of the World Mother and the emblem of birth. After wandering his appointed span among the hollows and glooms of Hades, or the Inferno, he passes into the Heaven of the gods through the celestial Gate of Capricorn, by the side of which stands Saturn, the Reaper, symbolic of time and age. Thus the two gates of the underworld are respectively the womb which leads in and the tomb which leads out.

In the underworld Æneas and Dante beheld the sorrows of the lost souls, the agony of the damned, and the curses of sin, lust, and degeneracy. According to the Mysteries, these are the self-generated sufferings which man must

(*Continued on Page 26*)

Notable Reprint

The Druid Ceremony of Stonehenge

The Grand Conventional Festival of the Britons. From *"The Costume of the Original Inhabitants of the British Islands," by Samuel Rush Meyrick, L.L.D. and F.S.A. and Charles Hamilton Smith, Esq. William Bulmer and Co., London, 1815.* (The following being a description and reproduction of Plate XI, Ed.)

The superstition of the Druids corresponded with that of the world in general, not only in its theology, but also in the ceremonies by which the deities were worshipped. The penetrating and accurate Cæsar, marking this similarity, does not hesitate to affirm that they adored Mercury, Apollo, Mars, Jupiter, and Minerva, adding, *de his eandem fere, quam reliquae gentes habent opinionem;* "their opinion respecting these nearly coincides with that of other nations." Dionysius informs us, that the rites of Bacchus were duly celebrated in the British islands; and Strabo cites the authority of Artemidorus, that "in an island close to Britain, Ceres and Proserpine are venerated with rites similar to the orgies of Samothrace." As it is then an historical fact that the mythology and rites of the Druids were the same in substance with those of the Greeks and Romans, as well as of other nations which came under their observation, we shall have pretty good authorities for the representation of them, if with the ancient Bardic poems in our hands we attentively scrutinize the mythological sculptures of the Egyptians to assist in the composition.

This plate therefore represents Stonehenge, the Gwaith Emreis, ambrosial work, of the ancient Britons, in its original splendour, and decked out for the celebration of the Helio-arkite ceremonies. Stone circles in Ireland are called Caer Sidi; the British Bards apply the same appellation. But this is also the name of the zodiac, and as these temples were constructed on astronomical principles, they either represented that celestial zone, solar cycles of sixty, and thirty stones, or the lunar one of nineteen. But these temples had reference to the terrestrial as well as celestial objects of adoration, and therefore typified the ark, which Taliesin particularly terms Caer Sidi, "the enclosure of the just man." As that sacred vessel contained all the animated world so this its representative was in reference to it, called "the mundane circle of stones."

This Mawr Cor Cyvoeth, "great sanctuary of dominion," is represented as it probably appeared "on the morn after May-eve, when the song of the Cuckoo convened the appointed dance over the green," when "it was rendered complete by the rehearsal" of ancient lore, the chaunting of "hymns" in honor of the British divinities, and the interpretation of their will by the birds of the mountain." At this time the huge stones of the oval adytum, which represented the mundane egg, "were covered with veils," on which were delineated the history of "the dragon king." On the principal trilithon of these appeared "the gliding king with expanding wings, before whom the fair one retreats," or Jupiter in the form of a dragon about to violate Proserpine, and become the father of Bacchus. On another the serpent entwining two phalli,

The Grand Cerem

Stonehenge

representing the sun entering the sign Gemini. On a third again the serpent between the sun and moon showing that both are affected by eclipses. Similar devices were exhibited on others. Thus was pourtrayed "Hu the distributor, as presiding in the mundane circle of stones, the glaring Hu, the sovereign of Heaven, the gliding king, the dragon, the victorious Beli, Lord of the honey island of Britain;" and now we see "rapidly moving in the course of the sky, in circles, in uneven numbers, Druids, and Bards unite in celebrating their (dragon) leader."

Taliesin describes the preparation for the solemn periodical rite performed on this day, viz. the removing of the shrine out of the cell in the Arkite island, which seems to have been surrounded only at high water. In his account we may remark a ritual observation of the time of flood, alluding to the deluge; a fanatical rite of piercing the thigh so as to draw blood; and a ceremonial adorning of the sacred rock, which was at that time to display the countenance of the Arkite god. Again, that this was done at the dawn, that the Helio-arkite god might be coming forth from the cell at the precise hour of the sun's rising. That this rock was the chief place of tranquillity, for here the divinity was supposed to reside, excepting at the time of the solemn procession; and lastly, that this patriarchal god, the supreme proprietor, was he who received his family exiled from the world into his ark or sanctuary. Aneurin thus details the different days' ceremonies: "In the festival on the eve of May they celebrate the praise of the holy ones (the helio, and lunar-arkite deities) in the presence of the purifying fire, which was made to ascend on high. On Tuesday they wear their dark garments (in allusion to the darkness of the ark, during the patriarch's confinement.) On the Wednesday they purified their fair attire, (typifying Noah's restoration to light.) On the Thursday they truly performed their due rites. On the Friday the victims were conducted round the circles. On the Saturday their united exertions were displayed without the circular dome. On the Sunday the men with red blades were conducted round the circle, and on the Monday the banquet was served." In the festival of May-eve, however, the more immediate rites of the lunar-arkite goddess took place, as those of the solar divinity did in the morning. Thus Taliesin, speaking of the cows which drew her chest, exclaims, "Eminent is the virtue of the free course when the dance is performed. Loud is the horn of the lustrator, when the kine move in the evening." But from the Egyptian sculptures we are led to suppose that her shrine also accompanied that of the Helio-arkite god on the following morning. On this glorious morn the Druids welcomed the rising sun, the Rhwyv Trydar or "leader of the din," with frantic shouts of joy, accompanied with a vocal hymn and instrumental music, and during this "the priests" within the adytum "moved sideways round the sanctuary, whilst the sanctuary was earnestly invoking the gliding kind." Just behind the altar appears the presiding Druid, "with the circle of ruddy gems on his golden shield," the image of the Caer Sidi. This he occasionally struck with the thyrsus or "bush-topped spear," to have probably the same effect as the horrid din with which the heathens pretended to save the moon at the hour of her eclipse. He presides in the bloody area of the altar, about, in his character of Ysadawr or sacrificer, to slay the victim. Behind are his attendants, "overshading the Bardic mysteries with the banners of the Bards." Near at hand is "the spotted cow," in whose collar are entwined "the stalks of the plants about to be drenched with gore, which procured blessings. On a serene day she bellowed (as a warning presage of the deluge) and afterwards she was boiled" or sacrificed. To the left appears "a Bard seated on a grey steed as governor of the festival." "A thick-maned steed is under the thigh of the fair youth, his shield light and broad hangs upon the slender courser. His blue and unspotted weapon (hasta pura) was the assuager of tumult," being the emblem of peace. "This spear of quartered ash he sometimes extended from his hand over the stone cell of the sacred fire," as he rode about the temple. Conspicuous in the center stands the "bull or brindled ox, with the thick head-band having seven score knobs on his collar." This animal was the symbol of the patriarch in his character of husbandman. It was attended by three priests termed Garan hir, lofty cranes, from their attendance also on the water mysteries. Hence this deity was called Tarw Trigaranau, "Tarvos Trigaranos," and sculptured with three cranes on his back. This animal in the Triads is termed "The yellow ox of the spring," in commemoration of the sign Taurus, into which the sun entered at the season when the Druids celebrated the great arkite mysteries; the brown ox which stopped the channel, from the promise which Noah obtained that no future deluge would occur; and the brindled ox with the thick headband. Such is the "animal which the silver-headed ones" or hoary Druids protect." In front of this is another symbol of the divinity, "the eagle raised aloft in the sky in the path of Granwyn" or Apollo (the ecliptic) "before the pervading sovereign" or rising sun.

Such appears the temple within; but Taliesin asks, "Who approaches the Caer with white dogs, (Druids,) and large horns?" We must therefore examine the grand procession.

First of this band appears the divining Bard with his hudywydd or magic wand, followed by the Bards striking their tuneful harps: whose number was sometimes "seven score." Next follows the shrine of Ceridwen, or "curvatures of Kyd (the ark) which passed the grievous waters, stored with corn, and borne aloft by serpents" or attendant priests. On the preceding eve this shrine had been drawn by cows and attended by torch-bearers, whence Ceres was represented as having wandered over the earth with lighted torches. Now it is attended only by three priests, the Hierophant who represented "the great Creator;"—"one bearing a torch" who personated the sun, and the herald, who as the especial minister of the goddess was regarded as a symbol of the moon. Next comes 'the house" or shrine of the Helio-arkite god, "recovered from the swamp," which is preceded by "the assembled train dancing after their manner, and singing in cadence, some with garlands" of ivy "on their brows," others with cornute caps. "These are the oxen of Hu the mighty, with part of his chain," the symbol of his confinement, and his five attendants which we now behold with golden harness of active flame." These have drawn the Avanc or huge monster from the lake, during which the attendants sing a piece of music still known to a few persons in Wales, called "Cainc yr Ychain banawg," which was an imitation of the lowing of the oxen, and the rattling of chains. The hunched oxen which the Druids employed in this rite were probably of the finest breed which the country afforded, but distinguished either by the size of their horns, or some peculiar mark, and set apart for sacred use. They are now drawing the Avanc to where Taliesin intimates the diluvian patriarch found rest, viz. the spot on which the spotted cow was sacrificed. Originally three oxen drew the Avanc, and probably represented the sons of the patriarch, but as Ham incurred the displeasure of his father, so one is said to have been unequal to the task, and consequently left behind. But "the two oxen of distinguished honour put their necks under the car of

[19]

the lofty one Majestic were they, with equal pace they moved to the festival." Thus we see the Avanc was the car or shrine of the Diluvian god which was drawn from the lake or representative deluge to his temples and sanctuaries upon firm ground, by which he was invested with the empire of the recovered earth. These yoked oxen also refer to the deity himself; for Taliesin, speaking in his name, says, "I was subjected to the yoke for my affliction, but commensurate was my confidence, the world had no existence were it not for my progeny." "This house, recovered from the swamp, is surrounded with crooked horns," some of the dancers before carrying the double pateras, and those who follow sounding "loud the horns of the lustrator." It is also followed by others bearing "crooked swords in honour of the mighty king of the plains," and the whole is closed by the "circular revolutions performed by the attendants and white bands in graceful extravagance," and those "with curved swords and clattering shields."

On the rampart surrounding the temple are assembled the representatives of the people, the heads of tribes and families, with their standard bearers, while the people themselves, who, Cæsar says, *"nullo adhibetur concilio,"* were never admitted into the assemblies, are viewing the procession in groups on the plains.

The Unsuspected Cause

I am convinced that the great majority of those complaints which are considered purely mental, such as irritability and irascibility of temper, gloomy melancholy, timidity and irresolution, despondency, etc., might be greatly remedied, if not entirely removed, by a proper system of temperance, and a very little medicine. On this account, medical men often have it in their power to confer an immense boon of happiness on many valuable members of society, whose lives are rendered wretched by morbid sensitiveness of the mind, having its unsuspected source in morbid sensibility of the stomach, bowels, or the nervous system. From numerous facts, indeed, which have come within my own observation, I am convinced that many strange antipathies, disgusts, caprices of temper, and eccentricities, which are considered solely as obliquities of the intellect, have their source in corporeal disorder. By a temporary gastric derangement many an enterprise of "vast pith and moment" has had its "current turned awry," and "lost the name of action." The philosopher and the metaphysician, who know but little of these reciprocities of mind and matter, have drawn many a false conclusion from, and erected many a baseless hypothesis on, the actions of men. Many a happy and lucky thought has sprung from an empty stomach! Many an important undertaking has been ruined by a bit of undigested pickle—many a well-laid scheme has failed in execution from a drop of green bile—many a terrible and merciless edict has gone forth in consequence of an irritated gastric nerve!
—*Dr. Johnson.*

# Questions & answers·

A Department Maintained for the Convenience of the Reader

Question. Can you tell me the names of the great generals who never lost a battle? G. S.

Answer. There are only three important military leaders of whom history records no defeat. They are Alexander the Great, Julius Cæsar, and the Duke of Wellington.

Q. Is it true that one of the Popes was a Freemason? If so, will you kindly give his name? F. L.

A. A number of bishops and cardinals and two or three saints have been accredited with Masonic affiliations, but it is difficult to prove absolutely that they were initiated into the Freemasonic Order. The Masonic Pope was Pius IX, who was initiated into the Order while a young man. Pope Boniface IV is also suspected of Masonic affiliations because of his kindly attitude toward the Masonic Order.

Q. What is the true meaning of the legend of St. Patrick driving the snakes out of Ireland? F. C.

A. The early Celts worshipped the serpent god which had been introduced into Ireland by the Phœnicians, the Chaldeans, and the Atlanteans. In the ancient world it was customary to name the priests of a cult after the deity whom they served. Therefore the priests of the serpent god were themselves called "snakes." It is well known that the Druids were often referred to as "serpents" and they used the eggs of snakes in the preparation of their magical medicines. St. Patrick, while not the first Christian missionary to Ireland, is accredited with having been the first great power among the Irish in the establishment of Christianity. The legend that he drove the snakes from Ireland signifies that St. Patrick destroyed the pagan cult of serpent worship and drove its priests from their temples.

Q. Will you please give us the names of the greatest of the Greek philosophers? K. G. F.

A. The foremost thinkers of the Greek School are Orpheus, Pythagoras, Plato, Aristotle, Euclid, and Erastosthenes. Of these Thomas Taylor writes that Orpheus, Pythagoras, and Plato are the great triad. The Greek Mysteries were given out symbolically and mystically by Orpheus, enigmatically and through images by Pythagoras, and scientifically by Plato. (See *The Mystical Hymns of Orpheus.*) There were at least four great Greeks who bore the name of *Orpheus.* It was the first of these who is now recognized as the great and illumined sage who brought the principles of Greek mythology from India thousands of years before the Christian era. Socrates is often included among the first minds of Greece, but as none of his writings are in existence and nothing is known concerning him save through the writings of Plato, there is a certain element of doubt both concerning his true identity and the exact nature of his philosophy. Of course there are many great Greek thinkers, but those named above have by the outstanding nature

[21]

of their doctrines been most widely accepted as founders and patrons of science and philosophy.

Q. Do animals go to heaven? And what is the difference between the spirit of an animal and the spirit of a man? J. T. S.

A. A few months before his death, Mr. Luther Burbank told me that if his little dog could not go to heaven, he did not want to. The heaven of the orthodox thinker apparently has no place in it for the animal, for man is very selfish; he creates a universe for his own convenience or rather he tries to prove that God did. Up to a short time ago the Christian world believed that the sun, the moon, and the stars had been hung in the sky by God for the convenience of man, and therefore in his theology—which is as selfish as himself—man has conceived a heaven which will exclude all who disagree with him and denies immortality to everything that is different from himself in form, in nature, in intelligence, and in principle. In this the Mohammedan is more generous than the Christian, for in the Koran it is written that ten animals have been admitted into the eternal Paradise: the dog of the seven sleepers of Ephesus; the ass which rebuked Balaam; Solomon's ant; Jonah's whale; the ram of Ishmael; the ass upon which the Queen of Sheba rode; the camel of Saleb; the Queen of Sheba's dove; the ox of Moses; and an animal called Al-Borak, upon which Mohammed ascended to heaven. Occasionally the ass upon which Jesus rode into Jerusalem is added or substituted for one of the other animals. Philosophy teaches that the Eternal Essence which we call God and which is the sum and origin of all things is as much in the animal as it is in man and therefore the plant of the field or the animal that roams among the hills is as surely an immortal creature as is man. The difference between the various forms of life which we see is not in the invisible spiritual nature which is within but is rather a difference of unfoldment of the objective vehicles by means of which the invisible nature manifests itself. As the animal has not the rational faculties of man, man's heaven would be inconceivable and far from a divine place to the plant or the animal. But the law of evolution is gradually unfolding the potentialities of the lower kingdoms of Nature and in time the animal will unfold its consciousness to a degree fully as great as that of man, and all together the mineral, the plant, the animal, and the man are being swept along to endless stages of growth and unfoldment until finally all attain to that perfection which is the ultimate condition of unity with Eternal Life. We do not know what heaven awaits the animal and we are far from sure just what heaven awaits us, but we are certain that in the infinite wisdom of Nature all have equal opportunity and equal compensation.

Q. Will you kindly tell us why roosters are so often put on weather vanes and the towers of old churches? D. E.

A. The practice of placing the rooster in prominent positions and on the peaks of towers is based upon an ancient pagan custom. The rooster is a phallic symbol and sacred to the sun. It was accepted by the Greeks as the emblem of Ares (the Roman Mars) and typified watchfulness and defense. Its presence indicated that the gods watched over and defended that house. It was placed in the center of the weather vane to signify the sun which was in the center of the four corners of creation. The Greeks sacrificed a rooster to the gods at the time of entering the Eleusinian Mysteries and the last words of Socrates were: "Crito, we owe a cock to Æsculapius. Discharge this debt therefore for me, and don't neglect it."

Q. What became of the Nails of the Crucifixion? A. R. S.

A. There are many legends concerning the Crucifixion Nails, none of which take into account the probable facts that the nails, if actually used, were almost certainly wooden spikes. There is a legend to the effect that the Emperor Constantine used one of the Passion Nails for a bridle bit. This would rather demonstrate a lack of piety on his part. Another of the nails, according to popular tradition, was used in the construction of the famous Iron Crown, which Napoleon—without benefit of clergy—placed on his own head at the time of his coronation. The presence of the nail is supposedly proved by the fact that a certain part of the metal of the crown will not rust. In late years there has been a miraculous multiplication of sacred relics, and many Passion Nails of doubtful authenticity are to be found in different parts of the world. But it is quite certain that the whereabouts of the actual spikes or pegs is unknown.

Q. If philosophic idealists believe in the sacredness of life, declaring it to be a cardinal sin to destroy even the smallest creature, do they have any philosophic solution to the problem of what to do with vermin, bugs, and poisonous insects? L. M. S.

A. Some scribe or Pharisee, with malice aforethought, submits the above! In all matters of this kind it is wise to realize that we are most truly philosophic when we accomplish the greatest good to the greatest number. Very often by obeying the letter of the law we crucify the spirit. The Jains, a very strict East Indian religious sect, employ a man to stand with a broom in front of their temple in Calcutta and tenderly whisk to one side all creeping and crawling things that may chance to stray across the pavement so that no living thing will be injured or stepped on by passersby. If after the individual has used every precautionary measure, such as cleanliness, tidiness, etc., it becomes a matter where various pests are a menace to the community, it is then necessary to destroy them in order to accomplish the greatest good to the greatest number. For example, rats are very often the carriers of plagues and epidemics, which will sweep through whole districts and exact a terrific toll of human life. It is quite impossible for an individual to live an absolutely harmless life: the very air he breathes contains minutes organisms which must die in order that he may continue; the growing tree absorbs into itself the life of lesser plants and creatures and thus lives at the expense of the weaker; the water we drink is a mass of animaliculae that are just as surely alive as horses, dogs, and cattle. We may, and should, reduce our destructiveness to a minimum, but we cannot become entirely free of other lives which must be sacrificed for our survival. The point is this: if we must kill, it is also our duty to give life; if we must destroy, there is only one reason for our perpetuation—that we produce more than we destroy; if multitudes of lives must be sacrificed for our continuance, we owe to Nature a debt which we can only liquidate by making the best possible use of the time which is given to us at so great a cost to other things. The most foolish and wicked person in the world is the one who doesn't realize what must die that he can live. Therefore if we must kill to live, let us not live to kill but, using the energy which is given to us, dedicate our lives to constructive labors by which all humanity and Nature may be benefited. In this way we justify our existence. As the lesser is sacrificed for man, so man, in turn, must be willing to be sacrificed for something still greater and in the cause of that divine power which is as far above man as man is above the reptiles and the vermin.

Q. Is perpetual motion a scientific possibility? J. H. J.

A. In celestial dynamics perpetual motion, or something so nearly akin to it that man's mind is incapable of differentiating between them, is an absolute reality. Up to the present time, however, no practical method has been devised for harnessing universal energy in a mechanism created out of material substances for use in a material world. The ancients claimed to possess perpetual motion machines, and while their claims may be attacked the great lapse of time makes it as impossible to deny their assertions as it is to prove them. Fortunes have been spent in the search for a perpetual motion machine. These have been so uniformly unsuccessful that the United States Patent Office will not even give attention to applications for patents on perpetual motion devices unless accompanied by a working model. The somewhat facetious attitude with which the modern world views the perpetual motion idea is summed up in a definition which appears in Dietrich's essay on the subject: "The question of perpetual motion is reduced to the finding of a weight that is heavier than itself or an elastic force having a greater elasticity than it possesses!" In time, perpetual motion will probably be discovered along with many other ideas rejected by the scientific world. In fact, there is one device at the present time which may prove to be an interesting element in the problem. It is a machine which will run indefinitely in any climate where there is a variation of temperature of two degrees in 24 hours. This change in temperature is sufficient to keep the machine in perpetual motion.

Q. Is there any literal truth in the story of Samson's hair being the source of his strength? J. R.

A. Of course the Biblical allegory of Samson is based upon the phenomena of the equinoxes and the solstices as these were observed by ancient astronomers. Samson was the sun and the house of Delilah the Constellation of Virgo which, when the sun enters it in the fall months, loses its strength by having its rays (hair) cut off by the Celestial Virgin. There is undoubtedly a certain amount of truth in the theory that the strength of the body is depleted by the cutting of the hair. There are certain etheric emanations which escape through the open ends of cut hair and science has rather thoroughly established that baldness is almost the inevitable result of continuously cutting the hair. There is little baldness among those nations who wear their hair long. Nature is economical and only supplies man with those parts and members which time has proved to be essential to his survival. People who are incessantly removing and eliminating what they consider to be "spare parts" may either live or die regretting it. While it may not be noticed as such, hair cutting and shaving are as surely surgical operations as the disentanglement of an appendix or the forcible removal of a kidney.

Q. Will you kindly publish Herbert Spencer's definition of God? R. S.

A. The reference is not at hand, but if our memory does not play us false, the definition is approximately as follows: "God is infinite intelligence, infinitely diversified through infinite time and infinite space, manifesting through an infinitude of ever-evolving individualities."

BOOK EXCHANGE
Rare·Philosophical·Occult Items

This department in our new monthly magazine is established to meet what we feel to be a great need. The great philosophical, religious, and symbolical books of the 15th, 16th, 17th, and 18th centuries are now to be obtained only after a search often involving years. Being in a position to know where many of these volumes can be obtained, we will list them in this column so that other students needing these works for reference or other purposes may have the opportunity of purchasing them. This department is not being maintained for the purpose of profit, and the books are priced at cost plus the actual expense of handling. All books listed will represent the best available material on the various subjects. Those acquainted with the rarity of the volumes will understand the reason for their apparent exorbitant cost.

If you have any rare books on these subjects which you wish to dispose of, we shall be glad to list same on this monthly page.

Calmet's Dictionary of the Holy Bible. 3 vols., original calf (rebacked). Extremely fine plates, engraved by C. Taylor. London, 1800-1801. Price $10.50. Note: The volumes contain the autograph signature of Bushrod Washington, Supreme Court Justice of the United States and nephew of George Washington.

Lives of Alchemystical Philosophers, to which is added a Bibliography of Alchemy and Hermetic Philosophy, by A. E. Waite. London, 1888. Cloth, perfect condition. Price $10.50.

Monumental Christianity or the Art and Symbolism of the Primitive Church, by John P. Lundy. New York, 1876. Original cloth, binding somewhat loose. Price $6.00.

The History of the Holy Cross. Reproduced in Fac-simile from the Original Edition printed by J. Veldener in 1483. Text and Engravings by J. Ph. Berjeau. London, 1863. Cloth, fine copy, with rare Masonic interest. Price $10.50.

The Mystical Hymns of Orpheus, demonstrated to be the Invocations which were used in the Eleusinian Mysteries. Translated from the Greek by Thomas Taylor. London, 1896. Cloth, sound copy, with some extra pages bound in. Price $5.50.

The Indian Religions or the results of the Mysterious Buddhism and the Divinity of Fire, by Hargrave Jennings. London, 1890. Cloth, fine copy. Price $7.50.

The True Ahriman Rezon, or a Help to all that are or would be Free and Accepted Masons. First American Edition, with curious frontisplate, by Lau. Dermott. New York, 1805. Price $7.50.

The Migration of Symbols, by Count Goblet D'Alviella. A remarkable and invaluable work published in Westminster in 1894. Cloth, splendid copy, with numerous plates. Price $25.00.

Address "Book Exchange," care of The All-Seeing Eye.

(*Continued from Page 14*)

endure because he permits himself to be controlled by his own lower nature. All this Inferno is a dream and an illusion, like the Buddhist wheel, to which man clings although he would be free if his mind could but let go.

Hades is, therefore, the sphere in which those creatures dwell who are under the domination of the senses. Their agony is the agony of hopeless desire, useless selfishness, and the sorrow which results from the vain struggle after a mirage. Hades is the dwelling place of those who have never discovered themselves, who have never realized Reality, who have never attained self-consciousness. For when man finds himself, he rolls away the stone of his sepulchre and ascends from the realms of death.

The word *death* is a misnomer as we generally use it. Those are not dead who have laid aside this mortal coil—they really are dead who do not *know themselves*. Death is ignorance, for those who are ignorant are buried in the cold stone coffin of their own limitations, knowing nothing, appreciating nothing, realizing nothing, achieving nothing—the mindless have never lived.

Life is not merely animated existence. Life is thought; life is achievement; life is appreciation; life is recognition; life is realization; life is aspiration; and, most of all, life is understanding! To those who understand life, there can be no death; to those who do not understand the purpose of our sojourn here, there can be no life.

So, according to the Mysteries, the ignorant lie sleeping—sleeping through all eternity, sleeping as worlds are made, sleeping as worlds perish again, sleeping as nations rise, sleeping as empires fall. Surrounded by infinite opportunity and part of a plan based upon infinite growth, those who are not initiated into the mystery of Reality sleep in their narrow coffins of egotism, selfishness, and unawareness through all the eternities of time and being!

The Mysteries taught that there are two manner of men: those who are awake and those who are asleep. Those who are awake live in a world of infinite light, infinite wisdom, infinite beauty, infinite opportunity, and infinite progress. To such all things are good; to such there is no death, and gradually they ascend that ladder of stars leading to the footstool of Divinity itself. To these awakened ones the universe is home and the myriads of stars and heavenly bodies are kindred hosts of celestial beings. All the world is a laboratory of experimentation; every stick and stone preaches a sermon; every living thing teaches a lesson. But to the sleeping ones the world is a cold and dismal place; every man is an enemy; every plant is poisonous or thorny; every beast snaps and howls; every stone is sharp; every problem is a disaster; always the clouds obscure the face of the sun and the heavenly lights are darkened; life itself is a futile struggle against the inevitable and the grave its closing episode.

Immortality is not the perpetuation of the body. It is an innate realization of the perpetuity of spirit. Once man gains consciousness of Self, he can never lose it; once he has learned to live he cannot die, though his form may change. Life is the realization of life and death is the lack of that realization. Could Plato, initiated into the nothingness of death, ever die? Could Socrates ever cease to be who knew that by drinking the hemlock he was but liberating himself from the bonds and limitations of a world which could not understand? He realized that the fleshy house was not his real self but that he changed his bodies as he changed his garments. Having arrived at the realization of truth, he was immortal.

[26]

But what is truth? Whence comes that power which, when it is established in the soul of man, answers all things, solves all things, reveals all things, and supplies all things? What is that indescribable elixir which, when poured into the human soul, makes of the weakling a hero, of the poor man one of indescribable wealth, of the ignorant a divinely illumined sage, and of a man a god?

We hear much of truth. It is a word on every man's tongue but in few men's hearts. Can it be revealed by one to another? Is it a tangible, intellectual reality, or is it an indescribable recognition of the relationship between the individual Self and the Universal Self? What is this mysterious doctrine which lifts man from the ranks of the mediocre and carries him to the very footstool of Divinity? What is it that makes the martyr die with a smile upon his lips and with blessings for his executioners? What is it that inspires the artist to paint pictures which illumine the world? What is it that sounds as soft music in the ears of the great composer? What is it that moves the pen of the author that he may write books which will live forever in the hearts and souls of humanity?

The symbol of that great power is the *crux ansata*—the cross of life— that golden key which unlocks the mysteries of self, that golden key which all too often becomes a cross for the crucifixion of the illumined. And yet those who have this golden key smile at death, laugh at torture, and, retiring into the sanctuary of themselves, are sufficient for all their needs!

This great and mysterious power, this power of divinely revealed truth, is what man gains when he was accepted into the House of the Hidden Places, for it is said that the Mysteries either found a good man or made one, and though he started upon the road a scoffer he ended amazed and silenced.

True religion is not a mass of idle mummeries, contentions, and debates. It is not a series of codes to be accepted in spite of better judgment. It is not an institution obeying the dictates of God by damning unbaptized infants and burying its elect in hallowed ground. These things are the chaff that shall be tossed to the winds; these are the false doctrines—meaningless and useless —serving only as hindrances in the search for truth.

True religion is that institution established by antiquity for the purpose of so unfolding the heart and mind and hand of man that he may gradually grow into that divine realization which confers immortality. The real purpose of religion is to inspire into activity and objective existence that subjective power of understanding which lies latent in the hearts and souls of unillumined humanity.

And as the seekers after truth came from all parts of the ancient world, they beheld the mighty Pyramid rising before them as a looming miracle in stone, a glorious House—man's supreme offering to that definitionless Divinity that gives him the power of recognition! The Great Pyramid was built as an imperishable monument to the Divinity which lies buried in humanity. It is the tombstone of God lying dead in Nature, awaiting the day of resurrection. *It marks the grave of the builder.* It is the sprig of acacia, and he who entered its ancient portal was consecrated to the task of raising the dead God to life again—in himself.

There is a God sleeping in the soul of every man. This sleeping God is his own Divinity—a spark of Universal Divinity imprisoned in a sarcophagus not only of material clay but the clay of earthly thoughts, earthly desires, and wormlike attributes. Here in the House of the Hidden Places man was instructed how to awaken the sleeping God, how to summon into manifestation those latent potentialities which, when trained and unfolded, produce the perfected man.

The unfolding of man's spiritual nature is as much an exact science as astronomy, medicine or jurisprudence. It is not a haphazard procedure based upon a none too certain faith. The secret processes whereby the Divine nature of man may be resurrected and enthroned as the ruler of the human life—this is the secret science, this is the divine doctrine, this is the supreme arcana of all ages and of all peoples. It is to this end that all religions have been established; and out of religion have come science, philosophy, logic, and reason as methods whereby this divine purpose might be attained.

Religion, therefore, represents the Tree of Life. The Garden of Eden is the House of the Mysteries in the midst of which grows this Tree; and Knowledge and Understanding are the fruit of the Tree and he who eats of that fruit shall be a god, having eternal life. But lest this fruit be stolen, lest the foolish attempt to steal the prize belonging to the wise, the supreme mystery is concealed under the emblems and symbols meaningless to the uninitiated. For being the most priceless of all human possessions, truth is guarded more sedulously than any other secret. What is there in the world that is its equal? What more can man possess than understanding? All other things are impermanent, but understanding endures; all other things may be lost or destroyed, but understanding belongs forever to him who once possesses it!

Through the mystic passageways and chambers of the Great Pyramid therefore passed the illumined of antiquity. As *men* they entered its portal, as *gods* they came forth again. It was the place of the "second birth," the "womb of the Mysteries," and wisdom dwelt in it as God dwells in the heart of man. Somewhere in the depths of its recesses there resided an unknown being who was called "The Initiator,' or "The Illustrious One," robed in blue and gold and bearing in his hand the sevenfold Key of Eternity. This was the lion-faced hierophant, the Ancient of Days, the Holy One, the Master of Masters, who never left the House of God and whom no man ever saw save he who had passed through the gates of preparation and purification. It was in these chambers that Plato—he of the broad brow—came face to face with the wisdom of the ages personified in the Master of the Secret House.

But what does this mean to the material scientist? What does this solve for the geologist, who with his little hammer chips at the casing stones and tries to solve the problem of all ages with a microscope and a pestle? What does this mean to the Biblical historian, whose brows are knit over the problem of who built the world's great structure long before Adam and Eve must have been even remote conceptions in Jehovah's mind? Or what does it mean to the theologian who dares not peer over the edge of the King James' Bible for fear of endangering his eternal salvation? Only minds trained in the free range of philosophic thinking, uncurbed by creed or dogma, unfettered by the bonds of theology or the limitations of science, and whose God is a non-sectarian Deity can face this problem without prejudice and appreciate the magnitude of true religion as herein revealed.

Who was the Master of the Hidden House—whose many rooms signified the worlds in space—whom none might behold save those who had been "born again"? He knew the secret of the Pyramid, but He has departed the way of the wise and the house is empty. The hymns of praise no longer echo in muffled tones through the chambers, the neophyte no longer passes through the elements and wanders among the seven stars. The candidate no longer receives the "word of life" from the lips of the Eternal One. Nothing remains but the shell—the outer symbol of the inner truth, and men call the House of God a tomb. The Great Pyramid is not the only House of God worthy of that appellation!

Eager to receive this divine boon, the candidates accompanied by the Silent Voice, the Unknown Watcher, climbed the ancient steps which must have originally led up to the entrance of the Great Pyramid. What lay within he did not know. Whether he would ever come out again he did not know. He only realized that if he failed to meet the requirements of the Mysteries, he would forever vanish from the sight of men. But within that mighty pyramid of stone gleaming in the Egyptian sun he knew there dwelt a sacred and sanctified One—the Keeper of the Royal Secret. He was resolved to reach that One and secure that secret or die in the attempt. The time of his trial had come. His previous life, his devotion to study, his sincerity of motive, his cleanliness of heart—all these had been thoroughly established.

As he approached the tiny gate, the solid wall before him parted, a great stone door hung on invisible hinges of granite swung open before him, and he passed into the darkness of the Secret House. The tests began. Surrounded by the gloom and cold of the Sacred Place, he passed through in succession the chambers and passageways which typified all the forms and experiences of mortal existence. Thus the labors of a lifetime were recapitulated in a few hours in the Great Pyramid Mysteries. Strange creatures confronted him. Temptations were ever about him. But at last his soul ascended as a bird up the chimneylike passageway leading to the place of light.

He passed through the dwelling-places of the Spirits of the Gods. The earth shook and thunders rumbled about him. At last the grand staircase of the Seven Breaths of the Seven Stars was reached and far above in the still unexplored pinnacle of the building was the dwelling-place of the Secret God ——the Unknown One Whose name could not be spoken, Whose nature could not be conceived, and Whose thoughts could not be interpreted.

The details of the ceremonial are entirely a matter of speculation, for nothing is actually known concerning them save to a few—and they are not permitted to speak. But as far as can be ascertained, the King's Chamber was the scene of the great climax of the initiatory drama. Here crucified upon a St. Andrew's cross, the candidate was suspended like the solar god upon his cross of the equinoxes and the solstices.

After the solar crucifixion had been performed, the candidate was laid in the great stone coffin and for three days his spirit—freed from its mortal coil— wandered at the gateways of Eternity. His *Ka* as a bird flew through the spiritual spheres of space. He passed upward through the Seven Gates and stood before the mighty throne of the Empyreum. He discovered that all the universe was life, all the universe was progress, all the universe was eternal growth.

He also realized himself to be an integral part of this eternal plan, that no more could he cease to be than the sun and the moon and the stars could cease to be. He conversed with the immortals. He was then brought into the blinding presence of the Living Word, and then realizing that his body was a house which he could slip out of and return to without death, he achieved actual immortality.

It is probable that peculiar atmospheric conditions, the temperature of the King's Chamber, and the dull cold of the coffin formed an important link in the chain of circumstances which permitted the consciousness of the neophyte to escape from his body and come into the presence of the Great Illuminator. At the end of three days he returned to himself again and, having thus personally and actually experienced the great mystery, he was indeed an Initiate —one who beheld and one to whom religion had fulfilled her duty by bringing him into the light of God.

The new initiate, wearing the insignia and symbol of his accomplishment, was now brought into the presence of the Great Illuminator—the Master of the Secret House. He beheld the august patriarch whom no eyes ever saw save those who had passed through the Mystery of the "philosophic death" and who had been "born again" out of Time into Eternity.

Mystically, there are two births. In physical birth man is born from Eternity into Time, and through the span of his earthly struggle battles desperately against inevitable conquest by Time. In the Mysteries there is the philosophic death and the second birth out of Time back again into Eternity, and the new initiate no longer struggles against the corroding influences of Time but dwells in the perfect realization that past and future are gone and that in the Mysteries there is but one time—and that of infinite duration— eternally posited in the ever-present NOW.

By this sage Illuminator—the Master of the Secret House—the technique of the Mysteries was unfolded. The power to know his guardian spirit was revealed to the new initiate; the method of disentangling his material body from his divine vehicle was explained; and to consummate the Great Work, the Divine Name—the secret and unutterable designation of the Supreme Deity, by the very knowledge of which man and his God are consciously one —was solemnly revealed. With the giving of The Name the new initiate was himself a *pyramid*, within the chambers of whose soul numberless other human beings might also receive enlightenment. Having achieved the Great Work, having accepted the hierophant of the Secret House as his spiritual father—the one who had given him that light which is the life of men—and having made the final offering—his own life—to the service of the Secret House, the initiate was ushered forth again into the glare of the desert sun.

When he entered he had gazed up at the mystery of the great stone pyramid; and now he gazed again, but no longer at a mystery. He beheld a great stream of light which descended from the heavens upon the pyramid. He saw it break up into numerous paths and, coming down the walls in all directions, diverge like the branches of a tree. He realized that he himself was a branch, for the life of the tree was in him—nay, he was more than a branch, he was actually a fruit of the pyramidal tree. So, Pythagoraslike, he took the three seeds of the tree which was within the fruit of his own soul and, going forth, he planted them. And another tree grew up from the seeds, which tree also bore the golden fruit of Life and all those who partook of it, lived.

So we still chip at the walls of the Pyramid, filled with wonder why men should have built such a structure, and what great urge inspired the herculean labor. We hear men say: "It is the most perfect building in the world;" that it is the source of weights and measures; that it was the original Noah's Ark; that it is the origin of languages and alphabets; that it is the origin of the scales of temperature and humidity; that it is the only structure upon the face of the earth that actually squares the circle; and that it stands as the absolute dividing line between the land and water surfaces of the earth. We wonder at all these things, but if we really understood the purpose for which this mighty House was built, we would wonder still more or, more likely, we would scoff. For it seems incredible to this generation that there was ever a time when men knew more than men know now. Though the modern world may know a million secrets, the ancient world knew *one*—and that one was greater than the million; for the million secrets breed death, disaster, sorrow, selfishness, lust, and avarice but the *one* confers life, light, and truth.

The time will come when the secret wisdom shall again be the dominating religious and philosophical urge of the world. The day is at hand when the doom of dogma shall be sounded. The great theological Tower of Babel, with its confusion of tongues, was built with bricks of mud and the mortar of slime. Out of the cold ashes of lifeless creeds, however, shall rise *phoenix-like* the ancient Mysteries. No other institution so completely satisfied the religious needs of humanity, for since the destruction of the Mysteries there has never been a religious edifice wherein Plato could have worshipped!

The Dying God shall rise again! The secret room in the House of the Hidden Places shall be rediscovered! The Pyramid shall yet stand as the ideal emblem of solidarity, aspiration, inspiration, resurrection, and regeneration! As the passing sands of time bury civilizaton upon civilization beneath their weight, the Pyramid shall remain as the visible covenant between that eternal wisdom and the world. The time may yet come when the chants of the illumined shall be heard again in its ancient passageways and the Master of the Hidden House await in the Silent Place for the coming of the seeker after that spiritual truth which the modern world needs so badly and of which it knows so little.

In an ancient fragment accredited to Hermes but by some supposed to have been written by Apuleius, is a remarkable prophecy concerning the future of Egypt. Hermes is the speaker and Asclepius the one addressed. The work from which this extract is taken is called the Asclepian Dialogue, which has never been completely translated into English: "Are you ignorant, O Asclepius, that Egypt is the image of heaven, or, which is more true, a translation and descent of everything which is governed and exercised in heaven? And, if it may be said, our land is truly the temple of the whole world. Nevertheless, because it becomes wise men to foreknow all things, it is not lawful that you should be ignorant that the time will come when it may seem that the Egyptians have in vain, with a pious mind and sedulous religion, paid attention to divinity, and all their holy veneration shall become void and of no effect. For divinity shall return back to heaven. *Egypt shall be forsaken, and the land which was the seat of divinity shall be destitute of religion, and deprived of the presence of the Gods. For when strangers shall possess and fill this region and land, there shall not only be a neglect of religion, but (which is more miserable) there shall be laws enacted against religion, piety, and divine worship; they shall be prohibited, and punishments shall be inflicted on their votaries. Then this most holy land, the seat of places consecrated to divinity, and of temples, shall be full of sepulchres and dead bodies. O Egypt, Egypt, fables alone shall remain of thy religion, and these such as will be incredible to posterity; and words alone shall be left engraved in stones, narrating thy pious deeds. The Scythian also, or Indian, or some other similar nation, shall inherit Egypt.* For divinity shall return to heaven, all its inhabitants shall die, and thus Egypt, bereft both of God and man, shall be deserted. I call on thee, O most holy river, and predict to thee future events. Thou shalt burst forth with a torrent of blood, full even to thy banks, and thy divine waters shall not only be polluted with blood, but the land shall be inundated with it, and the number of the dead shall exceed that of the living. He, likewise, who survives, shall only, by his language, be known to be an Egyptian, but by his deeds he will appear to be a stranger. Why do you weep, O Asclepius? Egypt shall experience more ample and much worse evils than these, though she was once holy, and the greatest lover of the Gods on the earth, by the desert of her religion. And she who was alone the reductor of sanctity and the mistress of piety will be an example of the greatest cruelty. Then also, through the weariness of men, the world will not appear to be an admirable and adorable thing. This whole good, a better than which, as an object of perception, there neither is, nor was, nor will be, will be in danger, and will be grievous to men. Hence this whole world will be despised, and will not be beloved, though it is the immutable work of God, a glorious fabric, a good compounded with a multiform variety of images, a machine of the will of God, who, in his work, gave his suffrage without envy, that all things should be one. It is also a multiform collected heap, capable of being venerated, praised and loved by those that behold it. For darkness shall be preferred to light, and death shall be judged to be more useful than life. No one shall look up to heaven. *The religious man shall be accounted insane, the irreligious shall be thought wise, the furious brave, and the worst of men shall be considered a good man.* For the soul, and all things about it, by which it is either naturally immortal, or conceives that it shall attain to immortaliy, conformably to what I have explained to you, shall not only be the subject of laughter, but shall be considered as vanity. *Believe me, likewise, that a capital punishment shall be appointed for him who applies himself to the religion of intellect. New statutes and new laws shall be established, and nothing religious, or which is worthy of heaven or celestial concerns, shall be heard or believed by the mind. There will be a lamentable departure of the Gods from men; noxious angels will alone remain, who, being mingled with human nature, will violently impel the miserable men [of that time] to war, to rapine, to fraud, and to every thing contrary to the nature of the soul.* Then the earth shall be in a preternatural state; the sea shall not be sailed in, nor shall the heavens accord with the course of the stars, nor the course of the stars continue in the heavens. *Every divine voice shall be dumb by a necessary silence,* the fruits of the earth shall be corrupted, nor shall the earth be prolific, and the air itself shall languish with a sorrowful torpor. These events and such an old age of the world as this shall take place, such irreligion, inordination, and unreasonableness of all good. When all these things shall happen, O Asclepius, then that lord and father, the God who is first in power, and the one governor of the world, looking into the manners and voluntary deeds [of men,] and by his will, which is the benignity of God, resisting vices, and recalling the error arising from the corruption of all things; washing away likewise all malignity by a deluge, or consuming it by fire, or bringing it to an end by disease and pestilence dispersed in different places, will recall the world to its ancient form, in order that the world itself may appear to be an adorable and admirable production, and God, the fabricator and restorer of so great a work, may be celebrated, by all that shall then exist, with frequent solemn praises and benedictions."

SYMBOLICAL PHILOSOPHY*

YEARS ago we conceived the idea of gathering from the available archives of the ancient world the symbols and allegories which have played so important a part in the structure of civilization and of attempting to explain them in a simple manner to the modern world, according to the ideals of those who conceived their many interpretations. During the last year the plans for this tremendous undertaking have rapidly assumed definite shape, until we are now in a position to present to the public a volume containing an epitomized compilation of pagan and Christian symbolism to be used in interpreting the philosophic, scientific, and religious allegories of the ancient and modern worlds.

Not only will the work be a compilation of existing material, but it will also contain a great amount of original matter. Mr. Hall's private library, containing a large number of rare printed works and manuscripts, many absolutely unique, will form the basis of the research work. Over $25,000 worth of reference books are being used in compiling this volume. Translations have been made from the German, French, Latin, Hebrew, and Greek, and at the present time the store of material presents a fascinating fund of little-known information on vital subjects.

When completed, the volume will be 13 inches wide and 19 inches high, and will be supplied with a substantial slip case for its protection. It will contain nearly 300 pages of reading matter and plates, with 46 full page illustrations in three and four colors, and a digestive index which will greatly enhance the value of the book to the student. There will be 46 chapters, including many references from world authorities on symbolism, and numerous explanatory cuts throughout the text. The book is being planned by John Henry Nash, the foremost book designer on the American continent, and will be printed by one of the best-equipped printing establishments in the West. The entire book is being published with quality, permanence, and art as primary considerations. The binding is to be of double weight, especially reinforced, and of antique design. With reasonable care the volume should be in excellent condition at the end of two or three hundred years.

*Title, "An Enclopedic Outline of Masonic, Hermetic, and Rosicrucian Symbolical Philosophy," to which is added a Treatise on the Qabbalah of the Jews.

By MANLY P. HALL

Write for Information and Descriptive Literature

THE HALL PUBLISHING COMPANY,

301 Trinity Auditorium Building   Los Angeles, California, U. S. A.

THE · ALL· SEEING EYE

Being a Monthly Magazine
which is published in Los
Angeles on the Fifteen-
th day of every month
edited by
Manly P. Hall
and
devoted to the Search for the
Fundamental Verities Existing in the Educational
Systems · Religions
and Philosophies
of All Ages

J U N E
MCMXXVII

The ALL-SEEING EYE

DEVOTED TO THE SEARCH FOR THE
FUNDAMENTAL VERITIES EXIST-
ING IN THE EDUCATIONAL
SYSTEMS, RELIGIONS,
AND PHILOSOPHIES
OF ALL AGES

Vol. IV	JUNE, 1927	No. 2

PUBLISHED EVERY MONTH BY
THE HALL PUBLISHING COMPANY
301 TRINITY AUDITORIUM BUILDING,
NINTH AT GRAND AVENUE, LOS ANGELES, CALIFORNIA

MANLY P. HALL . . . . *Editor*
HARRY S. GERHART . . . . *Managing Editor*
MAUD F. GALIGHER . . . . *Associate Editor*
HOWARD W. WOOKEY . . . . *Art Director*

CONTENTS

Do You Know?

That in an old German town hall there stands a staircase made entirely of petrified wood.

That Stephen Girard, the founder of Girard College, by the terms of his will forbade clergymen of any denomination to enter the grounds of that college.

That the great composer, Beethoven, wrote some of his finest musical compositions and conducted large orchestras after he had become so deaf that he could not distinguish a single note.

That the custom of lifting the hat originated in the age of chivalry, when knights entering into a gathering of friends removed their helmets, thus signifying that it was unnecessary to defend themselves against their friends.

That Inez de Castro, queen of Portugal, was crowned after death. Her body was taken from its grave, placed upon a magnificent throne, arrayed in robes of royalty, and acclaimed by the populace.

That January 1st of the year A. D. 1 corresponds to the middle of the 149th Olympiad, the 753d year of the building of Rome, Anno Urbis Conditae (A. U. C.), and the year 4714 of the Julian period since the creation.

That the descendants of Confucius number over 40,000 and are separated from the founder of their house by over seventy generations. Thus they constitute the largest and oldest single family in the world.

That between the 12th and 18th centuries such animals and insects as rats, cows, dogs, locusts, caterpillars, etc., were tried by courts of the ecclesiastical law the same as human beings. In 1740, a cow was tried by jury, found guilty, and publicly executed.

That certain of the ancient Mexican peoples went to war with wooden swords and blunt spears so that they could not kill so many of each other. It was not for humanitarian motives, however, but so that a greater number might be captured alive and later offered as human sacrifices to the gods.

The EDITOR'S BRIEFS

The Bible Versus the Bible

It is daily becoming more evident that those who translated the Old and New Testaments from the ancient Hebrew and Greek did not possess sufficient understanding to cope with the intricacies of the archaic originals. As a result, Biblical students of the 20th century are confronted with so many self-evident contradictions that it is extremely difficult to determine just exactly what a good Christian should believe. Attempts to emphasize certain points in scriptural writings have already split the Christian church into scores of non-cooperative units. What is the theologian to fall back upon if numerous statements in his sacred book are irreconcilable? Or how can he convert the heathen if he cannot be certain that he himself properly understands his own spiritual code?

Let us first consider some of the things that the Bible has to say concerning God. In the 26th verse of the 19th chapter of Matthew the powers of God are described as follows:

WITH GOD ALL THINGS ARE POSSIBLE.

But in the 19th verse of the 1st chapter of Judges appears proof that all things were not possible with God, for it says:

AND THE LORD WAS WITH JUDAH, AND HE DROVE OUT THE INHABITANTS OF THE MOUNTAIN; BUT COULD NOT DRIVE OUT THE INHABITANTS OF THE VALLEY, BECAUSE THEY HAD CHARIOTS OF IRON.

In the 33rd verse of the 14th chapter of First Corinthians God is declared to be a peace-loving Deity, in the following words:

GOD IS NOT THE AUTHOR OF CONFUSION, BUT OF PEACE.

But in the 1st verse of the 144th Psalm He appears to have some warlike tendencies:

BLESSED BE THE LORD MY STRENGTH, WHICH TEACHETH MY HANDS TO WAR, AND MY FINGERS TO FIGHT.

The 11th verse of the 5th chapter of James declares God to be compassionate, with these words:

THE LORD IS VERY PITIFUL AND OF TENDER MERCY.

But in the 14th verse of the 13th chapter of Jeremiah God contradicts this with His own words:

I WILL NOT PITY, NOR SPARE, NOR HAVE MERCY, BUT DESTROY THEM. This would seem to indicate that He occasionally hardened His heart!

In the 13th verse of the 1st chapter of James, the Apostle defends the integrity of God as follows:

LET NO MAN SAY WHEN HE IS TEMPTED, I AM TEMPTED OF GOD; FOR GOD CANNOT BE TEMPTED WITH EVIL, NEITHER TEMPTETH HE ANY MAN.

This is difficult to reconcile with the 1st verse of the 22nd chapter of

Genesis where it is distinctly written:

AND IT CAME TO PASS AFTER THESE THINGS THAT GOD DID TEMPT ABRAHAM. Or that little place in the 11th verse of the 18th chapter of Jeremiah, in which that prophet quotes God as saying: BEHOLD I FRAME EVIL AGAINST YOU, AND DEVISE A DEVICE AGAINST YOU.

Apropos of this the 18th verse of the 6th chapter of Hebrews reads: IT WAS IMPOSSIBLE FOR GOD TO LIE.

But in the 11th verse of the 2nd chapter of Second Thessalonians it says: FOR THIS CAUSE GOD SHALL SEND THEM STRONG DELUSION, THAT THEY SHOULD BELIEVE A LIE.

In the 5th verse of the 20th chapter of Exodus appears those oft quoted words:

I, THE LORD THY GOD AM A JEALOUS GOD, VISITING THE INIQUITIES OF THE FATHERS UPON THE CHILDREN.

The prophet Ezekiel, however, in the 20th verse of the 18th chapter of his book begs to differ, saying: THE SON SHALL NOT BEAR THE INIQUITY OF THE FATHER.

The monotheists apparently base their conclusions upon the 4th verse of the 8th chapter of First Corinthians where it is distinctly stated: THERE IS NONE OTHER GOD BUT ONE.

But the polytheists also speak with the voice of authority, for the first, second and third verses of the 18th chapter of Genesis declare God to be three distinct persons:

AND THE LORD APPEARED UNTO HIM (Abraham) IN THE PLAINS OF MAMRE * * * AND HE LIFTED UP HIS EYES AND LOOKED, AND LO, THREE MEN STOOD BY HIM.

In the 13th verse of the 6th chapter of Hebrews it is written: BECAUSE HE (God) COULD SWEAR BY NO GREATER, HE SWORE BY HIMSELF.

According to the 34th verse of the 5th chapter of Matthew, however, God really shouldn't have sworn at all, for it is written: BUT I SAY UNTO YOU, SWEAR NOT AT ALL; NEITHER BY HEAVEN FOR IT IS GOD'S THRONE; NOR BY THE EARTH FOR IT IS HIS FOOTSTOOL.

There is a certain inconsistency between the statement appearing in the 4th verse of the 20th chapter of Exodus where it states: THOU SHALT NOT MAKE UNTO THEE ANY GRAVEN IMAGES, OR ANY LIKENESS OF ANYTHING THAT IS IN THE HEAVENS ABOVE, OR THAT IS IN THE EARTH BENEATH, and the statement which appears in the 18th to 20th verses of the 25th chapter of the same book: THOU SHALT MAKE TWO CHERUBIM OF GOLD * * * AND THE CHERUBIM SHALL STRETCH FORTH THEIR WINGS ON HIGH, COVERING THE MERCY SEAT WITH THEIR WINGS, AND THEIR FACES SHALL LOOK ONE TO ANOTHER.

No doubt prohibitionists accept as their motto the 1st verse of the 20th chapter of Proverbs:

WINE IS A MOCKER, STRONG DRINK IS RAGING, AND WHOSOEVER IS DECEIVED THEREBY IS NOT WISE.

[36]

On the other hand, those who believe in the cup that cheers can derive a slogan equally appealing from the same book, for in the 6th and 7th verses of the 31st chapter of Proverbs appearing the following:

GIVE STRONG DRINK UNTO HIM THAT IS READY TO PERISH, AND WINE TO THOSE THAT BE OF HEAVY HEARTS. LET HIM DRINK AND FORGET HIS POVERTY, AND REMEMBER HIS MISERY NO MORE.

In the 52nd verse of the 15th chapter of First Corinthians it is declared that the dead shall be raised:

THE TRUMPETS SHALL SOUND AND THE DEAD SHALL BE RAISED.

Job, being somewhat of a pessimist on this score, denies immortality in the 9th verse of the 7th chapter of his book:

AS THE CLOUD IS CONSUMED AND VANISHETH AWAY, SO HE THAT GOETH DOWN TO THE GRAVE SHALL COME UP NO MORE.

The New Testament contains many curious contradictions; for example, in the 52nd verse of the 26th chapter of Matthew it is written:

ALL THEY THAT TAKE THE SWORD SHALL PERISH BY THE SWORD.

But in the 36th verse of the 22nd chapter of Luke, that disciple records this admonition:

HE THAT HATH NO SWORD LET HIM SELL HIS GARMENT AND BUY ONE.

In the 30th verse of the 32nd chapter of Genesis Jacob declares:

FOR I HAVE SEEN GOD FACE TO FACE, AND MY LIFE IS PRESERVED.

In the 18th verse of the 1st chapter of John, appears a sweeping denial of the above:

NO MAN HATH SEEN GOD AT ANY TIME.

In the 12th verse of the 2nd chapter of First Timothy the fair sex is assailed in no uncertain terms:

I SUFFER NOT A WOMAN TO TEACH, NOR TO USURP AUTHORITY OVER THE MAN, BUT TO BE IN SILENCE.

God apparently had a better opinion of women than the author of First Timothy, for He declared:

AND ON MY HANDMAIDENS I WILL POUR OUT IN THOSE DAYS MY SPIRIT, AND THEY SHALL PROPHESY. (See Acts 2:18.)

It is quite evident that genealogists were somewhat inaccurate in early days, for in the 23rd verse of the 6th chapter of Second Samuel we find:

THEREFORE MICHAL, THE DAUGHTER OF SAUL, HAD NO CHILD UNTO THE DAY OF HER DEATH.

But in the 8th verse of the 21st chapter of the same book appears the following:

THE FIVE SONS OF MICHAL, THE DAUGHTER OF SAUL.

There also seems to be a little discrepancy in the story of Judas and his thirty pieces of silver, for in the 3rd verse of the 27th chapter of Matthew it is declared:

THEN JUDAS * * * BROUGHT AGAIN THE THIRTY PIECES OF SILVER TO THE CHIEF PRIESTS AND THE ELDERS.

But in the 18th verse of the 1st chapter of Acts it is written:

NOW THIS MAN PURCHASED A FIELD WITH THE RE-WARD OF INIQUITY.

There is a very curious contradiction in the book of John, for in the 18th verse of the 8th chapter it is written:

I AM THE ONE THAT BEAR WITNESS OF MYSELF.

But in the 31st verse of the 5th chapter of the same work it is stated:

IF I BEAR WITNESS OF MYSELF, MY WITNESS IS NOT TRUE.

Two other interesting contradictions appear in the book of John. In the 22nd and 30th verses of the 5th chapter it reads:

THE FATHER JUDGETH NO MAN, BUT HATH COM-MITTED ALL JUDGMENT TO THE SON * * * AS I HEAR I JUDGE.

And in the 47th verse of the 12th chapter this is contradicted in the following language:

I CAME NOT TO JUDGE THE WORLD BUT TO SAVE THE WORLD.

There also seems to be a certain amount of confusion concerning the end of the world, for in the 10th verse of the 3rd chapter of Second Peter it is affirmed:

THE EARTH ALSO AND THE WORKS THAT ARE THERE-IN SHALL BE BURNED UP.

This is in distinct variance with the 4th verse of the 1st chapter of Ecclesiastes which asserts:

BUT THE EARTH ABIDETH FOREVER.

Do not consider for a moment that these constitute all the contradictions and ambiguous statements which appear in the Scriptures. The Christian Bible contains literally hundreds of these examples of improper translation. The amazing thing is that Biblical scholars for centuries have permitted these inconsistencies to remain uncorrected! It proves conclusively that the Bible has failed in its purpose and that man worships the book and not its contents.

We believe that there would be no conflict between science and religion if we actually understood our scriptural writings, but the same attitude which has permitted the above contradictions to remain uncorrected for centuries also prevents the growth of religion by turning the thinking mind from the church. The most dangerous individual in all the world is the standpatter who boasts that he is the same yesterday, today and forever. We believe it was Emerson who said that consistency is the bugbear of little minds. There is a type of mind in the religious world which prides itself upon the fact that it accepts the Bible "from kiver to kiver." No jot or tittle of its contents must be changed lest its infallibility be questioned, yet while it is incorrectly translated its fallibility is daily demonstrated. We seriously need a new and scholarly translation of the Bible, but it is a grave question as to whether the world would accept the correct version if it were presented. We are in such hopeless servitude to precedent that we are more ready to accept the patent mistakes of our ancestors than we are new and corrected documents, even though their verity be demonstrated.

rientalism

Magic and Sorcery of the Far East

By MANLY P. HALL

The Orient has long been considered a land of mystery because the Western type of mind has never been able to understand the mental outlook of its people. People frequently say that the Hindu or the Chinaman is uncanny. This is the natural result of ignorance concerning the life and ideals of the Oriental. From the dawn of time, Asiatics have been suspected of possessing some subtle and unknown power beyond the comprehension of other races; India is still commonly referred to as the land of the living saints; and the gods are still supposed to wander the earth among the hills and valleys of Hindustan.

Magic, in general, is divided into two classes—transcendental magic and legerdemain. The first depends upon the knowledge and manipulation of certain intangible powers and processes in Nature by which a man can produce what is an apparent miracle. Transcendental magic itself is subdivided into many forms, the two most important of which are (1) black magic, which is the sorcery as performed by the Dugpas; and (2) white magic, which is the true wonder-working as performed by the Gurus, Mahatmas, and Arhats.

Legerdemain—the second and far more common form of magic—is otherwise known as conjuration, jugglery, and sleight of hand. This form of magic attempts, by purely mechanical means, to reproduce the miracles of true transcendentalism. Legerdemain has been raised to the dignity of a fine art by Eastern magicians and wandering fakirs, and while its effects are achieved through the medium of trickery they never fail to mystify those unacquainted with their modus operandi. The true miracle-workers of India are now seldom met with, for the ridicule and persecution resulting from their exhibitions have driven them into the fastnesses of the mountains and secluded temples far from the sight of the white man. Those who have traveled extensively in India realize that the Indian people as a mass firmly believe in the existence of certain venerable and illuminated sages, possessing the power of performing miracles and able to directionalize the invisible laws of Nature at will. In spite of every effort on the part of missionaries and educators to destroy the belief in miracle-working, this faith is so strongly imbedded in the Hindu nature that nothing can uproot it.

The purpose of this article is first to describe the feats of legerdemain which we have personally witnessed in China, Singapore, and India, and then to relate the descriptions given by reputable Brahmins of that type of magic performed by the true wonder-workers whose accomplishments are now seldom seen by Caucasians.

We first contacted Oriental legerdemain while stopping at the Grand Hotel des Wagons Lits, in Peking. One evening a Chinese juggler presented a program of his native sleight of hand tricks to a small group of guests who had found it too cold to wander on the streets outside. The conjurer erected a small tent in one of the hotel parlors and, using the tent to contain his apparatus, presented a series of remarkably clever illusions to the consternation of his audience. The magician was an elderly and venerable Chinaman, robed from head to foot in a magnificently brocaded Mandarin coat. He was a small man, his back bent with age, but his dexterity was bewildering.

Reaching the center of the polished parquet floor, the old man spread a beautifully embroidered foulard over his arms and suddenly, without the slightest warning, turned a complete somersault, landing on his feet and carrying in his arms a bowl of varicolored Chinese fish. The bowl was at least four feet in circumference and a foot in depth, and probably contained about five gallons of water. He did not spill one drop of the water and permitted the audience to convince themselves of its reality. The unusual degree of skill displayed by the magician is apparent from the fact that he had no stage complete with special accessories and the help of distance to assist in the illusion, but produced his mysterious effects on a hardwood floor, bare of carpet, and entirely surrounded by his audience.

When the consternation had subsided, the Chinaman brought from his little tent a large ornate bowl filled with clear water. This he placed in the middle of the floor and, sitting down beside it, produced from somewhere amidst the voluminous folds of his robe a native basket containing several pounds of gray sand. Picking the sand up in handfuls, he poured it into the water, stirring it until the water was of the consistency of thin mud. He then washed his hands and carefully dried them. Then, reaching into the bowl, he scooped up the mud from the bottom and, after muttering a few words, permitted it to pour from between his fingers back into the basket absolutely dry! This he continued to do until he had practically cleared the water. The moment he gathered up the sand it became as dry as it was when first taken from the basket.

Removing the bowl into the seclusion of his tent, the conjurer returned with a wax chrysanthemum, several small strips of tissue paper, and a lovely silk fan. Twisting the little bits of paper, he formed out of each a beautiful butterfly with outspread wings. When he thus fashioned four of these dainty creations, he laid them together on the open side of his fan. Then with a flick of the fan he tossed the paper butterflies into the air and began fanning them. So skilfully did he manipulate the pieces of paper that they never separated but, remaining within about a foot of each other, seemingly came to life. They rose in the air far above his head and, maintained by the motion of the fan, circled about the room and came to rest on the heads and shoulders of various members of the audience. At last after the butterflies had performed several remarkable feats of this nature, the magician called to them and under the direction of his fan the four butterflies finally came to rest together on the open blossom of the chrysanthemum which he held out.

The performance lasted for over an hour, each trick seemingly more difficult than its predecessor. Having at last exhausted the contents of his mysterious little tent, the Chinese juggler packed his equipment and, after passing around a China bowl, which returned to him containing a goodly assortment of coins, he hobbled away, leaving amazement and confusion behind him.

In the grounds of the Raffles Hotel in Singapore we saw one of the finest demonstrations of Oriental magic. We made a desperate effort to photograph the various tricks, but the failing light—for magicians prefer to work in the

The Boy in the Basket Trick

evening—to a certain degree thwarted our purpose. We did, however, succeed in securing a few snapshots of the famous boy-in-the-basket trick, the best of which is reproduced above. The boy-in-the-basket trick is a very famous example of Eastern legerdemain. It has been presented many times on the American stage, but it has never been done in America as well as in India, with the single exception of the troupe of Hindu conjurers who were brought to the World's Fair.

The equipment for the exhibition consists of a large basket, somewhat square and with a circular opening in the top; a cover containing a round hole which fits closely over the opening in the basket; a pointed stake which passes through the hole in the cover; a square of canvas or native cloth; a long, sharp sword; and a scantily-clothed native boy, generally about 14 years old. In the particular instance herein described a net was added to the general equipment. The trick is performed on the open ground with the audience entirely encircling the conjurer. This worthy first seats himself cross-legged upon the ground and plays several notes upon a strange flutelike instrument. After a few moments the native boy appears, generally clothed only in a loin cloth. The lad was securely tied up in a net, which was apparently drawn so tightly about him that he could not move in any direction, and then was forced into the basket, which was barely large enough to contain his body; in fact his head and shoulders extended considerably above the top of the opening. The magician then spread the cloth over the basket. The cloth did not reach entirely to the ground but hung over the rounded sides of the basket. The lid was next placed in position but would not entirely go down because of the protruding head and shoulders of the boy which could be seen through the folds of the cloth. Leaving the basket sitting in the midst of the audience, the conjurer again seated himself, playing a weird and pathetic melody upon his flute. After a few seconds, the lid of the basket slowly dropped into position. Allowing a short interval to pass, the magician then rose and, going over to the basket, inserted the stake in the opening in the lid and with a quick move drove it straight through to the bottom of the basket. The boy had apparently vanished. Withdrawing the stake, the juggler then took his sword and thrust it through all parts of the basket and, taking off the lid, he jumped into the basket and, stamping around, demonstrated its emptiness. Finally, he reached under the cloth and drew forth the net which had enclosed the boy. Allowing a few moments to pass, he replaced the net, returned the cover to its proper position and, sitting down, again played upon his flute. As soon as the first note was struck, the basket began to heave and move, and the lid rose again. Upon removing the cover and canvas, the boy was again found tied up in the net, and it required the assistance of two other men to extricate him from the basket. Observing the profound admiration created by the trick, the magician immediately sent the boy around with a half cocoanut shell to take the customary collection before the enthusiasm had time to cool! All through the evening the magician continued his exhibition until at last finding that he had exhausted the financial resources of his audience, he departed, followed by the members of his troupe.

The Victoria Memorial building in Calcutta is surrounded by quite a park where several snake-charmers can nearly always be found entertaining crowds of natives and tourists. Many people believe that the snakes used by these charmers are not really poisonous. This conclusion is erroneous, for while the serpents represent some of the most poisonous forms of reptiles known, the power which the natives possess over them is uncanny. Though it is undoubtedly true that many claiming to be snake-charmers are impostors, those who are actual representative members of the snake-charmer calling have attained an almost inconceivable degree of control over the snakes they handle. For example: Upon one occasion we saw a native turn a white rat loose among several snakes. One of the reptiles immediately coiled itself around the body of the animal and prepared to devour it. The magician watched closely and when the life of the rodent was just on the verge of being extinguished, he ordered the snake to release the rat. The serpent immediately unwound its coils and returned to its basket, and the magician, picking up the rat, demonstrated that the animal was not injured in any way. A young army officer, watching a snake-charmer one day and noting the impunity with which the native handled his reptiles, suddenly exclaimed: "Why, those snakes won't hurt anybody," and, leaning over, he picked up one of them. He was dead in just fifteen minutes, though every possible effort was made to save his life.

While wandering in the grounds of the Victoria Memorial building we met the interesting personage whose photograph accompanies this article. When first seen, he was sitting down, surrounded by his snakes and a troupe of small boys, the latter as irrepressible in India as in America. Noting the approach of a white man, which meant money, the Hindu prepared his performance. Motioning the boys to keep back, he stood up, his skin gleaming like copper in the humid Indian sunlight. His clothing consisted of a varicolored turban and a rag about his loins. He motioned to a young Mohammedan who stood nearby to loan him his slipper, and the youth with a laugh

A Hindu Snake Charmer

kicked off his scuffer which the juggler then picked up. The slipper consisted of a flat sole and a toe-cap—nothing more. With a quick move, the snake-charmer threw the slipper on the ground at my feet and as I watched there coiled from the toe of it an East Indian cobra at least five feet long. The snake coiled itself around the magician's neck and is the one which appears in this photograph. There is no possible means by which the snake could have been concealed in the toe of a slipper and the scanty clothing worn by the conjurer makes the trick still more difficult of solution.

Benares is a city remarkable for its interesting places and people. The bathing Ghats are famous all over the world and to Benares come the holy, the great, and the good from all over Hindustan. As the evenings are sultry, few care to wander into the dusty streets of the native section of the city, and it is far more pleasant to sit in the hotel grounds and be entertained by some wandering theatrical troupe, a trained elephant, or skilful acrobats.

It was in Benares that we witnessed that most famous of all Oriental illusions—the growing of the mango tree. While there is hardly a country in the world where the story of this trick has not been told, yet, strange to say, the intimate details of it have seldom been described. After placing a number of eggs in a basket and causing them to instantly hatch, the magician next turned to the preparation for the mango tree trick. Finding a suitable place where the ground was smooth and hard, he invited his audience to draw their chairs up closer and detect—if they could—the method by which the illusion was accomplished. The preparation for the trick consisted in securing three sticks about four feet long, which he arranged in the form of an American Indian tepee, covering them to the ground with a large white cloth. He then lifted up one side of the cloth so that it was possible to watch what was going on within the tentlike structure.

Then from his "little bag of tricks" the conjurer produced a large oblong mango seed, which he passed around for careful examination, afterwards requesting one of the audience to carve his initial on the seed pod. This having been done, the magician next produced an empty flower pot which he filled with earth and in which he planted the seed. He then thoroughly watered the earth with a sprinkling can, placed the flower pot with its contents within the tepee-like tent and, dropping the flap, sat down beside the tent and played upon his flute. After about five minutes he lifted the side of the tent and there, protruding from the earth, was a tiny green shoot. Closing the flap again, he continued to play. After a few moments he once more lifted the flap, and a mango bush about a foot in height was growing in the pot. Again he closed the tent and after a few seconds reopened it, revealing a full grown mango bush in blossom. He dropped the flap still another time and when he finally removed the tent entirely the mango bush was covered with ripe mangoes, which he picked and tossed to his audience. Then suddenly he tore the plant up by the roots and, shaking off the dirt, showed the open pod still clinging to the roots and still bearing the initials inscribed thereon at the beginning of the experiment.

The foregoing illusions are representative of the marvelous ingenuity acquired by the Oriental juggler. None of the illusions described involve any use of supernatural power, however; they are all explainable to those acquainted with the artifices of legerdemain, but to the uninitiated they are a never-ending source of wonder. I have discussed with these conjurers the methods by which they attain these remarkable results and it is interesting to note that, while admitting themselves to be only tricksters, they all realize that it is possible to accomplish these illusions without the aid of legerdemain. These very magicians realize that among their own people there are certain illuminated Masters and holy men, capable of growing a tree in fifteen minutes by processes totally unknown to the Western world. The conjurer admits that his illusions are copied from the sacred magic of the East Indian Wise Men. But while these holy ones perform their experiments only in the seclusion of the temple for the purpose of demonstrating to disciples the cosmic principles underlying biology and physics and consequently the multitudes are denied the sight of these marvels, the trickster—with his legerdemain—produces the same effects for the amusement of the populace.

But let us now consider the transcendental magic of the Hindus—that part of their wisdom which has nothing to do with sleight of hand but which demonstrates that certain ones among them do possess a knowledge of superphysics.

While in Calcutta, three examples of true transcendental magic were related to us by a native Brahmin of irreproachable reputation, a well-educated man, a graduate of the Calcutta University, and able to converse in several languages. He did not lie, but described a number of instances which occurred while he was under the guidance of an eminent Hindu holy man recognized not only as one of the true miracle-workers and philosophers but indeed as a living saint.

The young man told me that upon one occasion he retired into the foothills of the Himalayas for a two-year period of meditation and renunciation.

Growing the Mango Tree

One day as he was wandering barefoot through the undergrowth, his Master who was 2,000 miles away suddenly appeared before him and pushed him aside just as he was about to place his foot upon a death-head cobra. I questioned him carefully concerning the details of the incident and he seemed amazed that the entire affair should not be readily conceivable; in fact he asked me if things like that did not happen in America! He further declared that his Master appeared to him in full daylight not once but many times; in fact that by means of telepathy he talked at least once a week with his Teacher who was 2,000 miles away and received satisfactory answers.

The same young man described an experiment in which his Master, in order to explain a certain point in the organic constitution of animals, picked up a rabbit and in the presence of his disciples caused the animal to turn into a rat and then back again. The transformation took place in clear sight in a fully lighted room, and was gradual so that every detail of the process might be carefully analyzed. What is most interesting, the young man could not understand why such an occurrence should be regarded as unusual. He declared that such things were done every day by the holy men of India, but never for curiosity-seekers—only for the edification of their own disciples.

This young man also told a story—which was later verified by others—to the effect that at stated times offerings to the Goddess Kali are made in a certain secluded spot in the foothills of the Himalaya Mountains. The young man's father who had been present at one of these ceremonials had repeated it to him in detail, and we believe that this is the first time the ceremonial has ever been described in English.

On a certain day the holy men gather in a secluded pass, bringing with them offerings of grain, fruit, and goats. The grain and fruits are piled in the midst of an open space and the goats are tethered near by. The holy men then seat themselves in a great circle surrounding the offerings and begin a chant, which continues for a considerable period of time. The ceremony consists of an offering and invocation to the Goddess Kali, asking her to accept the gifts as recompense for the sins of the people and as a peace offering against evil. When a certain point is reached in the chant, a black swirling cloud appears over the distant mountains, resembling, as far as can be ascertained, a miniature cyclone funnel. Swirling and twisting, this funnel approaches nearer and nearer and, finally hovering over the offering, causes the light of the sun to be darkened. In the midst of this funnel stands the Goddess Kali, a gigantic figure with six arms, each carrying an appropriate symbol. In one of her hands the goddess carries a mace or battle-axe and, leaning over, she strikes with it the heaped-up offering. The dark cloud then passes slowly from view, leaving the holy men in sacred ecstacy.

When the chant is finished, the holy men arise and upon reaching the altar of offerings, discover that the goats have all been killed, the fruits and vegetables have all been parched and withered, and of the grain nothing but chaff remains. This is a strange story and several times hints concerning it have reached me, but this is the only complete account that I have ever been able to secure of it. As to the veracity of the story, we have only the word of the natives themselves, for no white man has ever beheld the ceremony. It is inconceivable, however, that the whole population of India should believe implicity in the supernatural, testifying almost to a man that they have personally beheld experiments and demonstrations involving supernatural power, unless there is an element of truth underlying these stories.

I once discussed the problem of miracles with a very learned Brahmin Pundit, and his conclusions on the subject may be summed up as follows: "You Christians believe that Jesus Christ performed miracles. You believe that He turned water into wine; that He raised the dead; healed the sick; passed through a closed door; and multiplied the loaves and fishes. Do you believe that the day of miracles ended 2,000 years ago? Your Jesus told His disciples that greater things than He did they should do. Why, then, do you declare the miracle-working of India to be false? There are no such things as miracles, if you consider the meaning of the word in it last analysis. A miracle is in reality only an effect, the cause of which is unknown. For thousands of years our people have devoted themselves to the study of the invisible worlds and the forces and powers in Nature which are beyond the comprehension of any save those who dedicate their lives to service, asceticism, and virtuous living. We are specialists in matters pertaining to the invisible and the intangible, as you are specialists in those things pertaining to the visible and the tangible. We do not understand each other because our work is in different worlds; we only understand one another when we are engaged in similar labors. India is a land which in your estimation may seem very backward because it is concerned with things which do not interest you and which your people do not understand. Do not doubt or deny the knowledge possessed by Asia. But if you would pass judgment upon that knowledge, come and investigate it and we will show you the proof that you desire. Live as we tell you to live, think as we tell you to think, study with our wise men, and you will then realize that there are among our people certain ones who possess a knowledge which makes them capable of working miracles."

# Notable Reprint

Translated from the "Third Book of the Mathesis" of Julius Firmicus Maternus.

(Note: This work was translated into English in 1831 by Thomas Taylor, the eminent Greek and Latin scholar. The original work is shown in quotation marks, the material not in quotation marks or shown in parentheses being Mr. Taylor's commentaries.)

"O Lollianus, the glory and ornament of our country, it is requisite to know, in the first place, that the God, who is the fabricator of man, produced his form, his condition, and his whole essence, in the image and similitude of the world, nature pointing out the way."

Nature may be said to point out the way, because its forerunning energy is employed by Divinity in the formation of bodies. By *the fabricator,* in the above sentence, Firmicus means Jupiter, who is called the *Demiurgus* by Plato, in the Timæus.

"For he composed the body of man, as well as of the world, from the mixture of the four elements, viz. of fire, water, air, and earth, in order that the conjunction of all these, when they were mingled in due proportion, might adorn an animal in the form of a divine imitation. And thus the Demiurgus exhibited man by the artifice of a divine fabrication, in such a way, that in a small body he might bestow the power and essence of all the elements, nature, for this purpose, bringing them together; and also, so that from the divine spirit, which descended from a celestial intellect, to the support of the mortal body, he might prepare an abode for man, which, though fragile, might be similar to the world. On this account, the five stars (i. e. Saturn, Jupiter, Mars, Venus, Mercury), and also the sun and moon, sustain man by a fiery and eternal agitation, as if he were a minor world; so that the animal which was made in imitation of the world might be governed by an essence similarly divine. Hence those divine men Petosiris and Necepso (two of the most ancient writers of Egyptian astrology, which, in many respects, differs from that of the Chaldeans), who deserve all possible admiration, and whose wisdom approached to the very penetralia of Deity, scientifically delivered to us the geniture of the world, that they might demonstrate and show that man was fashioned conformably to the nature and similitude of the world, and that he is under the dominion of the same principles by which the world itself is governed and contained, and is perennially supported by the companions of perpetuity."

By *the companions of perpetuity,* Firmicus means the stars, whose nature, and motions, and influences are perpetual. Hence, in the Orphic Hymn to the Stars, they are invoked as "Th' *eternal* fathers of whate'er exists."

"According to Æsculapius, therefore, and Anubius (of the astrological Æsculapius, I have not been able to obtain any information; and of Anubius nothing more is to be learnt than that he was a most ancient poet, and wrote an elegy de Horoscopo.), to whom especially the divinity Mercury committed the secrets of the astrological science, the geniture of the world is as follows:

"They constituted the Sun in the 15th part of Leo, the Moon in the

15th part of Cancer, Saturn in the 15th part of Capricorn, Jupiter in the 15th part of Sagittary, Mars in the 15th part of Scorpio, Venus in the 15th part of Libra, Mercury in the 15th part of Virgo, and the Horoscope in the 15th part of Cancer. Conformably to this geniture, therefore, to these conditions of the stars, and the testimonies which they adduce in confirmation of this geniture, they are of opinion that the destinies of men, also, are disposed in accordance with the above arrangement, as may be learnt from that book of Æsculapius which is called Myriogenesis, (i. e. Ten Thousand, or an innumerable multitude of Genitures,) in order that nothing in the several genitures of men may be found to be discordant with the above-mentioned geniture of the world.

"We may see, therefore, how far or after what manner a star accommodates the testimony of its radiation to the luminaries. For the luminaries are the Sun and Moon. But Saturn first conjoins himself with the Moon: for he follows the condition of the Moon. He does this, however, because, being constituted in a feminine sign, he diametrically receives the rays of the Moon, which is also constituted in a feminine sign."

The feminine signs are, Taurus, Cancer, Virgo, Scorpio, Capricornus, and Pisces; but the masculine signs are, Aries, Gemini, Leo, Libra, Sagittarius, and Aquarius.

"But when the same Saturn, in that geniture, makes a transition to the sign Aquarius, he again conjoins himself to the Sun by a similar radiation, and is again disposed in the same condition as that of the Sun. For being constituted in a masculine sign, he associates himself by an equal testimony of radiation, since he diametrically looks towards the Sun, with radiation similar to that with which he regards the Moon. After this manner also Jupiter is constituted in Sagittary, and through a trigon affording a testimony to the Sun, first conjoins himself to his condition, and on this account being constituted in a masculine sign, and associating with the Sun, who is constituted in a sign of the same kind, first follows the power of it; but when he has made a transition to Pisces, he again conjoins himself in a like condition to the Moon. For he, in a similar manner, being posited through a trigon in a feminine sign, looks towards the Moon, who is constituted in a sign of the same kind, with an equal radiation of condition.

"In like manner also the planet Mars, being constituted in Scorpio, because he is in a feminine sign, through a trigon, affords a testimony to the Moon; but when he comes to Aries, he affords a testimony to the Sun, and making a transition, being placed in a masculine sign, he conjoins himself by a trigonic radiation with the Sun. This mode, however, is changeable; for Mars being constituted in Libra, which is a masculine sign, yet he affords a testimony to the Moon through a square aspect; but when he has made a transition to Taurus, being constituted in a feminine sign, and looking towards the Sun by a square radiation, he again affords a testimony to it. These [divine]men, however, were of opinion that the planet Mercury is common in the above-mentioned geniture, this star affording no testimony either to the Sun or Moon by a square, or a trigon, or a diameter; nor does it conjoin itself by radiation either with the Sun or Moon. But if Mercury is a morning star, he is delighted by day with the Sun, but if an evening star, by night with the Moon. All that we have here said, these men were of opinion ought to be observed in the genitures of men, and thought that they could not discover the destiny of man, except those radiations were collected by a sagacious investigation."

It may not be altogether foreign to the purpose to adduce in this place, what is said by Hermes in his Treatise de Revolut. Nativit. lib. i. p. 215. A Latin translation only is extant of this work, and it is uncertain whether the author of it was the celebrated Hermes Trismegistus, or a Hermes of more modern times. This author says that "the dominion of the planets over the ages of man is as follows: The Moon governs the first age, which consists of four years. Mercury governs the second, which consists of ten years. Venus the third, and this extends to eight years. The Sun the fourth, and this age consists of nineteen years. Mars the fifth, and this consists of fifteen years. Jupiter, the sixth, consists of twelve years; and Saturn governs the seventh age, and this extends to the remaining years of human life."

Proclus, also, in his admirable Commentary on the First Alcibiades of Plato, observes that the different ages of our life on the earth correspond to the order of the universe. "For our first age (says he) partakes in an eminent degree of the Lunar energies, as we then live according to a nutritive and physical power. But our second age participates of Mercurial prerogatives, because we then apply ourselves to letters, music, and wrestling. The third age is governed by Venus, because then we begin to produce seed, and the generative powers of nature are put in motion. The fourth age is Solar, for then our youth is in its vigour and full perfection, subsisting as a medium between generation and decay; for such is the order which vigour is allotted. But the fifth age is governed by Mars, in which we principally aspire after power and superiority over others. The sixth age is governed by Jupiter, for in this we given ourselves up to prudence, and pursue an active and political life. And the seventh age is Saturnian, in which it is natural to separate ourselves from generation, and transfer ourselves to an incorporeal life. And thus much we have discussed, in order to procure belief that letters, and the whole education of youth, are suspended from the Mercurial series."

"Lest, however, the fabulous device (Firmicus calls the geniture of the world a *fabulous* device, because it supposes the mundane periods to have had a temporal beginning, though they are in reality eternal. For in a fable, the *inward* is different from the *outward* meaning.) of these men should deceive you, and lest some one should think that this geniture of the world was contrived by these most wise men, without a cause, it is requisite that we should explain all things particularly, in order that the great sagacity displayed in this device, may, by the most diligent expositions, be intimated to all men.

"The world had not a certain day of its origin, nor was there any time in which the world was formed by the counsel of a divine intellect, and providential Deity; nor has the eager desire of human fragility been able to extend itself so far as to conceive or explain the origin of the world, especially since the greater apocatastasis of it, which is effected by a conflagration or a deluge, consists of 300,000 years."

In the greater apocatastasis of the world, which is effected by a deluge or a conflagration, the continent becomes sea, and the sea continent: "This, however," says Olympiodorus, (in his Scholia on the first book of Aristotle's Treatise on Meteors,) "happens in consequence of what is called *the great winter,* and *the great summer.* But *the great winter* is when all the planets become situated in a wintry sign, viz. either in Aquarius or in Pisces. And *the great summer* is when all of them are situated in a summer sign, viz. either in Leo or in Cancer. For as the Sun alone, when he is in Leo, causes summer, but when he is in Capricorn winter, and thus the year is formed, which is so dominated, because the Sun tends to one and the same point, for his restitution

[49]

is from the same to the same,—in like manner there is an arrangement of all the planets effected in long periods of time, which produces the great year. For if all the planets becoming vertical, heat in the same manner as the Sun, but departing from this vertical position refrigerate, it is not unreasonable to suppose that when they become vertical, they produce *a great summer*, but when they have departed from this position, *a great winter*. In *the great winter*, therefore, the continent becomes sea, but in *the great summer* the contrary happens, in consequence of the burning heat, and there being great dryness where there was moisture." At the end, too, of this first book of Aristotle on Meteors, Olympiodorus observes, "that when *the great winter* happens, a part of the earth being deluged, a change then takes place to a more dry condition, till *the great summer* succeeds, which, however, does not cause the corruption of all the earth. For neither was the deluge of Deucalion mundane, since this happened principally in Greece." See the volume of my Aristotle containing this Treatise on Meteors, p. 478, etc. Firmicus, therefore, is mistaken in asserting that a deluge follows a conflagration; since the contrary is true. For it is obviously necessary that places which have been inundated should afterwards become dry, or they would no longer be habitable.

"For the mundane apocatastasis is accustomed to be accomplished by these two events; since a deluge follows a conflagration, because substances which are burnt can not otherwise be renovated and restored to their pristine appearance and form, than by the admixtions and the concrete dust of the ashes, which are a collection of generative seeds becoming prolific. Divine man, therefore, following the example of mathematicians in the genitures of men, have prudently devised this, as if it were the geniture of the world. Hence I deem it expedient to explain the contrivance of that divine composition, in order that the admirable reason of the conjectural scheme may be unfolded according to the rules of art.

"These divine men, therefore, wished so to constitute the Moon [in the geniture of the world], that it might conjoin itself with Saturn, and might deliver the dominion of periodical revolutions. Nor was this improperly devised. For because the first origin of the world [i. e. the beginning of the first mundane period] was uncultivated and rude, and savage through rustic association, and also because barbarous men, having entered on the first vestiges of light, and which were unknown to them, were destitute of reason, in consequence of having abandoned humanity, these divine men were of opinion, that this rustic and barbarous time was Saturnian, that, in imitation of this star, the beginning of life might be characterized by barbaric and inhuman ferocity. After Saturn, Jupiter received periodical power. For to this planet the Moon was conjoined in the second place, in order that pristine and squalid rusticity being deserted, and the ferocity of rude association being laid aside, human life might be cultivated through the purification of the manners. In the third place, the Moon conjoining herself with Mars, delivered to him the power of periodical revolution; so that mortality having entered into the right path of life, and inhumanity being subdued by a certain moderation, all the ornaments of arts and fabrications might originate from this conjunction. After Mars, Venus received predominating power, in order that, human disciplines gradually increasing, prudence and wisdom might adorn mankind. Hence they were of opinion that this time, in which the manners of men were cultivated by learning, and naturally formed to rectitude by the several disciplines, was under the dominion of Venus; so that being protected by the majesty of this joyful and salutary divinity, they might govern their erroneous actions by the ruling power of Providence. But [these divine men] conceived the last period to be under the dominion of Mercury, to whom the Moon in the last place conjoins herself.

"What can be found more subtle than this arrangement? For mankind being purified from rude and savage pursuits, arts also having been invented, and disciplines disposed in an orderly manner, the human race sharpened its inventive power. And because the noble genius in man could not preserve [uniformly] one course of life, the improbity of evil increased from various institutes, and confused manners and the crimes of a life of wickedness prevailed: hence the human race in this period both invented and delivered to others more enormous machinations. On this account these wise men thought that this last period should be assigned to Mercury, so that, in imitation of that star, the human race might give birth to inventions replete with evil." (Is not what is here said about the last period verified in the present age?)

"That nothing, however, may be omitted by us requisite to the elucidation of this subject, all things are to be explained, which prove that man was formed in the imitation and similitude of the world."

Man, says Proclus, is a microcosm, and all such things subsist in him partially, as the world contains divinely and totally. For there is an intellect in us which is in energy, and a rational soul proceeding from the same father, and the same vivific goddess, as the soul of the universe; also an ethereal vehicle analogous to the heavens, and a terrestrial body derived from the four elements, and with which likewise it is co-ordinate.

"And that the mundane apocatastasis is effected through a conflagration and a deluge, we also have asserted, and is confirmed by all men. The substance likewise of the human body, the course of life having received its completion, is, after a similar manner, dissolved. For as often as, through the natural ardour of heat, the human body is too much relaxed, it evaporates in consequence of the inundations of humours; and thus it always suffers a decoction from a fiery ardour, or is dissolved by excessive desudation. Nor do the wisest interpreters of the medical art assert, that the substance of the human race is dissolved by a natural termination in any other way, than by either moisture dissolving fire, or again heat predominating, fire being inwardly and deeply extinguished, is left without moisture. Thus the artificer, Nature, constituted man in an all-various imitation of the world, so that whatever dissolves, or forms the essence of the world, this also should be the cause of the formation and dissolution of man."

Labor

He that in his studies wholly applies himself to labor and exercise, and neglects meditation, loses his time: and he that only applies himself to meditation, and neglects labor and exercise, only wanders and loses himself. The first can never know any thing exactly; his lights will be always intermixed with doubts and obscurities: and the last will only pursue shadows; his knowledge will never be certain, it will never be solid. Labor, but slight not meditation; meditate, but slight not labor.—*Confucius.*

MYSTIC CHRISTIANITY

PHILOSOPHY SCIENCE & RELIGION

The Secret Key to *Mystic* and *Masonic* Christianity

By MANLY P. HALL

It may yet be demonstrated that Christianity is not only ethical but, like all other great World Religions, is both philosophic and scientific.

For 2,000 years the theory of Christianity has been promulgated and its ethics emphasized; yet it is becoming ever more apparent that Christendom is actually without a religion.

Before going further, however, let us define *religion* as distinguished from theology, ecclesiasticism, ritualism, dogma, and those other forms which constitute the composite structure of *Churchianity.*

True religion embraces the arts, sciences, philosophies, and crafts of all races and all nations. Religion is the art of living, the science of being, the philosophy of life, and the truly religious person is the master craftsman.

True religion is therefore impossible without exact knowledge. When theology, divorcing logic and reason, attempted to maintain isolated individualism it forged the first link in a chain of causation which will ultimately destroy the institution of the church.

Christianity awake to its latent powers is indestructible; but Christianity asleep, mumbling idle words which it does not understand or sermonizing from texts whose deeper meanings are unknown, cannot cope successfully with the growing scientific materialism of the 20th century.

The purpose of this article is not to belittle Christianity; it is rather to call attention to the tragic fact that the exponents of Christianity continually and consistently belittle their own faith, by ignoring the true purpose for which Christianity was founded and the ends which it must accomplish if it is to survive.

We are living in an age which has absolutely no time for the consideration of spiritual abstractions. Men and women of today demand facts, not fancies; verities, not conjectures. The universalizing of education has placed intellectual weapons in the hands of every individual, and thus armed man attacks the structure of superstition and theory.

People are no longer afraid to think, and that form of modesty prevalent in past generations which made people fear to discuss subjects about which they understood little is fast disappearing. The serf not only dares to criticise his king but does not hesitate to shout his viewpoints from the house tops. Every man and woman in the modern world is awakening to the realization that he not only has the prerogative of personal opinion but that he also has the right to express that opinion.

This growing individualism sounds the death knell of dogma. · It is no longer a case of follow the leader; each feels within himself the germ of leadership and strikes out for himself into the unexplored byways of thought. Men no longer gather to listen with awe and trembling to the words of the mighty; they now gather to demand their own right to be heard.

If religion is to survive—and religion must survive, for it is the moral structure of humanity—it must survive in harmony with the progressiveness of the age. It must be an active, virile element in society; it must keep pace with the growing minds of men; it must be the energizing power which is always spurring man on to greater and nobler accomplishments.

This does not mean that theologians must gather and evolve a new creed or discover a new religion; it merely means that the time has arrived when humanity is qualified to consider and know the deeper issues of religion— those profound aspects as yet unrevealed to the multitudes.

If theology does not open its gates and reveal to man that knowledge now indispensable to the spiritual culture of humanity, then mankind will rise and storm the citadel of theology, demanding its divine birthright and opportunity to know and understand the secret workings of Nature.

Theology for centuries has manifested an exclusive spirit, whereas the fundamental principle of true religion is inclusiveness. But the day is at hand when the walls of creeds and cults must crumble and the human soul be ushered into a new concept—Universalism.

The keynote to the religion of the future will be that man himself is the maker of his destiny. Religion will then reveal to man his divine potentialities and, equipping him with the knowledge of the true nature and purpose of his existence, send him forth to achieve individual immortality through accomplishment. We were once accused of being an individualist because we believed that each individual must work out his own salvation. The thought of being personally responsible for the actions and attitudes of self, of being forced unassisted and alone to work out the destiny of self, of being required by Nature's infinite plan to attain with infinite toil the salvation of self may overwhelm that type of mind which for ages has leaned upon the clergy and permitted others to dream for them, think for them, live for them, and—all too often—die for them!

We affirm that Christianity contains a doctrine acceptable to the progressive minds of the 20th century; Christianity contains a doctrine sufficient to meet not only the needs of today but the needs of uncounted centuries to come, and so exact that it complements science and philosophy.

Religion, philosophy, and science form a great trinity. Alone each is incomplete; together they constitute knowledge. Real knowledge is the understanding of the whole of a thing; ignorance is a partial understanding of the parts of a thing. No scientist can ever attain to true knowledge unless he adds to science religion and philosophy. No theologian will ever understand religion until he adds to his theological thought the findings of science and philosophy. The religious institution of tomorrow will be a structure housing under one roof the laboratory, the university, and the church.

The first step toward a true understanding of Christianity is the realization that there is something in that faith as yet unknown; that beneath its popular concepts is concealed a profound something as yet unrecognized by the mass of mere churchgoers.

Some may say, "Why hasn't Dr. Jones ever mentioned this fact?" or, "It can't be so or my minister would have told me." Alas! in all probability, the minister did not know, for the secret doctrine is not discussed in theological seminaries and those who should understand it best know least about it. Again, there are some who, realizing its existence, fear to speak lest a misunderstanding world reward them as it rewarded the great thinkers of the past by boiling them in oil or breaking them upon the rack and wheel.

Do not imagine that the secret doctrine of Christianity is known to only one or two; it is known to many, but the discovery of it generally follows a period of agnosticism in which the mind, recognizing the fallacy of the existing system and rebelling against organized religious ignorance, seeks in its own way to understand the mysteries of life.

The body of Christianity is twofold in its structure. These divisions may be likened to the two persons who make up each individual. If you will consider yourself as double instead of single, there is first the you which is visible and which may be termed the personality, and then there is the you which is invisible or the real and intangible self. The visible, mercurial you is born and dies; it passes through joy and sorrow, limited in its expression to the visible world in which it dwells, but the invisible you is immortal, unchangeable and unlimited. As the invisible you is the real you, so the invisible church is the real church.

Accordingly, the rituals and ceremonials of religion bear the same relation to the spirit of religion that your hands and feet bear to that invisible and intangible divinity within yourself. The church is the material body of Christianity as your physical form is the house of your spirit. Foolish people, looking at the house, believe that your body is really yourself; but the wise, looking not at the body but through the body, see the divine spark of God enthroned within each form of clay.

As the body of man is born, grows, ages, and dies, so great world religions come into being, remain for a short time, and then pass out of existence. But as the spirit in man does not die though the body perish, so the spirit of religion remains indestructible and immortal through all its metamorphoses of form. Truth is not extinguished with the downfall of its house any more than man perishes with the death of his body.

All the great world religions have promulgated the same doctrine, which was divided into two parts—one part constituting the body and the other the spirit of the faith. The sacred books preserve the body and tangible parts of a religious doctrine; the spiritual and intangible parts of every faith are never committed to writing but are communicated orally to a few illumined minds in each generation. This unwritten part is the spirit or the secret doctrine of every religion.

While the body of each faith differs radically from the bodies of all other faiths, the secret doctrine of all faiths is identical. The same analogy exists in the constitution of man, for whereas there is an infinite multiplicity of personalities the spirit of every creature is composed of but one substance— namely the nature or essence of God Himself.

It is sad to realize that in this 20th century so many of the great religions have forgotten that within their constitution is concealed a secret doctrine— the spirit of their faith. Religionists have forgotten that the letter of the law killeth but that the spirit of the law giveth life. They are unaware that the real purpose for the existence of any religion is to perpetuate this secret doctrine and disseminate it to those qualified to sense its profundities.

This article is devoted to outlining the nature and purpose of this secret doctrine concealed beneath the rubbish of dogma and creed; it is devoted to the proposition that beneath the emblems, allegories, myths, parables, and symbols of every religious system is concealed a certain divine teaching, the understanding of which constitutes a proper religious education.

First of all, we must realize that the literal explanation of the mysteries of religion is not the true one, and those who are satisfied to accept hollow words without inquiring into their hidden meaning will never attain to the secret doctrine of religion.

Before it is possible to approach this hidden mystery of religion, the mind must also become acquainted with certain forms of specific knowledge indispensable to properly estimate spiritual realities. The untrained mind cannot think intelligently and dispassionately. The insurmountable obstacle in theology is the astigmatic mental vision of its exponents.

All too often, faith paralyzes reason, for what we believe we do not think about, and what we accept without thought is, in the last analysis, valueless! The major failing of theology is its total indifference to the claims of logic and reason. For centuries the religious world has been taught to regard as unpardonable heresy man's divine prerogative of honest doubt. Thus the theologically-trained person is at a decided disadvantage, for he has lost the use of those God-given intellectual faculties which enable him to discriminate between the verities and the illusions of religion—the essentials and non-essentials of salvation.

Faith and belief are indispensable qualities of the soul, but all faith and no thought produces the religious fanatic and the theological bigot who, knowing nothing, declares ignorance—which he misnames faith—to be the supreme ideal of religion!

The secret doctrine in Christianity may be briefly summed up in the following words: There is an exact science by means of which man can come into harmony with the laws of Nature, which laws manifest the will of God for His creation. It is not only possible to study the visible world with its flora and fauna, but it is also possible to study with equal accuracy the invisible world which is the original and the ultimate home of the spiritual nature of man. Sin, suffering, sickness, and death, are the inevitable result of spiritual ignorance. While to a certain degree they can be controlled by material knowledge, they can never be entirely eradicated until the individual understands the exact nature of himself.

In the New Testament much emphasis is laid upon the fact that man is the living temple of the living God. This thought is of far greater import than the average person comprehends. It implies that the ceremonies and rituals enacted within places of worship obscurely signify certain processes and adjustments which must take place within the body of every individual who would become religious.

Christianity was the outgrowth of the ethical teachings disseminated by that illustrious Son of Man—Jesus the *Christ*-ened. Jesus was a member of the Essene Order. The Essenes were a community of holy men, living in a rambling lamasary or monastery on the side of Mt. Tabor. This community was a branch of a much older organization having its headquarters near Lake Maoris in the heart of ancient Egypt.

The abstract origin of the Essenes has been a matter of much controversy. Some believe them to have been of Brahmin or Buddhistic extraction, while others claim that they were the outgrowth of Pythagorean speculation. Be that as it may, the Essenes were an ascetic group bound together by mutual ideals and aspirations. They existed in the Holy Land as evidence of disagreement with the orthodox interpretation of Jewish theology. Their purpose was to study and interpret the writings of Moses and the prophets according to the secret doctrine which they realized existed beneath the popularly accepted version of the Scriptures.

Little doubt exists that Jesus was educated by the Essenes, instructed in their secret teachings, and afterwards initiated into the Essene Mysteries. The Gospels preserve the story of his initiation in their description of the wanderings and temptation of Jesus in the wilderness.

Robed in the white seamless garment of the Essenes, with his hair and beard uncut according to the fashion of the Essenes, Jesus wandered forth preaching and teaching the secret doctrine of the Jews, and—because of the knowledge of the inner workings of Nature which come to those who under-stand the law—performing miracles and possessing powers beyond the com-prehension of ordinary men.

In the simplicity of their lives and the loftiness of their ideals the Essenes represented the true principles of mystic Christianity. They also represented pristine Christianity inasmuch as they were renowned throughout Asia Minor for their wisdom and integrity. Learned in medicine, law, astronomy and music, the Essenes were employed by the Roman officers stationed in Judea in the capacity of scribes, tutors, and general instructors of the young.

The Essenes were Orientalists in their methods of living: they prayed, meditated, and fasted like the holy men of the Far East and they attained spirituality by consecrating themselves to the service of humanity and the impersonal dissemination of truth and righteousness.

The first ideals of Christianity were concerned with healing the sick, cleansing the lepers, raising the dead, and casting out demons, by which the early Christians desired it to be understood that they healed those who were spiritually sick; that they cleansed man from the leprosy of sin; that they raised him from the death of ignorance; and that they cast out of him the demons of avarice, and lust, and passion.

During the first centuries of Christianity the Christian faith—like the pagan doctrines in the midst of which it was established—was celebrated in the form of Mysteries. Gradually the church grew up about the Mystery until this secret doctrine in Christianity was apparently lost sight of, at least it disappeared from the sight and cognition of the world.

Realizing in common with the true philosophic minds of all generations, that all religions are in reality steps in the unfoldment of Universal Truth as a whole, it becomes apparent that Christianity preserved within the structure of its outer doctrine the same secret teachings which were the prized possessions of the Egyptians, Persians, Greeks and Brahmins.

All arts, religions, philosophies, and sciences may be divided into two general divisions—theory and practice. In other words, religion may be considered as twofold: speculative and operative. We have had nearly 2,000 years of speculative Christianity. During this period atrocities unmentionable have been perpetrated in the name of the lowly Nazarene; a thousand times has Christ been crucified by His church.

Speculative Christianity has sent Christian nations at each other's throats in war and conflict; it has persecuted heathendom; it has blessed the munitions of war in its cathedrals; it has forced the Prince of Peace to march at the head of armies whose avowed purpose was conquest and plunder.

Speculative Christianity has resulted in the faith promulgated by the man Jesus being split up into countless contending factions, who by their lack of charity for each other demonstrate their lack of understanding. Specu-lative Christianity has become a vast material institution, already deeply enmeshed in the bonds of commercialism, competition and crystallization.

While speculative Christianity seems hopeless involved in its theories and notions founded upon the shifting sands of theological opinion, operative Christianity represents the exact science of salvation.

Consider, if you will, the profundity of the thought, *the exact science of salvation*. All over the world the cry goes up: "What does God expect of me?" No one seems to know and those who teach are as ignorant as those who listen. The time has come when the world must realize the true function of religion and just what position it occupies in the plan of human progress. The world must now consider religion from a hitherto unfamiliar viewpoint: it must consider religion in the light of an exact science and must not cease its search after the fundamental principles of religion until it has discovered the keys to the mystery of life, as these lie buried under the debris of theology's fallen house.

Space will only permit a consideration of one of these secret keys: namely, the place occupied by the functions and parts of the human body in relationship to the exact science of individual salvation.

According to the secret teaching, each individual must work out with diligence his own destiny and salvation. As the Christian and Essene Mysteries were fundamentally similar to those of the Greeks, we will clothe our story in the terminology of the Greek Mysteries, bearing in mind, however, that the material set forth actually represents part of the Mystery doctrine incorporated into Christianity but now practically lost.

The universe is divided into three distinct parts which are called the three worlds: that is, heaven, earth and hell. The triple tiara of the Pope is symbolic of Christianity's sovereignty over these three worlds. As the words *heaven, earth,* and *hell* have lost their original meanings, it may be better to substitute for them names whose meanings are more apparent. We will therefore call heaven the *supreme* world; earth, the *superior* world; and hell, the *inferior* world. The supreme world is spirit; the superior world is soul, or mind; and the inferior world is matter. The ruler of the supreme world is called the *Father;* the ruler of the superior world, the *Son;* and the ruler of the inferior world, the *Holy Spirit.* Thus the creative Trinity of Father, Son, and Holy Spirit, represents the personified attributes of these three worlds.

The supreme world is the home of the gods: that is, the personifications of the immortal principles. The superior world is the home of the demigods and heroes: that is, the gods who partake of mortality and the men who partake of immortality. It is also the home of the ministering spirits: that is, the personifications of natural law. The inferior world is the physical universe, and is the home of humanity and several kingdoms of subhuman life. The inferior world is under the control of Pluton, or Father Dis, the regent of the dead, for by analogy the inferior world is the *hell* of orthodox Christianity.

As the universe consists of these three universal planes—the supreme world, the superior world, and the inferior world—so man, constructed in the image of the universe, is likewise a triune being existing in three worlds or spheres of consciousness. The divine spirit of man, being composed of the substance of the immortal gods, exists in the supreme sphere. The soul and mind of man, being composed of the substance of the immortal heroes and mortal gods, exists in the superior sphere. The body of man, being composed of the substance of the material universe, exists in the inferior world. These three parts—spirit, soul-mind, and body—each existing in its own sphere, when compounded together result in the partially rational immortal-mortal: man.

According to the Mysteries, the supreme sphere in man corresponds to a secret area within the intricacies of the human heart. Within the heart is the flame composed of the immortals. Thus the heart represents the temple of Olympus, within the halls and galleries of which dwell the twelve gods. These twelve, by their combination, constitute the Supreme Intelligence referred to as the *Father*.

The superior sphere corresponds in man to the brain, which is the dwelling place of the god-men who hide themselves within its structure as the holy men of India hide themselves within their caves at the head of the Ganges River.

The inferior world has its human correspondent in the generative system, for the material world exists solely through the generative processes, and the generative processes of Nature are epitomized in the generative processes of man.

A momentary digression will show how the analogy works out. The Holy Spirit is sometimes called the *Holy Ghost*. A ghost is the shadow of a reality. We generally consider it to be an intangible form—a wraith or specter. A moment's consideration, however, will demonstrate that the material world and all the forms that exist within it are the ghosts, or shadows, of the divine, intangible spiritual natures of existing things. Thus the universal form is called the Holy Ghost—the shadow of Divinity. The generative processes by means of which the ghosts of form are brought into temporary existence are said to be under the Holy Spirit, or shadow-building power of Divinity.

In Masonic emblemism the same fact is presented but in a slightly different manner. The three kings—or actually two kings and a cunning workman—represent the threefold spirit of man manifesting in the three worlds or spheres of existence and engaged in the construction of a threefold temple in man. The order may be considered as follows: the supreme sphere is the dwelling place of the Universal Spirit, designated in Masonry *King Solomon;* the superior sphere is the dwelling place of the Individual Spirit, designated *King Hiram of Tyre;* and the inferior sphere is the dwelling place of the Personal Spirit, designated *Hiram Abiff.* Thus King Solomon represents the activity of spirit in the spiritual world; King Hiram of Tyre represents the activity of spirit in the intellectual, or soul, world; and Hiram Abiff —the widow's son—represents the activity of spirit in the material world.

Hiram Abiff is the master-builder. He represents that form of divine energy which, obeying the laws of the Creative Mind, organizes matter into the Universal Temple. In other words, Hiram Abiff is the Universal Spirit of material organization. All forms are the result of his handiwork and every form is a Solomon's Temple, for whether it be a grain of sand or a solar system it is a house built in honor of, and as a habitation for, the living God.

From earliest times the various secret schools of the Mysteries have had as their supreme allegory the myth or legend of the "dying god"—the supreme creature who descended into the worlds of men and was murdered for the sins of humanity. In India it was Krishna; in Greece, Prometheus; in Scandinavia, Balder the Beautiful; among the Central American Indians, Quexalcoatl. This god, dying upon the cross, is the Masonic Hiram Abiff murdered by the elements of the inferior world, among the essences of which he has been commissioned to erect the Eternal House.

Hiram Abiff—the Masonic martyr—is not only Plato's divine man who was crucified when the worlds were formed, but is also that part of man's spirit which he calls I AM and which enters into matter at the time of physical birth. Therefore, at the very moment of birth the builder is murdered and the body which he has formed becomes his tomb. This body—the living house of the "martyred" god—is therefore well termed "the holy sepulchre." Man's physical form, controlled by his passions, his greeds, his selfishness, and his animal nature, is the holy sepulchre of the Templars, which is indeed in the hands of the infidel.

Recognizing that at the moment of physical birth the blow with the mallet is delivered and the spirit is buried over the brow of the hill (the diaphragm) upon which stands the temple (the heart), the activities of life must then be devoted to the resurrection of the dying god.

Jacob Boehme symbolizes the germ or seed of the martyred builder as being planted in the heart. When man, by an absolute and technical knowledge of the process of human regeneration, actually begins the labor of raising the dead builder, the seed in the heart grows into a mighty tree which reaches upward and blossoms in the brain. This is the Tree of Life which grows in the midst of the Garden of the Lord and which bestows immortality.

Thus the secret teaching is to the effect that the murdered builder—or, to be more exact, the builder who was buried alive in the temple which he had built (the body)—is by a technical knowledge preserved from remote antiquity brought to life again. This resurrection of the dead is termed in Christianity the "second coming of Christ" and is the consummation of a religious life.

The above represents only an infinitesimal fraction of the stupendous structure of religion. Religion is the master science of all ages, for the mastery of its complexities requires a profound knowledge of all arts, all philosophies, and all sciences. The day is at hand when religion must recognize the dignity of its own estate.

STATEMENT OF THE OWNERSHIP, MANAGEMENT, CIRCULATION, ETC., REQUIRED BY THE ACT OF CONGRESS OF AUGUST 24, 1912,

Of The All-Seeing Eye published monthly at Los Angeles, California, for April 1st, 1927.

STATE OF CALIFORNIA, } ss.
COUNTY OF LOS ANGELES }

Before me, a Notary Public in and for the State and county aforesaid, personally appeared Harry S. Gerhart, who, having been duly sworn according to law, deposes and says that he is the Managing Editor of The All-Seeing Eye and that the following is, to the best of his knowledge and belief, a true statement of the ownership, management (and if a daily paper, the circulation), etc., of the aforesaid publication for the date shown in the above caption, required by the Act of August 24, 1912, embodied in section 411, Postal Laws and Regulations, printed on the reverse of this form, to-wit:

1. That the names and addresees of the publisher, editor, managing editor, and business managers are:
Publisher, The Hall Publishing Company, Los Angeles, Calif.
Editor, Manly P. Hall, Los Angeles, Calif.
Managing Editor, Harry S. Gerhart, Los Angeles, Calif.
Business Manager, Harry S. Gerhart, Los Angeles, Calif.

2. That the owner is:
The Hall Publishing Company, Manly P. Hall, 301 Trinity Auditorium Bldg., Los Angeles, Calif.; Maud F. Galigher, 301 Trinity Auditorium Bldg., Los Angeles, Calif.

3. That the known bondholders, mortgagees, and other security holders or holding 1 per cent or more of total amount of bonds, mortgages, or other securities are: None.

4. That the two paragraphs next above, giving the names of the owners, stockholders, and security holders, if any, contain not only the list of stockholders and security holders as they appear upon the books of the company but also, in cases where the stockholder or security holder appears upon the books of the company as trustee or in any other fiduciary relation, the name of the person or corporation for whom such trustee is acting, is given; also that the said two paragraphs contain statements embracing affiant's full knowledge and belief as to the circumstances and conditions under which stockholders and security holders who do not appear upon the books of the company as trustees, hold stock and securities in a capacity other than that of a bona fide owner; and this affiant has no reason to believe that any other person, association, or corporation has any interest direct or indirect in the said stock, bonds, or other securities than as so stated by him.

HARRY S. GERHART, Managing Editor.

Sworn to and subscribed before me this 2nd day of May, 1927.

(SEAL.)   MAY MILLER.
(My commission expires March 26, 1931.)

uestions & answers·

A Department Maintained for the Convenience of the Reader

Q. Do you advocate people who think along progressive lines joining various organizations and brotherhoods promulgating certain religious, philosophical, and ethical codes? If so, will you kindly give the names of such sects and groups as you could recommend.—M. M. S.

A. This question must be considered from several angles. In the first place, it has often been said that in organization there is strength. But is it not also true that this strength is of the organization and not of the individual? Groups of people—either in communities or in organizations—depending upon each other for mutual support and mutual enlightenment, all too often lose both their individuality and their independence. Thus while the strength of the entire is continually increased by new recruits, it is a question just what effect is produced upon the recruit.

In the second place, motive is the deciding factor in many of these problems. Why does an individual join an organization? Is his purpose to lean upon or to be leaned upon? If he is weak, he will lean upon any strong personality with whom he comes in contact; and if he is strong, it will not be long before the greater part of an organization will be leaning upon him and he will be denounced by that vast number of leaners who will immediately become envious of his intelligence if he possesses any. Most people who join religious and philosophical organizations do so for what they can get and not for what they can give, and a large group composed of individuals with axes to grind has very little to offer to an active, independent intellect.

In the third place, organizations have a consistent habit of being inconsistent and inconstant in their doctrines and tenets. Today you may be able to vouch for everything they do; tomorrow their policies may be widely at variance with your ideals. Most organizations, moreover, do not contain more than one real mind. This mind is reflected in the membership. When this individual mind changes its opinions, the membership—chameleonlike—changes its mental and spiritual shades to match the background. Those who will not change, branching out, form a new society until what was once a single train of thought becomes a seven-headed Hydra with all the heads biting at each other.

In the fourth place, organizations are segregative and separative. If you join an organization, the world considers you as championing the doctrines and codes promulgated by that group with which you have associated yourself. The saddest part of this feature is that the world also considers you as being opposed to and irreconcilably against those other organizations and individuals whose ideals are at variance with the cult that you have accepted. In other words, the world says that if you are for one thing you must be against all else, or if actual animosity does not exist there must be at least a dangerous indifference.

In the fifth place, it is a well known fact that crystallization is the keynote of the physical world and vitalization the keynote of the spiritual world. Organizations seemingly cannot exist without crystallization nad crystallization gradually produces in spiritual movements the same condition that it produces in the physical body: age, disease, suffering and death. Death is the separation of conscious life from a vehicle no longer capable of giving its expression. All spiritual truths die when their vehicles become crystallized, and no organization has yet been formed which has been able to escape the inevitable dissolution resulting from crystallization. If the organization could die without involving the individuals who compose it, things would not be so bad. When the mind has followed and accepted dogma and creed for a certain length of time it becomes incapable of individual estimation, and the decay of the organization—by destroying the crutch upon which those lean who have lost the power to stand alone—leaves its component parts hopeless, helpless, and useless.

In the sixth place, the modern world lacks the solidarity of antiquity. We are a generation of superficial thinkers and therefore the products of our thought are superficial and impermanent. The organizations and institutions of antiquity stood for centuries because their founders and members represented the highest types of intellect. The ranks of the ancient educational and spiritual orders were not composed of easy believers. Each member dared to think his own thoughts, live his own life, and doubt anything that did not seem reasonable to his senses. Ancient religion was not a process of acceptation; every theory advanced was discussed and accepted or rejected upon the basis of its intrinsic merit. If modern organizations were of a standard conformable to those of the ancients, they would be of vastly greater value, although being organizations they must meet the inevitable fate of organizations—crystallization. Modern cults are all too often the brainstorms of honest but mentally incompetent persons who, fired with aspiration but lacking logic, reason, and philosophical education, are not properly qualified to finish the task they have begun.

In the seventh place, we are unfortunately living in an age of commercialization, which as surely has permeated our philosophical world as it has our material sphere. A great number of cults and creeds have been foisted upon the public not by philosophers and mystics but by financiers. Many of these have been eminently successful, as the disillusioned members will testify after the bubble has burst. In this respect it may be truthfully said that the devil has quoted Scripture with profit. Indeed, it has become quite a problem now to decide when joining an organization whether it will lead you to heaven or to the poor farm.

In the eighth place, spiritual and philosophical societies are the breeding grounds for the most dangerous forms of hero-worship extant. It is positively amazing to note how quickly half a dozen foolish people can make a demigod out of a seventh poor sinner. It is our firm belief that no person who ever worshipped a man understood him, but nearly all groups of people seem concerned with the perpetual deification of some poor, hard-working, long-suffering human being who may have died of starvation, whose words are quoted as Scripture, and whose accomplishments form the axis of the organization.

Having considered the arguments against affiliation with religious and philosophic organizations, it is only fair to present the other side of the proposition. There are two outstanding reasons why affiliation with the right kind of a group may attain a definite and constructive end.

(1) In an age which organizes and incorporates all forms of activity,

it is almost impossible for religion, philosophy, and ethics to survive unless they combat material organization with spiritual organization. Single individuals are overwhelmed by the mass movement of a materially organized civilization. Unless those interested in maintaining the high standards of culture absolutely indispensable to the survival of the race pool their strength, modern commercialism may totally obliterate creative idealism.

(2) Man's mind is tremendously influenced by what takes place about him. A child will study more faithfully at school than at home because in the schoolroom there are numbers of other children doing the same thing. There is also a certain amount of vanity involved. No individual likes to exhibit less capacity and intelligence than the person next to him. Thus organization offers a twofold motive for greater accomplishment: the stimulus of environment and the stimulus of personal vanity.

There are several organizations of a philosophic, religious and fraternal nature in America and other parts of the world that are actually accomplishing a great amount of good. Our position does not permit us to actually name them, nor could we conscientiously assume the personal responsibility of deflecting the mind of another person into any prescribed channel of thought and activity. Therefore, we can only suggest that in matters pertaining to organization an acid test be applied. We will suppose that you feel an inward urge to associate yourself wtih some group interested in philosophic or religious studies. You should investigate the matter very carefully, realizing that in all probability many of your future actions will be influenced by the code promulgated by that particular cult.

Do not be in haste to join new movements that have not had an opportunity for time to pass upon their merits. Time is the heartless critic, continually denouncing and exposing weakness, falseness and inconsistency. On the other hand, do not condemn that which is new but, restraining both enthusiasm and criticism, judge all things by their works.

There are good organizations, bad organizations, and indifferent organizations. Good organizations are in every case progressive, altruistic, educational, non-commercial and impersonal. They seek to build individual characters, teaching men how to think rather than what to think.

Bad organizations are usually non-progressive, penurious, bigoted, commercial and personal. They are usually built up about some individual who believes that he can increase his own power and position by having an organization back of him. In many cases such individuals depend on superstition for the attainment of their ends. They have long and curious names, weird and hair-raising mysteries. They conceal themselves behind a barrage of meaningless bombast so that those entering the cult cannot get close enough to find out how little the great man knows!

Indifferent organizations are those which, being neither hot nor cold, meet the sad fate prescribed for such: the Lord speweth them out of His mouth.

If you desire to join an organization for spiritual, philosophic or ethical betterment, feeling that you have not yet reached the place where you are qualified to decide for yourself that which is best for your immortal soul, we suggest that you search out an organization as loosely organized as possible, for many a noble enterprise has been hobbled by its own red tape. Go to a group that makes no profession that it is wiser or greater than others but in modesty and simplicity is diligently striving to work out its salvation. Shun as you would the plague deep and profound secrets, unutterable mysteries, and ten-dollar admission fees. Beware of mechanical cults which grind out "initiates" in strings like sausages. If possible, find a group that is in some way connected with the ancient systems of philosophy and thought. Eschew exclusiveness and permit yourself to be involved in nothing that isn't big enough to recognize the good in all men, the wisdom in all religions, and that truth belongs to no man. Beware, most of all, of any group or cult which is the self-appointed and sole custodian of truth, for all groups or individuals who believe that they are the only ones to whom God has communicated His divine knowledge brand themselves false prophets.

Classical Humor

The whale who had just swallowed Jonah discovered the prophet to be decidedly indigestible. The entire structure of the great amphibian was torn with internal unrest. "Oh-h-h," muttered the whale, "If I had only kept my mouth shut this would never have happened."

This month's popular scientific note is of intense practical value. In simple words, an amoeba is a microscopic Protozoa of the class Rhizopoda. The class Rhizopoda, including the orders Lobosa, Foraminifera, Heliozoa and Radiolaria, is remarkable for its pseudopodia.

Once upon a time there was a man who did not read his Bible very often. Like a great many other good Christians, he kept the Book on his table as a paper weight. One day this backslider was moved to pick up the Bible, and his eyes fell on a few words at the top of one of the pages. He read, "And Judas went out and hanged himself." He turned a few more pages and glanced at the words. This time it said, "Go thou and do likewise." And the man read no further.

Once a poor man desired to join a very fashionable church. (We don't know why.) He called upon the rector and expressed his wish. The reverend gentleman looked the shabbily dressed man over very critically with a mental picture of the effect of this man's appearance among the elite of his congregation. The minister then said: "Before you take this important step I think you should go home and pray for a week or two. When the Lord has made known His will in the matter, come back and we will talk it over again." Very well pleased with his diplomacy, the rector ushered out his visitor.

Two days later the poor man called again, to the dismay of the minister. The poor man spoke: "You need not worry, I had a long talk with God, and I am no longer trying to join your church. I told God I wanted to get into your church and He told me it was no use, that He had been trying to get in Himself for ten years."

LECTURE PROGRAM

The Church of the People

Trinity Auditorium   Ninth Street and Grand Ave.

MANLY P. HALL

Friday, May 20th, 8 P. M.

"The Mysteries of Light, Color, and Sound"

Mr. Hall's first lecture on this subject in Los Angeles

Sunday, May 22nd, 10:30 A. M.

"The King of Kings"

Sunday, May 29th, 10:30 A. M.

"The Platonic Solution of the Riddle of Life"

Sunday, June 5th, 10:30 A. M.

Prologue: "Father Damien"
"St. Francis of Assisi—His Sermon to the Birds"

THE LYCEUM

Beginning May 22nd, 9:30 A. M., the Lyceum will move to the left wing of the main floor of Trinity Auditorium. "The Purpose and Possibilities of a Lyceum"—Manly P. Hall will speak.

You Are Cordially Invited to All These Lectures
Come and Bring Your Friends

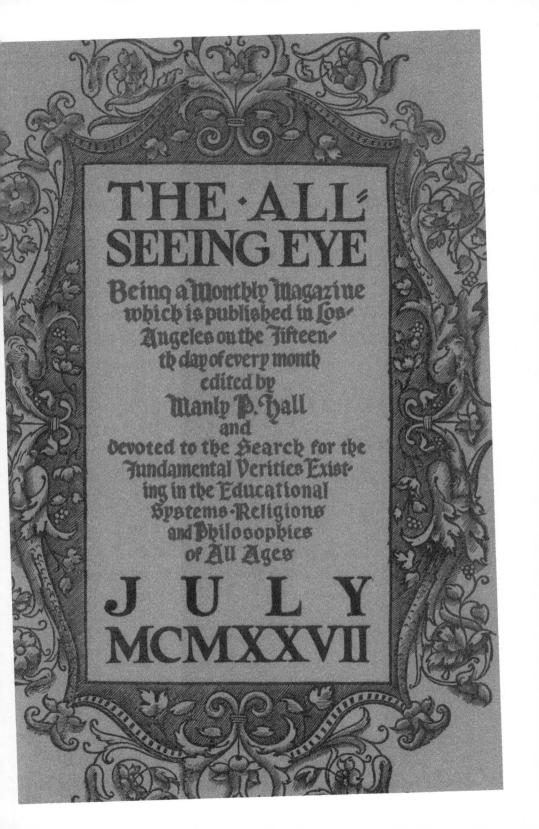

THE · ALL· SEEING EYE

Being a Monthly Magazine
which is published in Los-
Angeles on the Fifteen-
th day of every month
edited by
Manly P. Hall
and
devoted to the Search for the
Fundamental Verities Existing in the Educational
Systems-Religions
and Philosophies
of All Ages

J U L Y
MCMXXVII

The ALL-SEEING EYE

DEVOTED TO THE SEARCH FOR THE
FUNDAMENTAL VERITIES EXIST-
ING IN THE EDUCATIONAL
SYSTEMS, RELIGIONS,
AND PHILOSOPHIES
OF ALL AGES

VOL. IV	JULY, 1927	No. 3

Published Every Month by

THE HALL PUBLISHING COMPANY

301 Trinity Auditorium Building,
Ninth at Grand Avenue, Los Angeles, California

Manly P. Hall . . . . *Editor*
Harry S. Gerhart . . . . *Managing Editor*
Maud F. Galigher . . . . *Associate Editor*
Howard W. Wookey . . . . *Art Director*

CONTENTS

Change of address must be in this office not later than the first of the month preceding issue. Please give both old and new addresses.

Copyright, 1927, by the Hall Publishing Company

*Entered as second-class matter February 11, 1927, at the post office at Los Angeles,
California, under the act of March 3, 1879*

Per Copy, 25c—Six Months $1.00—One Year $2.00
Foreign, Six Months $1.15—One Year $2.25

Do You Know?

That punctuation marks were first used about 250 B. C. by Aristophanes of Alexandria.

That the original brazen serpent which Moses raised in the wilderness is supposed to be in the Church of St. Ambrose, at Milan!

That when pins were invented in the 14th century the maker was only permitted to sell them on the first and second day of each January.

That there is a newspaper in China that has been issued regularly for nearly one thousand years. It was originally printed from hand-carved wooden blocks.

That one of the first and most important Christian hymns was composed by the pagan Emperor Hadrian. The hymn was later paraphrased by Alexander Pope.

That the horseshoe became a symbol of good luck because it resembled in shape the metallic halos or glories which were so often placed behind the heads of saints.

That the little child whom Jesus called unto him, as related in the second verse of the eighteenth chapter of St. Matthew, was Ignatius, Bishop and martyr of Antioch, according to existing tradition. .

That the word "bedlam," which is popularly interpreted to mean confusion and uproar, was a corruption of the word "Bethlehem," a name given to one of the first insane asylums in London.

That Giles de Laval Marshal de Retz, who was born in France about 1396 was the original Bluebeard. The partially destroyed bodies of forty-six victims were found in his castle at the time of his arrest. He had given himself to the practice of black magic.

The EDITOR'S BRIEFS

Smashing Shams

Strange letters come in the early mail. We received one yesterday from a gentleman who took issue with us on a number of subjects, declaring— among other things—that our Sunday morning sermon, "The Platonic Solution of the Riddle of Life," was devoid of spirituality and comparatively meaningless to him.

We fully realize that to a mind unfamiliar with our platform, many of our statements might have sounded like heresy of the most dangerous type, especially since this was the first time the gentleman had ever attended one of our lectures.

This friend disputed our right to question the authenticity or inspired source of any of the scriptural writings, evidently overlooking such infamous proceedings as those which took place at the Council of Nicæa, through which no book—however sacred—could have passed intact.

Our correspondent also evidently has not traced the origins of religious faiths or studied their growth and unfoldment through all the generations of the past. Like millions of others, he has accepted as literal truth statements which cannot fail to mislead unless their inner meanings be accurately interpreted.

Investigation has proved beyond any reasonable doubt that the scriptural writings of nearly all nations have been tampered with and their true meanings distorted. Though it may shock our correspondent, we affirm that the opening chapters of the book of Genesis are not only inadequately translated but the text is hopelessly disfigured and the order of the verses and chapters inextricably mixed. If he does not wish to take our word for this, we would recommend that he consult any authority on archaic Hebrew, who will tell him that if he beheld an accurate translation of the document it would be unrecognizable. It will probably be impossible ever to restore completely the original meanings of such books as Genesis and Revelation, but no one acquainted with ancient languages and the idiosyncrasies of the early priestcrafts can rationally accept as infallible the existing versions of the various sacred books.

We have been accused of being unchristian in our attitude toward religion; in fact, an eminent local divine once declined to debate the evolution problem with us on the ground that we were not a Christian. Since our opinions when first heard may appear rather "heathenish," we shall take this opportunity to define our true position in this matter.

We believe in Christianity but we can never be made to accept the false doctrines now palmed off as fundamental elements in Christianity. There is no sacred book which today possesses sufficient authority to convince us of the existence of the orthodox hell. We can never be convinced that the damnation of any creature is possible in a universe ruled over by a beneficent Father, nor has it ever seemed reasonable to us that any individual should lose his soul because he was not baptized or that his soul could be saved by joining any church.

Centuries before the Christian Era, Gautama Buddha tore the veil from the Brahmin temple and preached a doctrine which emancipated the *Sudras* (slaves). The holy man with the yellow robe hurled his thunderbolts at the institution of caste, declaring that the Creator of the universe had intended all men to see the light of truth and to live in the luminance of hope. In Greece Pythagoras initiated his own slaves, who then became famous exponents of his philosophy.

Five hundred years later a lowly Syrian, son of a carpenter, overturned the caste system of the Jews and brought down upon his head the wrath of those who had long maintained themselves upon the ignorance of their fellow men.

There are two kinds of people in the world seeking for wisdom. The first desire to know that they may be greater than their brothers and use this superiority for the attainment of personal ends. The second desire to know that they may disseminate this knowledge and thus supply all men with the key to self-emancipation.

Sometime in the infancy of humanity those who sought to enslave mankind so that they could make of human creatures beasts of burden forged chains of fear to shackle minds and bodies. Thus came into being that man-made demon *Superstition* which transformed God's beautiful universe into a hellish phantasmagoria.

Down through the ages selfish persons discovered that they could control the lives of the ignorant and materially profit thereby by peopling the elements with imps and goblins or by threatening damnation to those untutored souls who did not realize that God, being all of creation, could not consistently permit parts of Himself to roast on some infernal grate!

With malice aforethought man fashioned a devil in his own image and gave it the name and appearance of the leading deity in the pantheon of some rival cult. Christianity, for example, realizing that Pan was the most universally revered of the Greek deities, metamorphosed him—horns and hoofs—into the lord of *Pan*demonium. Under the character of Satan it also ridiculed the pagan Saturn, and the Jews after their return from the Captivity fabricated Beelzebub to show their scorn for the leading deity of the Babylonians. So much for the geniture of the devil! He is anybody's concept of God except our own.

Devil-worship usurped the position once occupied by religion. Man no longer served God so much for the sake of good as through fear of evil. Places of worship became havens of refuge where benighted souls huddled together, fearing to sally forth lest they be swallowed up by the yawning jaws of perdition. Otherwise intelligent persons shuddered at the sight of their own shadows, believing that green-eyed, fork-tailed monsters, with the wings of bats and the feet of roosters, lurked in every dark corner ready to snatch away their immortal souls if their words or thoughts smacked of heresy.

Let us consider those things regarded as heresy. For some it was heresy to cook on Sunday; for others to laugh on the Sabbath day. To question the orthodox interpretations of the sacred writings was to insure eternal damnation; to doubt the efficacy of dogma was to earn a brimstone pit. In fact, to think at all was sufficient provocation to consign the thinker to excruciating torture through all the uncounted aeons of the hereafter.

We believe that the *love* of God is the foundation of religion; we do not believe that the *fear* of God is the beginning of wisdom. The inconsistent, irascible, intolerant, merciless, belligerent, anthropomorphic Deity—created by the crafty and venerated by the foolish—exists nowhere save in superstition-ridden minds.

Let us go back and consider the original teachings of the great World Emancipators—those who have brought to humanity a message of liberation from the servitude of superstition and intolerance. In every case you will find simple and direct moral or philosophical codes, without cults, creeds, dogma or sham. Take, for example, the lofty idealism of Buddha, a natural philosopher, whose simple tenets brought hope and freedom to the burdened slaves of India. He taught neither of gods nor of devils, but one branch of his church today has nearly 80,000 deities, most of whom are demons. With a few exceptions, the exalted and divinely beautiful faith which he established is now the hotbed of degrading superstitions.

Living in the 20th century, we may flatter ourselves with the thought that we are free from the mummeries of the ancient and medieval worlds. If we indulge ourselves in such Pharisaical boasting, we are due for a rude awakening, for the entire fabric of our religious systems—both Christian and so-called heathen—is permeated with superstition. There is a good reason why religion is losing its hold upon the minds of this generation: the educated faculties of the modern thinker no longer will permit him either to worship a Deity whose moral character is inferior to his own or to fear a devil of whose existence there is no possible evidence.

It is difficult to realize the hold which fear and superstition still retain upon the minds of the race. The entire structure of modern religious thought is erected upon the foundation of superstition and, being founded upon the shifting sand of unreality, that structure must eventually topple and fall into cosmic oblivion.

A great number of people are looking forward to the coming of another World Teacher—that intellect or group of intellects who will deliver the keynote to the next era of progress. The question has been asked many times, "What will be the dominant note of the next great message to mankind?"

We can only judge the future by the past. Looking back over the annals of history, it is notable that the great World Teachers have attained their ends by a process of elimination. In each case they tore down some false and unnatural impediment to the onward march of truth. They struck at great world attitudes and delivered man from the false creations of his own mind; for man needs not to be delivered from evil but from his own false mental concepts of evil.

MAN IS SAVED WHEN HE IS DELIVERED FROM BONDAGE TO HIS OWN NOTIONS!

For thousands of years the caste system paralyzed progress, and by its elimination mankind was brought out of the darkness of an institution that had outlived its usefulness. Since the dawn of time man has been oppressed by fear and superstition, and we believe that the next great Teacher will direct the smashing hammer blows of his divinely-given power against the most subtle, the most terrible, and the most paralyzing influence in the world today—the fear of the unknown.

There will come a voice crying in the wilderness, "God is good; life is eternal. In all the world what is there to fear?" This messenger will

[69]

tell humanity that the great system of theology is a lifeless, meaningless superstition—a fabric venerated for ages but in reality the substance of a dream. This messenger will show man that the universe is supremely good, that the unknown Fabricator of it is supremely wise, and that all things are combining together to work for the ultimate good of the whole.

Let us analyze some of the superstitions that must be destroyed before religion can grow to perfect flower and fruitage.

(1) The first superstition is the belief that man is capable of making up the mind of God. No man can say whether God be one, three, five, seven, or a multitude; nor is God's immutable nature changed by any man-made conclusion regarding Its number. "I AM THAT I AM," saith the Lord. "He is what I make him," says man. But the Deity remains unmoved and unchanged by all these things. Furthermore, God has delegated to no man the prerogative of damning in Its name the greatest or the least thing in the universe. No man has more *pull* with God than another nor is God closer to one man than to another. The man does not live who has seen the full magnitude of the Deity. God is not a man nor made in the image of a man, and all theories concerning God's appearance are mere notions. God is the eternal Principle of Good, the active power of the universe, impersonal and eternal. It bows to no man, favors no man above another, and forgives no man more than another. Being in equal proximity to all creation, It needs no mediator between Itself and humanity, for It is humanity, and no man needs to beg audience with that power which is in reality himself.

(2) The second superstition is the belief that God is sectarian in Its religious viewpoints. No place of worship exists that is big enough to include It or small enough to exclude It. To God there is neither Jew nor Gentile, Christian nor heathen. Such preferential distinctions are as inconceivable as would be the controversy of the cells of the human body over a place of worship. All churches—if they be true to the principles of Universal Truth—are churches of God; and all churches which deviate from Universal Truth cease to represent it in the world. We take note of the "heathen," failing to realize that the Spirit of God is omnipresent in every stone or piece of clay that enters into the construction of our buildings. As everything that exists is God, the only real heathen is he who does not realize that God is universal and no respecter of persons.

(3) The third superstition is the invention of *heaven* and *hell*. "Where does man go when he dies?" is the question. Wherever it be, it is in God's universe; therefore in God Itself. The belief in a power of evil and its ability to control the universe is founded upon nothingness. There is no place for *hell* in the nature of the Supreme One; he who believes in *hell* and a *devil* blasphemes his God.

It was Buddha who said, "If God does not prevent evil, He is not good; and if He cannot prevent evil, He is not God." Against this argument nothing can prevail; from this logic there is no appeal.

We are not attacking religion nor do we discredit the faith of any man—we are attacking those shams and superstitions which have crept into the faiths of mankind and made them unworthy representatives of God in the world. We believe that the major part of the structures of modern religions is not only useless in the spiritual evolution of the race but also widely at variance with the tenets of their founders. We are worshipping

(Continued on Page 83)

PHILOSOPHY SCIENCE & RELIGION

The Mysteries of Light, Sound and Color

By MANLY P. HALL

"Light," writes Dr. Edwin D. Babbitt, "reveals the glories of the external world and yet is the most glorious of them all. It gives beauty, reveals beauty and is itself most beautiful. It is the analyzer, the truth-teller and the exposer of shams, for it shows things as they are. Its infinite streams measure off the universe and flow into our telescopes from stars which are quintillions of miles distant. On the other hand, it descends to objects inconceivably small, and reveals through the microscope objects fifty millions of times less than can be seen by the naked eye. Like all other fine forces, its movement is wonderfully soft, and yet penetrating and powerful. Without its vivifying influence vegetable, animal and human life must immediately perish from the earth, and general ruin take place. We shall do well, then, to consider this potential and beautiful principle of light and its component colors, for the more deeply we penetrate into its inner laws, the more will it present itself as a marvelous store-house of power to vitalize, heal, refine and delight mankind."

The Pythagoreans declared the body of God to be composed of the substance of light, and among nearly all ancient peoples the sun was accepted as the embodiment of the Principle of Good. Even the most untutored and primitive types recognized the solar orb as the distributer of life, light, and heat. In order to symbolize the solar activity the Egyptians frequently pictured the sun's rays as ending in human hands. Such a representation may be seen on the throne chair of Tut-ankh-Amen. It is noteworthy that the initiated priestcraft recognized the true relationship existing between the visible sun and an invisible spiritual source, for they often portrayed the sun as a shield upon the arm of the God of Day. Upon this shield the light of the invisible spiritual Divinity was focussed and reflected into the lower worlds.

As light is the basic physical manifestation of life and bathes all creation in its radiance, it is important to realize in part at least the nature of this divine power. What we call light is really a rate of vibration causing certain reactions upon the optic nerve of the human eye. Few realize how they are walled in by the limitations of the sense-perceptions. There is not only a great deal more to light than anyone has ever seen but there are also unknown forms of light which our optical equipment will never permit us to register. There are unnumbered colors we cannot see, sounds we cannot hear, flavors we cannot taste, odors we cannot smell, and substances we cannot feel. Man is thus surrounded by a universe of which he knows nothing because he has no center of reaction within himself capable of responding to the rates of vibration of which this universe is composed.

Consider briefly the nature of space. Great is the riddle of that solid emptiness which men call space—that limitless area of life lying outside the narrow range of our senses. Space is a vast expanse of crisscrossing energies, swirling eddies of force, and blending clouds of varicolored light. Space is a great world peopled with countless beings and containing inconceivable hierarchies of evolving lives. We are as uncognizable to these invisible universes as they are to us, for our habitation is to them the emptiness of space as their habitation is to us the emptiness of space.

Even science has recognized that space is not a vacuum, for it has postulated a mysterious element called *ether* to serve as the medium between force and form. This ether may be likened to the hard rubber phonograph record upon which is imprinted sound in the form of tiny little ridges and hollows. Ether preserves the individuality of vibratory waves and, although unable to see or analyze their hypothetical medium, science realizes that such a medium must exist; that space is not really what it seems to be but is a vast field of organized activity incessantly animated by ripples of energy which cause the tiny molecules to dance and vibrate with an exuberance of cosmic force.

Vibration is the supreme manifestation of the Incomprehensible Divinity. It is the key to individualization and the mainspring of both sentient and insensate life. Thrilling the entire fabric of existence, it maintains Gods, men, and molecules in vibrant animation. While recognizing vibration as the underlying cause of the phenomena of being, modern thought is as yet unable to comprehend either the nature of this mysterious force or the relationship it occupies to the Universal Creator.

The Mysteries taught that in the beginning the Infinite One circumscribed an area in eternity, building around it the intangible yet imperishable wall which has been designated the *universal egg*. The space existing within this egg was permeated with the nature of Deity; therefore, being filled with Divine Life, no emptiness could exist within it. As gradually the divine essences entered into the sleep of material creation and worlds were fabricated within the nature of the supreme God-filled space, a division took place— matter came temporarily into existence. Matter is the negative pole of being and, while intrinsically divine, is actually the least cognizable degree of spirit. Thus matter—being farther separated from spiritual energization than space —in reality is relative emptiness in the midst of absolute fullness.

Both spirit and matter are rates of vibration, one of which is always battling against the other. Spirit, being higher in its vibratory rate than matter, is continually vivifying and vitalizing those bodies with which it comes in contact, thus heightening their vibratory power and resulting in their growth, evolution or refinement. On the other hand, matter—being grosser and less mobile—absorbs into itself the vibratory rates of spirit and, because it is slow to respond, swallows up or partially nullifies the powerful forces of spirit. Ultimately, matter will be reabsorbed into the nature of spirit and the two rates of vibration blended in the condition of the higher. By analogy the material constitution of man will ultimately be reabsorbed into his spiritual nature as previously it was exuded from it. Life was prior to form and will exist after form has returned again to its own source. Spirit is all-pervading; matter is an impermanent condition of spirit and eventually must retire into its conditionless source. Therefore, mortality is a material—and not a spiritual—condition, for matter is the only substance capable of dissolution.

The three rulers of the universe—the first and eternal Trinity—consist of one subjectified and two objectified powers, each existing in a sphere of being like unto its own nature. For convenience these three powers may be clothed in Christian terminology and be called the Father, the Son, and the Holy Spirit. The first power—the Father—dwells in abstract space. It is

One, perfect and eternal, the source and summit of the many, the first and invisible Monad, the Hidden One, indescribable, Whose name is unutterable, Whose nature indefinable, Whose supremacy inconceivable, and Whose absolute life permeates the entire area circumscribed by the wall of the *universal egg*. By the Pythagoreans It was symbolized as a point—the dark germ, the seed from which will spring forth the inverted tree of objective creation. As the source of sound, It is soundless; as the source of color, It is colorless; and as the source of light, It is lightless. This first person of the Divine Triad is the dark flame of which all things bear witness but which bears witness of nothing. Its dwelling place is the first world and It is inseparably and eternally one—Father, Mother, and Child; in Its nature there is no division.

The second power—the Son—is Light Spirit Which came forth out of Dark Spirit and bears witness to Its Father, of Whose substance It is formed and of Whose nature It partakes to a certain degree. As Dark Spirit was the point, so Light Spirit is the line which comes forth from the point and is the outpouring of the One into the many. Within It is the nature of the Father and whosoever beholds it beholds the radiance of the Father, for It is Light born of Life. It is called the second person because It is posterior to Its own Source, for if light be removed life remains, but if life be removed there can be no light. Now the light of the Son is white—the all-inclusive ray—containing within Its nature the spectrum and being opposite to Its own Source—the impenetrable black of the Father. The dwelling place of the Son is the second world, the intellectual sphere, which connects the abstract darkness of the Father with the elemental darkness of the lower world. This is the white ray that takes up Its abode in the elemental darkness that the darkness may be redeemed. This is the second flame. Of the colors It is all; of the musical notes It is all; and Its ultimate condition or state is reabsorption back into the nature of Its Father.

The Son may be likened to the flame of an oil lamp and the dark hidden Father to the oil or the fuel of the lamp, for the wick of the Son is deep in the eternal substance which is the Source of all life. All that is good partakes of the nature of light; all that inspires growth, attainment or understanding may be appropriately symbolized as radiant and glorious. The lamp has long been the symbol of learning and it is said the olden philosophers studied their sacred books with the aid of a waxen candle whose steady glow signified that light within the soul which makes the nature capable of understanding the truths set forth upon the written page. Fire is the most sacred of the elements because it radiates light and has its source in the one flame by which the universe is animated. The life of all things partakes of the natures of light and fire, and the bodies of all things partake of the natures of water and earth. Water is the sacred medium of fire and the germinal life of fire is accepted into the nature of water, wherein it germinates and later comes into expression as one of the many forms of organized activity. This is the real key to the symbolism of the Madonna. The baby Sun-God is the solar life— the Divine Seed—and the Virgin Mother is the watery, or humid, element which is the carrier or vehicle of the Seed.

The third power—the Holy Spirit, the Demiurgus of the world, the Fabricator and Controller of the inferior spheres—may be likened to a prism upon which the white light of the Son is broken up into seven streaming colors. The sum of these seven may be termed the *Lord of Form,* whereas the source of them—which is above the sphere of form—is the golden-white light of the Son. As the Father was the point and the Son the line, so the

Holy Spirit is the circumference of the mystical and spiritual circle of existence. Being the substance from which the lower world is fabricated, all terrestrial nature exists within Him; His consciousness, dwelling in the highest sphere of terrestrial substance, breaks itself up into a multiplicity of powers which were termed the angels, archangels, and the mundane deities of the ancients; and these under His direction move upon the face of the deep and organize the essences of the third world—the inferior sphere—into the dwelling place of material forms. Thus He is called the *Lord of the Underworld.* His scepter is vibration, by means of which He manipulates the gross elements of His universe. His three primary and four secondary parts become personified in the planets, in the colors, in the musical notes, and in all the septenary divisions of Nature. He is the third flame and, combined with the two previous aspects of the Trinity, constitutes the triple flaming Godhead worshipped under the mysterious monosyllable A.U.M. Such is briefly the divine structure of the universe. From an analysis of its septenary constitution the ancients created a language dealing principally with the abstractions of occult cosmogony and clothed these abstractions in the language of color and sound which—because their divisions correspond with the divisions of the universe during its creative processes—were appropriate types of cosmic activities.

Light is the universal symbol of Truth. Darkness, on the other hand, is the symbol of the lack of that Truth. Therefore, the great battle between light and darkness in reality is the struggle of wisdom to overcome its adversary—ignorance. The sun is the flaming altar in the center of the solar system, about which the planets with their attendant moons circle in the rhythmic dance of the spheres. Dancing was originally a sacred art created to express the harmonious motion of the world. In the midst of the dancers stood the great God Pan, lord of the mundane sphere, whose pipe of seven reeds signified the septenary division of celestial harmonics. The modern world has never been able to completely unravel the Pythagorean mystery of planetary harmony designated by the Greeks as the "music of the spheres."

Everything in Nature has a triune constitution composed of (1) a color, (2) a sound or tone equivalent, and (3) a form, although in the last analysis the color and sound are both form. Any creature can be profoundly influenced if its keynote or key color first be ascertained. In fact, it is possible to disintegrate any known substance by its key tone. This is not necessarily limited to animate life, for even such objects as glass, wood, steel or stone may be splintered or shattered if their keynotes be sounded. In the same way, the invisible constitution of each individual has a predominating key color. Two people with the same key color cannot influence each other, but one can overpower and overshadow the life of another if a powerful color value in his nature has a weak correspondent in the nature of the person he seeks to overcome. A practical demonstration of this may be discovered from a study of nurses and physicians. It is impossible for a nurse to be successful with a patient if the color values in her invisible constitution be inharmonious with those of the patient. A doctor will experience the same difficulty. The knowledge of these color values is frequently employed in transcendental magic, especially black art or sorcery.

The theory of music may have been discovered in either India or Egypt—in all probability, the former. It is quite possible that Orpheus, the founder of the Hellenic School, was a Hindoo; if not, he certainly studied with the illuminated minds of Asia. Orpheus is accredited with having constructed a seven-stringed instrument, upon which he played such perfect melodies that the wild beasts and birds gathered around him captivated by his harmonies.

After the lapse of those centuries which divide the modern world from the first Greek civilization, it is impossible to describe with any degree of accuracy the Orphic system of music. In fact it is quite probable that the seven-stringed lyre was not an instrument but merely a symbol of the Orphic system of philosophy which was founded upon a septenary division of the universe. The Greeks did not consider music to be a basic art. They regarded it as dependent upon mathematics. In fact, among the ancients the most important school of music was not harmonic but canonic, the Canonic School affirming that harmonies were governed by mathematics and that intervals which did not conform to the mathematical key to natural law were not harmonic, regardless of how pleasing they might be to the ear. As a result the Greeks made use of several tone intervals now considered discordant and rejected others incorporated into the modern theory of harmony.

The Greek Mysteries included in their doctrines a remarkable concept concerning the relationship of music to form. The elements of architecture, for example, were considered as comparable to musical notes or as having a musical counterpart. Consequently when a building was erected in which a number of these elements were combined, the structure was then likened to a musical chord, which chord was harmonic only when it fully satisfied the mathematical requirements of harmonic intervals. Thus a certain chord was said to be the *keynote* of the edifice. The late Enrico Caruso used to demonstrate this principle of the keynote with a glass tumbler. First striking the tumbler several times to ascertain its tonal pitch, he would then reproduce it with his own voice. After singing for a few seconds, the glass would be shattered to bits. In all likelihood, this is the true explanation concealed in the story of the walls of Jericho which fell when the trumpets of Israel were sounded. By applying the same principle in a manner now unknown, a disciple of Pythagoras once prevented a guest from murdering his host. After striking a few notes upon a lyre, the angry man with drawn sword trembled like a leaf and was unable to move until the musician ceased his playing.

Every element in Nature has its individual keynote. When these elements are combined in a composite unit the result is a chord which, when sounded, will disintegrate the compound into its integral parts. In like manner, each individual has a keynote which, when sounded, will destroy him. An organ pipe was recently manufactured which cannot be sounded alone without its vibration destroying not only the organ itself but also any building in which it might be placed. Such is the power of vibration.

In the construction of their temples the Greeks made use in remarkable ways of their knowledge of the principle of vibration. A great part of their rituals consisted of invocations and intonements. Special sound chambers were constructed and the sound waves reverberating through them were so intensified that a word whispered by the high priest would cause the entire building to sway and be filled with a deafening roar. The very wood and stone used in the construction of their sacred buildings eventually became so thoroughly permeated with the sound vibrations of their religious ceremonies that when struck they would yield the same tones repeatedly impressed into their substances by the rituals. It will yet be demonstrated by a logical process that one man—if he possessed the power—could with a single word destroy the world by intoning the harmonic chord of the mundane spheres.

Pythagoras is accredited with the discovery of the musical intervals of the diatonic scale. In his *Life of Pythagoras,* Iamblichus describes the curious incident which first led the seer of Samos to evolve the theory of musical steps or intervals. One day Pythagoras chanced to pass a brazier's shop where workmen were pounding out a piece of iron upon an anvil. By noting the difference in pitch between the sounds of the different hammer blows and their resultant harmony or discord, he gained his first clue to the musical intervals of the diatonic scale. Entering the shop, he found that the difference in pitch was due to the difference in size of the hammers. After carefully examining the tools and making an accurate estimate of their weight, he returned home and constructed an arm of wood to extend across the room from one wall to the other. At regular intervals along this arm he attached four cords, all being of the same composition, size, and length. At the lower end of each cord he then tied weights of different magnitude to correspond to the different sizes of the hammers. To the first cord he attached a 12-pound weight, to the second a 9-pound weight, to the third an 8-pound weight, and to the fourth a 6-pound weight. He then discovered that the first and fourth strings when sounded together produced a symphony diapason, or the octave, for doubling the weight produced the same effect as halving the string. The weight of the first string being twice that of the fourth, their ratio was said to be 2 : 1, or duple. By similar experimentation he ascertained that the first and third strings when sounded together produced the symphony diapente. The weight of the first string being half again as much as the third, their ratio was said to be 3 : 2, or sesquialter. The second and fourth strings having the same ratio as the first and third, when sounded together also produced another symphony diapente. The first and second strings when sounded together produced a symphony diatessaron. The weight of the first string being a third again as much as the second, their ratio was said to be 4 : 3, or sesquitertian. The third and fourth strings having the same ratio as the first and second, when sounded together also produced another symphony diatessaron. The second and third strings were said to have the ratio of 9 : 8, or epogdoan.

Having thus developed the system of musical steps for his diatonic scale, Pythagoras invented a number of musical instruments based upon the octave and its harmonic intervals, applying his system not only to stringed instruments but also to bells and flutes.

It is of special note that the Pythagoreans regarded music as the key to the mystery of life, for having discovered the existence of certain harmonic intervals in Nature Pythagoras thereupon proceeded to establish the harmonic relationships of the planets, constellations, and elements to each other. The outgrowth of his efforts was the formulation of that most important—but least known—of his doctrines: the *music of the spheres.*

Pythagoras also applied the newly discovered harmonic principle of music to the art of healing, developing a form of vibrotherapy which produced almost miraculous results. He also composed songs for various purposes: some to relax the nerves, others to produce sleep, and still others to increase the mental capacity. His experiments with the effect of music upon the human body also led to the discovery of the healing value possessed by certain poems, and he often cured his disciples of various ailments by reciting poetry to them. The Pythagoreans made a wide application of the principle of vibration and to the Pythagorean system of spiritual, intellectual, and material culture the modern world will yet pay its full measure of tribute.

(Continued on Page 84)

Notable Reprint

An Illustration of the Deep Principles of Jacob Behmen

THE TEUTONIC THEOSOPHER, IN THIRTEEN FIGURES,
LEFT BY THE REVEREND WILLIAM LAW, M. A.

Number 1:

God, without all Nature and Creature. The Unformed Word in Trinity without all Nature. The Eternal Unity, or Oneness, deeper than any Thought can reach. Alpha and Omega; the Eternal Beginning and the Eternal End, the First and the Last. The greatest Softness, Meekness, Stillness, etc. Nothing and All. Eternal Liberty. Abyss, without Ground, Time, and Place. The Still Eternity. *Mysterium Magnum* without Nature. Chaos. The Mirror of Wonders, or Wonderful Eye of Eternity. The first Temperature, or Temperature in Nothingness; a Calm, Serene Habitation, but without all Luster and Glory. The Trinity Unmanifest, or rather, that Triune Unsearchable Being, which cannot be an Object of any created Understanding.

I H V H

Number 1

Number 2:

The three first. (Sal, Sulphur, and Mercury.) The Triangle in Nature. The inferior, restless Part of Nature. The Properties of Darkness. The Root of Fire. The Wheel of Nature. The three Properties on the Left Hand, appropriable in a Sense unto the Father, Son, and Spirit. The Hellish World, if in a Creature divorced from the Three on the Right. *N. B.* Virgin. . . . Opposite to what in the Light World is called Virgin Wisdom.

Number 3:

The Fourth Property of Eternal Nature. The Magic Fire. The Fire World. The First Principle. The Generation of the Cross. The Strength, Might and Power of Eternal Nature. The Abyss's or Eternal Liberty's Opening in the dark World, breaking and consuming all the strong Attraction of Darkness. The Distinguishing Mark, standing in the Midst between three and three, looking with the first Crack [impact] (made in the first, gross and rough Harshness) into the Dark World; and with the second joyful Crack [impact] (made in

[77]

the second, soft, watery or conquered Harshness) into the Light World; and giving unto each what it is capable of, viz. Might, Strength, Terror, etc., unto the former, but Light, Splendor, Luster and Glory, unto the latter.

Number 4:

The three Exalted, Tinctured, or Transmuted Properties on the Right Hand. The Kingdom of Love, Light, and Glory. The Second Principle. The Second Temperature, or Temperature in Substantiality. The Trinity manifested, which only now can be an Object of a created Understanding. Byss. Wisdom. Tincture.

Number 5:

The four first Figures were, in some Manner, to show (according to the deep and wonderful Manifestation of the Divine Spirit, given to *Jacob Behmen)* the Generation of Eternal Nature, which has a Beginning without Beginning, and an End without End. This fifth repre-

Number 2

sents now, that this great Royal Residence, or Divine Habitation of Glory of GOD the Father, GOD the Son, and GOD the Holy Ghost, was replenished at once with innumerable Inhabitants, All Glorious Flames of Fire, All Children of GOD, and All Ministering Spirits, divided in three Hierarchies (each of such an Extent, that no Limits can be perceived, and yet not infinite) according to that Holy Number Three. But we know the Names only of two of them, which are *Michael* and *Uriel,* because only these two, with all their Hosts, kept their Habitation in the Light.

Number 6:

Here now one of those three Hierarchs, even the most glorious of them, because he was the Created Representative of GOD the Son, commits High Treason, revolts, lets his dark proud Will-Spirit, in a false *Magia,*

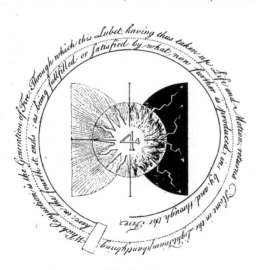

Number 3

without any Occasion given him from without, out of his own Center fly up on high, above God and all the Hosts of Heaven, to be himself All in All; but he is resisted, and precipitated down, and falls through the Fire into eternal Darkness, in which he is a mighty Prince over his own Legions, but in Reality a poor Prisoner, and an infamous Executioner of the Wrath of God; and may now well be reproached, and asked, How art thou fallen from Heaven, O *Lucifer,* Son of the Morning? To which Question a profound, prolix, distinct, most particular and circumstantial Answer is given, in the *Auroră,* to his eternal Shame and Confusion, which he had hid and covered from the Beginning of the World.

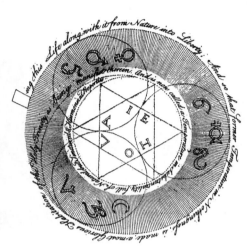

Number 4

Number 7:

When *Lucifer* by his Rebellion had brought the whole Extent of his Kingdom into such a desolate Condition, that it was, as *Moses* describes it, without Form and Void, and Darkness was upon the Face of the Deep, that whole Region was justly taken away from under his Dominion, and transformed into such another meaner and temporary Condition, that it could no more be of any Use to him. And when this was fully settled in Six Days' Time, according to the Six Active Spirits of eternal Nature, so that it wanted nothing more but a Prince and Ruler, instead of him who had forsaken his Habitation in the Light, *ADAM* was created in the Image and Likeness of GOD, an Epitome, or Compendium of the whole Universe, by the *VERBUM FIAT,* which was the Eternal Word, in Conjunction with the first Astringent Fountain-Spirit of Eternal Nature.

Number 8:

This *ADAM,* though he was indeed created in a State of Innocence, Purity, Integrity and Perfection, could not yet stand on that Top of Perfection which he was designed for, and would have been drawn up into, if he had stood his Trial, for which there was an absolute Necessity.

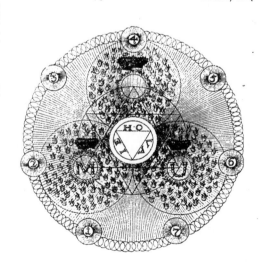

Number 5

Three Things there were that laid a Claim to *Adam,* and though they stood within him in an equal Temperature, yet did they not so without him, for *Lucifer* had made a Breach. These three Things were, (1) above him

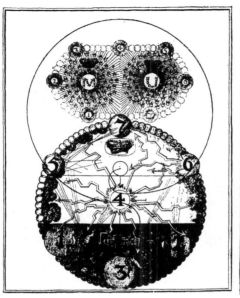

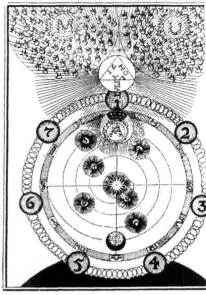

Number 6

Number 7

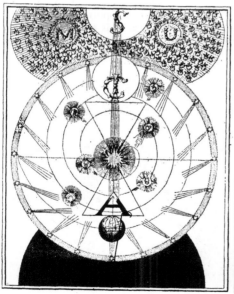

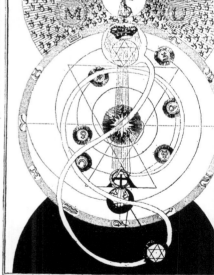

Number 10

Number 11

SOPHIA, called his Companion, and the Wife of his Youth. (2) SATAN, that uncreated dark Root in the Beginningless Beginning of eternal Nature. And (3) the SPIRIT OF THIS WORLD. And herein lies the Ground

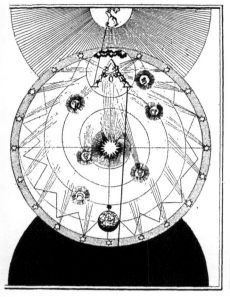

Number 8

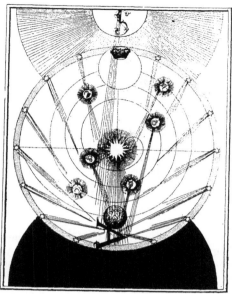

Number 9

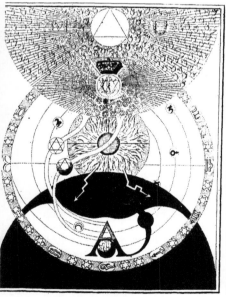

Number 12

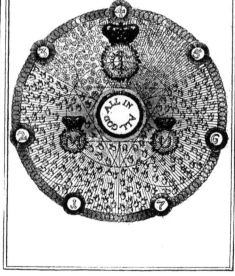

Number 13

of the Necessity of *Adam's* Temptation. In this Consideration the Devil comes not yet in, though he is not far out of the Way; nor the Tree of the Knowledge of Good and Evil; because this was but a necessary Consequence

of *Adam's* wavering, and dealing treacherously with the Wife of his Youth.
Number 9:

Here now is poor *Adam* actually fallen away from all his former Happiness and Glory, and has lost whatsoever was good and desirable both in himself and round about him: He lies as dead, on the outmost Borders of the Spirit of this World. SOPHIA has forsaken him, or rather he, having dealt treacherously, has forsaken Her, and the Holy Band of the Marriage-Covenant that was between them is dissolved: He is all over dark, and lies even under the Earth, over which he was to rule: All the Stars shoot their Influences upon him, of which the very best are but Death and Poison to that Life for which he was created: And nothing less could he expect, but that every Moment he should be quite drawn down and swallowed up in the Belly of Satan. This was his State and Condition after his Transgression, and before he heard the Word of Free Grace, *that the Woman's Seed should bruise the Serpent's Head.*
Number 10:

Here *Adam,* by that Word of Grace treasured up in his Heart, whose Name is JESUS, is raised again so far, that he can stand above the Earthly Globe, upon the Basis of a fiery Triangle [upright triangle] which is an excellent Emblem of his own Soul, and the Holy Name JESUS stands above him upon the Top of a watery Triangle [inverted triangle] and these two Triangles, which in *Adam's* Fall were divorced from each other, do now touch each other again, though (in this Beginning) but in one Point; that the Soul's Desire may draw down into itself the [inverted triangle] and that Holy Name may draw up into itself more and more the [upright triangle] till these two make up a complete [interlaced triangle] the most significant Character in all the Universe: For only then the Work of Regeneration and Reunion with *SOPHIA* will be absolved. And although, during this mortal Life, no such Perfection of the whole Man can be wrought out, yet is it attainable in the inward Part; and whatsoever seems to be an Obstruction, (even SIN NOT EXCEPTED,) must, for this very End, WORK TO-GETHER FOR GOOD TO THEM THAT LOVE GOD. Praised be his Triune Holy, Holy, Holy Name, in this Time, and throughout all the Extent and Duration of Eternity.
Number 11:

Here *Adam,* in the same Place as before, appears again, but in Union with Christ, which is to be referred to the Person of Jesus Christ, or of the Second *Adam* in our Humanity upon Earth; and is to show us the absolute Necessity of his Holy Incarnation, and immaculate Sacrifice for all Mankind, without which the great Work of our Regeneration and Reunion with SOPHIA could not have been wrought out to Perfection. In his Incarnation he brought that most significant Character, which the First *Adam* had lost, into the Humanity again, but first in his own Human Person, although it could not be visible in him from without, whilst he was upon Earth a Man like unto us in all things, Sins excepted. And, therefore, He, and even He alone, was able and sufficient to go for us into Death, to kill Death in his own Death, to break in his Passage the Hook and Sting of Satan, to enter into, and through his dark Territory, to bruise the Serpent's Head, and to ascend up on high, to take possession of his Throne, whereby the Prophecy of *Micah* was fulfilled, which *Luther* most significantly translated [Anglicized], The Breaker is come up before them.

Number 12:

From the Time in which that *Breaker,* prophesied of by *Micah,* was come up before us, the Gate stood open, that the First *Adam's* Children could follow him and enter into Paradise, which could not be done by any Soul before that Time. Holy Souls, both before and after the Deluge, that lived according to the Dictates of the Word treasured up in their Hearts, could, in their Departure from this World, go so far as to the Gate of Paradise, but Entrance could not be had by any one, till the First-Born from the Dead was entered in HIS own Person. Yet is there still a vast Difference between Souls in their Departure from this World; and this Difference wholly depends upon the real State and Condition of that significant Character, which was spoken of before; for those Souls that have attained it in this Life to Perfection, or in other Words, those that here have put on the Heavenly Substantiality of Jesus Christ, meet with no Obstacle in their Passage. Those in whom that Character is more or less defective, meet with more or less Impediment; and those that have nothing at all of it, cannot go any further than into that Region, which most significantly is called the Triangle in Nature. Oh that there were none such at all!

Number 13:

When the third Hierarchy, which *Lucifer* destroyed and depopulated, shall be completely filled again with Inhabitants from the Children of *Adam, Good* and *Evil* shall be separated, Time shall be no more, and GOD shall be All in All. This third Hierarchy, which, for good Reasons, was always hitherto represented as inferior to those of *Michael* and *Uriel,* is now here exalted again above them in the supremest Place: For as the Hierarch Jesus Christ, being the Brightness of GOD the Father's Glory, and the express Image of his Person, excels all the Angels, and has by Inheritance obtained a more excellent Name than they, who are all to worship him, and to none of whom HE ever said, as HE did to him, *Sit on my Right Hand, until I make thine Enemies thy Footstool,* so also all his Subjects in this Hierarchy, surpass all the Holy Angels in this, that they are Images of GOD, as manifested in all the three Principles, when the Holy Angels are only his Images, as HE was manifested in two of them: Wherefore, also they are distinguished from the Angels by this peculiar Character [interlaced triangle in circle] which is not contrived by human Speculation, but is written in the Book of Nature by the Finger of God; for it points directly, not only at the Creation of this third Principle in six Days; but also at fallen and divorced *Adam's* Reunion with the Divine Virgin SOPHIA. To those who are more like (though not in their outward Shape) the Animals of this World than Men, nothing is to be said of these and the like Things, because they are Spiritual, and must be Spiritually discerned.

SMASHING SHAMS

(Continued from Page 70)

superstitions—not God—and no matter how beautiful these superstitions may be, they will ultimately work our undoing if we do not rise above them and face facts, however prosaic and apparently non-spiritual those facts may appear. In the final analysis, that which is true is spiritual and that which is untrue is non-spiritual. The religion of the future must—and will—be founded upon realities, not upon illusions.

THE MYSTERIES OF LIGHT, SOUND, AND COLOR

(Continued from Page 76)

Chief among the symbolic inventions of Pythagoras was his *cosmic monochord*—an instrument of one string connecting heaven and earth, with its lower end attached to matter and its upper end to spirit. With this device he was able to demonstrate the principle of celestial harmonics. The planets were arranged by the Pythagoreans in a manner similar to that of the Jews, who used a seven-branched candlestick to represent the seven planets, placing the sun upon the central stem. While the Greeks symbolized the earth as the center of the solar system in their scheme of celestial harmonics, this was due solely to the fact that their calculations were made from the point corresponding to the earth. They were fully aware that the earth, together with its attendant moon, revolved—like the other planets—around a great central flame which they termed the *Altar of Vesta.*

Counting inward from the circumference, Pythagoras divided the universe into twelve parts. The first division was called the *empyrean,* or the sphere of the fixed stars, and the dwelling place of the immortals. The second was the sphere of Saturn, the third the sphere of Jupiter, the fourth the sphere of Mars, the fifth the sphere of the sun, the sixth the sphere of Venus, the seventh the sphere of Mercury, the eighth the sphere of the moon, the ninth the sphere of fire, the tenth the sphere of air, the eleventh the sphere of water, and the twelfth the sphere of earth. Because the octave consists of six whole tones, some authors have used a double octave to signify these twelve divisions.

According to the Pythagorean concept of the music of the spheres, the interval between the earth and the sphere of the fixed stars was considered to be a diapason, as the diapason was considered the most perfect harmonic interval. In other words, heaven and earth sustain the same harmonic relationship to each other as the string bearing the 12-pound weight bears to the string carrying the 6-pound weight. The arrangement most generally accepted for the musical sounds or intervals between the planet earth and the sphere of the fixed stars is as follows: From the sphere of the earth to the sphere of the moon, one tone; from the sphere of the moon to the sphere of Mercury, one-half tone; from the sphere of Mercury to the sphere of Venus, one-half tone; from the sphere of Venus to the sphere of the sun, one and one-half tones; from the sphere of the sun to the sphere of Mars, one tone; from the sphere of Mars to the sphere of Jupiter, one-half tone; from the sphere of Jupiter to the sphere of Saturn, one-half tone; from the sphere of Saturn to the sphere of the fixed stars, one-half tone. The sum of these intervals equals six whole tones or an octave. From the foregoing the harmonic relationship between the various heavenly bodies may thus be determined. For example: the harmonic chord between the sun and the earth is a symphony diapente; between the sun and the moon a symphony diatessaron, as is also the harmonic ratio between the sun and the sphere of the fixed stars. Upon these fundamental harmonics of the diapason, the diapente, and the diatessaron Pythagoras based his music of the spheres.

In the philosophy of the ancients heaven consisted of the greatest degree of spirit and the least degree of matter. Conversely, the earth was regarded as the greatest degree of matter and the least degree of spirit. Midway between these extremes of heaven and earth was the sphere or line of the sun, at which point the powers of the superior and the inferior worlds were perfectly balanced.

Spirit is active; matter, passive. In other words, spirit is the agent and matter the patient. Every organized form of life, visible or invisible, consists of a certain degree of activity operating upon a certain proportion of substance. Form, therefore, may be said to consist of a compound of spirit and matter, spirit serving as the cohesive power. When the spirit is withdrawn, disintegration takes place and form then returns to its original state of unorganized matter.

With the opposing forces of spirit and matter, creation was spun as a web, the upper end of the web being attached to the sphere of spirit and the lower end to the sphere of matter. The nobility, therefore, of any creature is measured by its proximity to the spiritual pole of existence and its ignobility by its proximity to the material pole of existence.

From the viewpoint of philosophy vibration was considered to be the action of spirit upon matter. When spirit was present to a greater degree than matter, higher rates of vibration obtained due to the presence of less material substance to impede the spiritual waves of force and the form composed of this combination was said to be of a high order. On the other hand, when matter was in excess of spirit and the spiritual impulses correspondingly feebler or impeded by a vast area of substance, the rates of vibration were slower and the form composed of this combination was said to be of a low order.

The longer a vibratory wave, the less spiritual its tone. Therefore, the lower notes pertain to the material world and the higher notes to the spiritual world. The higher the note the greater amount of activity also is manifested in its production. Some sound vibration waves are 70 feet long; others only a few inches. The short waves are the highest and the most spiritual.

The great Rosicrucian, Robert Fludd, uses two pyramids to demonstrate the proportional relationship between spirit and matter in the various planes of activity existing within the Universal Octave. His inverted pyramid with its base in the substance of spirit represents activity which, as it descends through the various worlds, gradually decreases in volume until the apex of the pyramid touches—but does not pierce—the surface of the element of earth, which point represents the least degree of spiritual activity. A second and dark pyramid symbolizes the substance of matter, which has its foundation upon the surface of the earth and ascends through the spheres until its apex touches—but does not pierce—the plane of pure abstract life.

As the pyramid of matter ascends from the surface of the physical universe upward through the various planes of superphysical substance, matter gradually decreases in density, this decrease being well represented by the converging lines of the pyramid. At the point designated as the orbit of the sun the forces represented by the two pyramids are equal. Below this point matter predominates, above this point spirit predominates.

The symbol of a monochord—divided into two octaves—is also employed by Fludd to signify the interval between heaven and earth, one octave consisting of the interval between the surface of the earth and the sphere of the sun and the other octave consisting of the interval between the sphere of the sun and the uppermost heaven world. According to this system the harmonic ratio between the earth and the sun is a symphony diapason and the ratio between the earth and the supreme heaven a symphony disdiapason, the entire distance between earth and heaven being twelve whole tones.

Let us now consider a simple method of demonstrating the law of mathematical proportions of the active and passive principles entering into the composition of the four elements. The elements may be considered as a pyramid and the key to the differences between the elements may be philosophically worked out as follows:

Earth consists of four parts of matter to none of spirit, inasmuch as the spiritual pyramid does not penetrate the sphere of the element earth. Water consists of three parts of matter to one part of spirit and is, therefore, less dense and more active than earth. According to the Rosicrucian theory, air consists of two parts of matter to two parts of spirit. Equilibrium, therefore, exists in air which is less dense and more active than water. Fire contains three parts of spirit to one part of matter. It is, therefore, the most mobile of the elements, being less dense and more active even than air, its incessant motion and lucidity bearing witness to the predominance of the active divine principle over the inactive material principle. The fifth element—spirit—contains four parts of spirit to no part of matter. Inasmuch as the material pyramid does not pierce the sphere of spirit, this fifth—and sacred—element completes the octave.

Using a monochord strung through the four elements, the harmonic relationships between the elements may be ascertained and the natural antipathies which certain elements bear to others found to result from the fact that according to the diatonic scale these antagonistic elements are not in harmonic ratio to each other. On this subject Fludd writes as follows:

"Thus in elementary music the relation of earth to the sphere of water is 4 to 3, as there are in the earth four quarters of frigidity to three of water; for only this part of the element fire, like the apex of the pyramid of light, is contained in the sphere of water; which if more parts of heat existed therein would become a more tenuous substance and be converted into air and would for that reason neither remain contiguous to the earth nor bear up as great a weight as it does. Since it has some heat it is fluid and clear, as heretofore mentioned. And on account of the above mentioned proportion of 4 to 3 (sesquitertia) earth is in agreement with water. But this combination is imperfect, because the parts of one are humid and those of the other dry. Nevertheless they have the Diatessaron consonance, because their predominant active qualities agree. So also the earth bears the double proportion to the spurious sphere of equality in which two parts are material and two igneous. That is, four parts of earth to two of that sphere; for the terrestrial nature produced the humid parts by virtue of the light compound with them. The sphere of equality is related to that of air in the proportion of two igneous parts of the sphere of equality to three of air. This gives rise to the igneous Diapente. And three igneous parts of air to four of the sphere of fire produce the Diapason. Earth, therefore, concords with water in Diatessaron, with the sphere of equality in Diapason. Water concords with the spurious sphere of equality in Diapente. The spurious sphere of equality concords with air in Diapason, because related in double proportion. Fire concords with air in Diatessaron, and with the sphere of equality in Diapason. Air concords with the sphere of equality in Diapente. The sphere of equality with water in double proportion or Diapason."

In philosophic symbolism the theory of music is dependent upon three essential elements: (1) a musician who produces the harmony by activity; (2) a medium by which the vibratory rates are actually set in motion; and (3) a sounding board or resonance chamber by which these vibrations are amplified and brought to their maximum power and quality.

In the universe God is the musician, the material sphere is the sounding board or resonance chamber, and the seven planetary strings are the media by which those tones are struck which will later vibrate throughout the structure of the instrument itself. The production of music depends primarily,

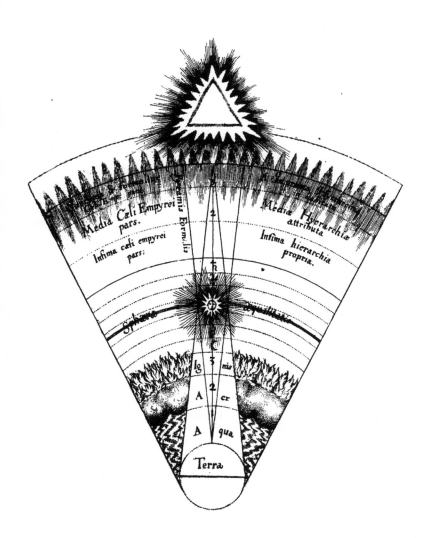

The Harmonic Intervals of the Spheres, according to Robert Fludd

therefore, upon two separate and distinct agencies combining together in perfect accord: namely, the musician and the instrument. Though the musician be skilled he cannot adequately express himself unless his instrument be of a quality commensurate with his ability. On the other hand, no matter how perfect the instrument, it is silent if the hands of the musician do not give it life or if played upon by the novice only discord will result.

In this there is a sublime analogy to the nature of man himself: Man's spiritual life—his consciousness—is a musician who depends upon his bodies to produce the harmonies imprisoned within his soul. Man's lower nature—that part of him visible to the sense-perceptions of others—is the instrument upon which the spirit must play. It is a popular but erroneous belief that if people become spiritual they are then able to give expression to these inner harmonies even though they neglect their own physical bodies. Though the individual's internal nature be developed until it is fired with divine enthusiasm and power, it can never do justice to the melodies in the soul unless the body be made a fine and perfect instrument to express the genius and technique of the spiritual nature playing through it. If the instrument be cracked or imperfect, it can never give forth those perfect tones which delight the soul and bring inspiration to life.

That color—like sound—is also a rate of vibration is now so thoroughly established as to make it unnecessary to advance proof of this fact. The waves of color which we recognize as color are much finer, however, than those cognized as sound. It is therefore quite evident that the phenomena of color exists primarily in man himself and that to a creature without an optical equipment similar to man's, color is merely an unsensed rate of vibration.

We are much better equipped to cognize sound than we are color vibrations. While the average person is capable of differentiating from nine to eleven octaves of sound, he can only cognize less than one octave of color. While many sound waves are a number of feet in length, color waves are so short as to require many thousands of them to make a line an inch long. In the last analysis, it is quite evident that if our sense-perceptions were fine enough we would discover that every color has both a sound and a bodily structure, and beyond that also a taste and an odor. There are breaks in the ascending scale of vibration for which man has no sense-perceptions of any kind. In future ages, however, as the human creature evolves its latent potentialities it will probably develop sense-perceptions capable of registering these unknown wave gaps. It is impossible to conjecture what response these rates of vibration will awaken in the nature of man and under what heading they will be classified. The science of color and its application to modern life is still a subject of the wildest speculation. While theories abound, there is very little actual knowledge concerning color other than that it is productive of powerful therapeutic and psychic effects.

Experiments with varicolored glasses, screens, and other appliances such as Babbitt's bottles, have proved color to be a most important factor in the life of humanity. Certain shades have been demonstrated to produce a powerful stimulating effect while others produce a depressive or sedative effect. It has also been proved that color can be used successfully to combat many forms of disease and that nearly all ailments have a color key by which their malignancy can be increased or decreased at will.

White and black are considered to be respectively the abundance and the privation of light. In philosophic symbolism that state both preceding and succeeding light was represented as black. Black was also employed to typify receptivity and white reflectivity. That which receives or absorbs light into itself was termed black, whereas that which reflects light from its own surface was termed white. For this reason the neophytes of the lower degrees of the Mysteries were often robed in black because, being students, they received intellectual light and were as yet incapable of radiating the information which they were absorbing. By way of contrast, the higher initiates were robed in white to represent the fact that they were radiant centers of intelligence, and instead of absorbing the condition of light descending upon them from the gods they reflected this light upon their disciples and the world which depended upon them for spiritual guidance. White is also the ancient symbol of day and black of night. As day was said to be ruled over by glorious beneficent spirits, its corresponding color tone was declared to be the symbol of good. On the other hand, night was said to be ruled over by the malignant infernal spirits and considered to be the fitting symbol of evil. The eternal warfare between good and evil was evidently based upon the alternation of day and night. For a similar reason white was considered to be the symbol of intelligence, wisdom, virtue, purity, and understanding; black, the symbol of ignorance, vice, perversion, intemperance, malignancy, and underhandedness. White and black were also the proper emblems of spirit and matter—the opposites between which organized creation existed.

The simplest division of color is into the primary and secondary colors. There are three primary colors—blue, yellow, and red—and four secondary colors—orange, green, violet, and indigo. For sometime modern science has tried to disprove the priority of blue, yellow, and red as the primary colors. Some affirm that orange is a primary color; others that green should be considered as one of the first three. It will yet be proved, however, that not only are there seven primary colors but that the colors which we see are not the real shades but merely complementary reflections of the actual colors.

For the sake of symbolism blue, yellow, and red have always been accepted as emblematic of the spiritual powers controlling the world and also of the three interpenetrating planes or worlds composing the occult constitution of the world. The white ray is the Divine Creator, and as this Being contains within Itself all the substances of the worlds which will be individualized within It so the white ray contains within itself all color. The sun is the source of color to this solar system and, therefore, color is most vivid in tropical countries and least vivid in the Arctic and Antarctic regions. Deprive a body of sunlight and you will gradually destroy its color. This fact can be very easily demonstrated by laying a board on the grass, for in a few days the area of grass covered by the board will be found to have turned white.

In this connection the question may be asked why the sun causes colors to fade if it is also the source of them. All living organisms pick up the color waves from the light and build them into their individual structures according to a definite rule, which is done with the assistance of a host of intelligences called the *Nature Spirits,* especially the gnomes and undines. It has also been found that if certain metal filings be placed at the roots of plants they will cause the blossoms to change color. When the roots of the plant absorb a certain amount of metal, they establish a metallic pole in the plant which draws the color wave corresponding with its own substance. Thus, iron has the power of drawing the red ray of Mars and a certain ruddiness will be found in those bodies containing a predominating amount of iron. Another interesting example of the effect of establishing a metallic pole is to be found in the time-honored practice of feeding iron to people who are run down or anemic. Metallic iron itself incapable of increasing vitality but does establish a pole for the Martial vibrations and thus accomplishes its intended purpose as Mars is the dynamo of the solar system and controls animation through its red ray. When a piece of cloth is dyed the coloring matter is merely imposed upon the substance of the cloth; there is no center of energy or force to replenish the coloring matter or cause it to grow. For this reason the rays of the sun pick up the coloring matter instead of depositing it, with the result that the color of the fabric is said to fade. The flower will preserve its original color in the strongest sunlight until it is plucked, when it begins to fade like the piece of dyed fabric because it is then deprived of the intelligent source regulating the distribution of chlorophyll.

The seven Creators of the lower worlds are often symbolized by the spectrum and also by the seven vowels. According to the celestial philosophy of the Temple, the spectrum of the sun is to be found in the planets. Each of the arts and sciences is capable of being used as a language for the expression of spiritual truths, for all Nature is controlled by one series of laws. Every product of Nature is an exemplar of these laws and an accurate analysis of any one structure will disclose the composition of all structures.

Let us now relate the various color harmonic values in order to demonstrate the interrelationship of the worlds. Beginning with the syllable *do* and ascending the musical scale, we find *do* corresponds to the color red, the planet Mars, and the emotional nature of man. The syllable *re* has its correspondences in the color orange, the sun, and the vital principle in man; *mi* in the color yellow, the planet Mercury, and the spiritual soul of man; *fa* in the color green, the planet Saturn, and the lower mind of man; *sol* in the color blue, the planet Jupiter, and represents the spiritual ego or auric sheath which encloses the constitution of man; *la* in the color indigo, the planet Venus, and the higher mind of man; *si* in the color violet, the moon, and the etheric double or shadowy counterpart of the physical body. (For details of this system see H. P. Blavatsky.)

In addition to the colors of the spectrum which we see there are a vast number of vibratory color waves, some too low and others too high to come within the range of registration by the human optical equipment. Some of these color waves can be caught by the sensitive photographic plate. The best known of these colors too elusive for human visualization are the infra red and the ultra violet, so termed not because they resemble either of these colors but because they are next to the shades for which they are named.

It will yet be proved that color—like sound—progresses by a series of octaves and that above the red of the spectrum is a spiritual red in symphony diapason. It is appalling to contemplate even for a moment the colossal mountain of ignorance which the mind of man must first surmount before it can conquer the abstract vistas of space. Yet still more appalling it is to realize how few there are in this age who interest themselves in these vital issues of life. As in generations past, man explored the unknown continents, so in the ages to come man, armed with curious weapons fashioned for the purpose, will explore the unknown fastnesses of light, color, and sound. It is impossible to conjecture with any degree of exactness what will be the discoveries resulting from these incursions into the realm of the unknown, but it is reasonably certain that these discoveries will complement the findings of the first great minds of antiquity—the illumined hierophants and initiates of the Mystery Schools of Greece, Egypt, and India.

uestions ⅋ answers·

A Department Maintained for the Convenience of the Reader

Question. What are the lost arts and sciences of antiquity? J. L.

Answer. This term is generally used to cover "Damascus steel," the "Tyrian dyes," and "malleable glass." The same term should be applied to alchemy and the process of manufacturing the fuel for the ever-burning lamps. Personally, we like to include both religion and philosophy, the operative keys to both of which have been lost. The modern world is just beginning to appreciate the profound knowledge possessed by the ancients concerning the spiritual constitution and life of man.

Q. It has come to my attention that Plato describes the lost continent of Atlantis in one of his *Dialogues.* Will you please tell me where this reference may be found? L. H.

A. In the *Critias,* one of the shortest of the Platonic fragments, the continent of Atlantis is described somewhat at length. Many suppose that the *Critias* was the last work of Plato and that he died without finishing it. In any event, the writing ends abruptly in the middle of a sentence. In the familiar translation of *The Dialogues of Plato* by B. Jowett, the description begins on the 599th page of the second volume.

Q. Will you clarify the distinction between Lucifer and Satan? R. E. B.

A. According to legend, Lucifer was one of the bright throne angels of the Lord and controlled the planet Ragnarok. Lucifer rebelled against the power of the gods and the flame of the sun personified in the Archangel Michael destroyed his planet, which then became the asteroids. Lucifer represents the individual intellect and will which rebels against the domination of Nature and attempts to maintain itself contrary to natural impulse. As you will read in the editorial of this month, Satan is merely the Greek god Saturn, who symbolizes the power of crystallization, whereas Lucifer signifies vitalization. According to the ancients, the planet Venus was the throne of Lucifer because it was the false sun or the bright light which came before the true light of the dawn. Mars is the dynamo of the solar system and Lucifer is supposed at the present time to operate upon humanity through the Martian ray. Samael is the regent of Mars and is the one who, according to the Qabbalistic Bible story, assumed the form of a serpent and tempted Eve. Lucifer is associated with temptation because he contributes impulsiveness to the human temperament, and man's impulsiveness often results in his own undoing. Lucifer, in the form of Venus, is the morning star spoken of in Revelation, which is to be given to those who overcome the world. The fall of Lucifer and his final resurrection is an allegory deeply involved in the mystery of humanity and the descent of man into the material spheres.

Q. I have been a student of psychology for some time but do not seem to get the spirit of it. What is meant by drawing information from the Universal Mind? All I have been able to learn I have dug out of a book. Can you suggest anything? E. F.

A. You have not been able to get the spirit of psychology because psychology as it is generally taught at the present time has no *spirit*. It is a bundle of contradictions held together by a string of discords. Psychology actually means the language of the soul, but as far as we have been able to determine the soul is one of the few elements which psychologists seldom— if ever—discuss. In the hands of experienced and educated men and women, psychology is capable of producing a great deal of good, but when disseminated by blundering enthusiasts little of value is accomplished. We would suggest that you cease what will ultimately prove to be a fruitless pursuit and turn your attention to some thoroughly established school of philosophy, such as the Platonic, Aristotelian or Baconian. These have withstood the test of time and if properly understood will reveal far more than you can hope to learn from modern psychology. Concerning the Universal Mind, we offer a simple illustration of the principle involved: The Universal Mind is the reservoir which contains all that has been, is or can be known. Man's individual intellect is an infinitesimal unit of Universal Mind substance which partakes of all but is limited in capacity for expression. The human mind may be likened to a little cup which is held out to be filled from the fountain of Universal Thought. Man can take from the fountain only as much as the cup will hold. Therefore the difference between the little mind and the great mind is in its capacity to receive and hold thought power. In other words, the ability to think is largely a matter of capacity. One tiny thought floods over and spills in a small mind while a great mind may circumscribe and contain an ocean of great and varied thoughts. Capacity is built by thought, by study, by observation, by comparison, and by mental toleration. By the last we mean that that mind has capacity which is capable of tolerating any thought, no matter how strange or wild it may appear. Big thoughts sprain little minds. A great number of people who are studying newer methods of religion and philosophy suffer from a form of mental indigestion. This results from taking in a vast number of thoughts and for lack of ability to digest them these thoughts set on the mind as a heavy meal sets on the stomach. Instead of trying to learn all that you can in a short time, strive to assimilate as much as possible of what you learn. This process of assimilation builds mental capacity. As the mind increases in capacity, bigger and better thoughts pour into it. When it is as great as the universe, then and then only is it *en rapport* with the Universal Mind. In time you will find that you can learn nothing from a book. Your learning will come from what you think about the thing you have read in the book. In the same way you will discover two great sources of information other than the printed page: the first is the world and the second is yourself. The study of these two will develop capacity rapidly and with safety.

Q. Is true gratitude a worthy sentiment or should one try to overcome it? Anon.

A. This question is a very difficult one because the worthiness of sentiments depends upon the plane of mental and spiritual consciousness of the one expressing these sentiments. At a certain stage of evolution sentiments constitute the highest possible expression of the soul. At another stage this is not the case. The elimination of sentiment generally leaves a nature cold and not a little cruel. The method of expressing sentiment also changes as the soul unfolds. In the highest form of humanity all sentiments take the form of constructive labor and that which we love we serve, thus demonstrating feeling without selfish emotion. While gratitude is not listed among the qualifications of the path, there is no doubt that this is a powerful influence for good if the real meaning of the word be understood. We know that a disciple can never pay his debt of gratitude to his Master and for this reason becomes to a certain degree the servant of the one who has brought him illumination. This form of gratitude is considered to be not only commendable but absolutely indispensable. Appreciation is the greatest incentive in the world. Personally, we take the attitude that there is no earthly reason why anyone should do anything for us. Therefore instead of accepting favors as a matter of course and wondering why people do not obey our wishes with greater alacrity, we are grateful for anything that others may do, realizing that there is no particular reason why people should do it except out of the goodness of their own hearts. On the other hand, we should not allow our gratitude to one person to prevent us from being kindly and thankful to those who have not put themselves out on our behalf. While emotions may be very plebeian, certain impersonal but kindly attitudes make life much more endurable for those souls that have not risen above a certain amount of personality. Those who have transcended the material world are very few in number and are too wise to deprive man of anything that assists him on the difficult path of accomplishment.

Q. Do you believe that impatience and such drawbacks in temperament neutralize or nullify conscious efforts to improve the character in other ways? S. C. T.

A. No effort which we make is lost. Every effort in time produces an effect equal in power to the effort that is expended. There is a homely demonstration of this point which may clarify the situation. A few years ago balloon ascensions were quite common in connection with county fairs. The nature of man may be likened to a balloon which would naturally leave the earth and ascend to the spiritual world. This is prevented, however, by the sand bags of ignorance, inconsistency, and those multitudinous faults and failings which serve as "ballast" for the human soul. When the time comes for the balloon to go up, it is first necessary to cast the bags of sand overboard. Various individuals evolve quite complicated methods for attaining this end but regardless of the manner employed the balloon will not rise until a certain per cent of the weight is removed. Every fault you conquer is ballast cast overboard. Those traits not conquered are ballast retained. The sand bags still in the balloon in no way detract from the importance of the others cast overboard. The ascent of man's nature toward its own spiritual source is augmented by the faults and failings cast overboard and hindered to a corresponding degree by those retained.

Q. Does a sudden change from a passive to an active interest in music indicate the awakening of a new center or the reawakening of an old one? Anon.

A. Approaching the subject from the standpoint of reincarnation, we realize that the predominating qualities and characteristics of one life are the result of attitudes and environments existing in a previous incarnation. It is impossible to state with absolute certainty whether a trait be the outgrowth of some impulse from the previous life from the meager description given, but it is generally possible to apply the following rule: Traits or inclinations which appear suddenly are almost always already awakened faculties readjusting themselves in a new environment. The awakening of a new faculty is a slow and tedious process, trying the patience to the utmost and is usually the result of necessity and not choice.

Q. Can Matt. 24:29-31 and 26:26-29; also Luke 22:19-20 be accepted literally and, if not, will you please give the true meaning? L. C. F.

A. We are at the present time carrying on investigation in an effort to prove which parts of the New Testament were added by later hands than the original authors. When this information has been arranged it will be possible to handle the subject with a great deal more certainty. The first statement—Matt. 24:29-31—concerning the end of the world is undoubtedly allegorical, for it appears in the ritualism of the Greek and Egyptian Mysteries and is not dissimilar to statements concerning Kali Yuga to be found in the great Brahman classic, Vishnu Puranas. These verses refer esoterically to the end of the material nature of all creatures, which is the inevitable result of the awakening and establishing of spiritual consciousness within the soul. The allegory of the blood and the bread from Matt. 26:26-29 and Luke 22:19-20 is borrowed from the Bacchic Mysteries, for among nearly all the pagans wine was symbolic of the blood of the Universal Spirit. Christ, symbolizing the soul of the world, distributes His life essence—the blood, or wine—and his formal substances—the body, or bread—throughout the lower worlds to leaven and redeem them. This story has a parallel in the body of Osiris which is broken up and distributed for the regeneration of the world and also in the story of Bacchus, the chosen personification of the wine. At various times articles will appear in this magazine which will cast further light upon this subject.

Q. What effect has the use of a so-called harmless drug such as sulphonal or trional on:
    1. The physical body.
    2. The inner bodies and centers.
    3. The evolution of the ego?   L. M. F. H.

A. Nearly all narcotic drugs directly affect the nervous system which is the link connecting the consciousness with the physical body. By forcing the condition of sleep they cause the separation of the higher etheric and astral bodies from the lower etheric and dense physical forms. The effect of all drugs upon the physical body is, to a certain degree, destructive. They cause a struggle in the system in which the life within the body battles against and finally overcomes the foreign substances introduced. In some cases, however, they are legitimate inasmuch as they prevent a greater struggle occurring as the result of pain or insomnia. They produce but a very slight effect in the invisible bodies and to a slight degree slow down temporarily the whirling vortices or centers, but of course no physical substance is capable of injuring the ego itself other than by a reflex. The only danger is the possibility of the drug causing a negative condition in the physical body which makes the active operation of the spirit through the body difficult.

Q. Please state the occult explanation of the Atonement? G. L.

A. This can be briefly answered by breaking the word itself into three parts, as follows: *At-one-ment.* The great sin of man is incompleteness. He redeems himself from sin by completing his own constitution, and by becoming at one with himself he atones for his symbolic fall into the state of ignorance or condition of separativeness.

Q. What is matter? Anon.

A. As evil is the least degree of good, so matter is the least degree of spirit. Matter is the crystallization of the true spiritual substance of the universe. It is exuded out of spirit and becomes a temporary vehicle for the manifestation of spirit. Matter is composed of an infinite number of tiny units which are called koilonic bubbles. The combination of these koilons into electrons, electrons into atoms, atoms into molecules, molecules into cells, and cells into organic and inorganic structures results in the organized forms which we are capable of seeing. Matter is primarily a homogeneity as spirit is a homogeneity, and forms return to the condition of homogeneous matter as individual lives return to the condition of homogeneous spirit.

Q. What is the explanation of the invisible friends whose company is enjoyed by so many imaginative children? Are they entirely the product of the imagination? I very clearly remember my own "friend," whom I called Imbyme. He was absolutely invisible, coming and going as a vibration in space, yet as palpable as any physical human (as far as awareness of his presence was concerned). I never heard his voice, yet I know his thoughts and wishes, and readily acceded to his suggestions. It was he who planned our games. When I was about seven years old he disappeared for the last time. D. L.

A. The creature which you cognized was undoubtedly an elemental one of a host of creatures especially concerned with vegetation, inhabiting the etheric body of the earth which interpenetrates the physical structure. The great number of children possessing the faculty of etheric vision is impressing upon the minds of the more prosaic adults the reality of those little folk which have been the heroes of myths and legends for uncounted generations. Your little playfellow was probably a gnome or earth spirit, whose body was composed entirely of the substance of ether. At the seventh year those vital energies which previously stimulated etheric vision became concerned in the process of growth and gradually the ability to see the tiny people of the earth is lost. It is also interesting to note that many children retain the ability to see the little people of the elements until the soft spot on the crown of the head closes. Generations to come will recognize the reality of the gnomes, undines, sylphs, and salamanders, and will concern themselves in enlisting the cooperation of these creatures in the attainment of certain peculiar physical ends, for the elemental spirits—working as they do with the etheric double or vitality body of all physical things—are capable of profoundly influencing the visible physical structure. We are indebted to Paracelsus of Hohenheim for the first classified knowledge pertaining to this remarkable subject. If you are interested in learning more about the people of the elements, we recommend to your consideration the *Count de Gabalis* by Abbe de Villars.

The most ancient of all things is God, for he is uncreated; the most beautiful is the world, because it is the work of God; the greatest is space, for it contains all that has been created; the quickest is the mind; the strongest is necessity; the wisest is time, for it teaches to become so; the most constant is hope, which alone remains to man when he has lost everything; the best is virtue, without which there is nothing good.—*Zoroaster.*

The basis of the world is power! It lives in us and in everything. From the beginning it came forth from God, and was uttered in the philosophies of great teachers and prophets of the ancient world. God has not placed it here to remain inactive, it strives, creates, institutes. So long as the world is filled with it so long will its efforts continue, for power expresses the will of God.—*S. F. Dunlap.*

ON A BOOK LOANED TO A FRIEND

I GIVE humble and hearty thanks for the safe return of this book which having endured the perils of my friend's bookcase, and the bookcases of my friend's friends, now returns to me in reasonably good condition.

I GIVE humble and hearty thanks that my friend did not see fit to give this book to his infant as a plaything, nor use it as an ash-tray for his burning cigar, nor as a teething-ring for his mastiff.

WHEN I lent this book I deemed it as lost: I was resigned to the bitterness of the long parting: I never thought to look upon its pages again.

BUT NOW that my book is come back to me, I rejoice and am exceeding glad! Bring hither the fatted morocco and let us rebind the volume and set it on the shelf of honour: for this my book was lent, and is returned again.

PRESENTLY, therefore, I may return some of the books that I myself have borrowed.—*Author unknown.*

Vital Statistics—If all the individuals who understand the full significance of the fourth dimension were to lie down in a line, the human chain thus formed would reach nearly six feet.

In Egypt the philosophers have a sublime and secret knowledge respecting the nature of God, which they only disclose to the people under the cover of fables or allegories. * * * All the Eastern nations—the Persians, the Indians, the Syrians—conceal secret mysteries under religious fables; the wise of all nations fathom the meaning of them, while the common people only see the symbols and the outside of them.—Origen.

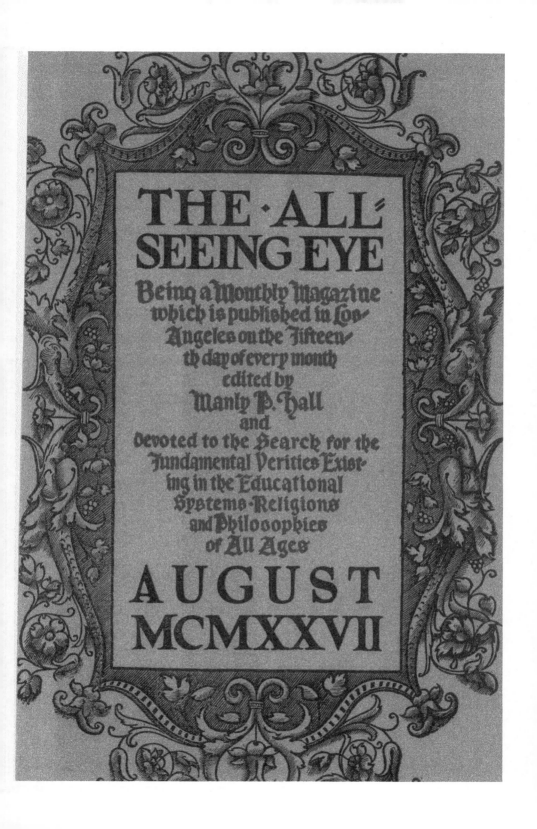

THE·ALL· SEEING EYE

Being a Monthly Magazine which is published in Los Angeles on the Fifteenth day of every month edited by

Manly P. Hall

and

devoted to the Search for the fundamental Verities Existing in the Educational Systems·Religions and Philosophies of All Ages

AUGUST
MCMXXVII

The ALL-SEEING EYE

DEVOTED TO THE SEARCH FOR THE
FUNDAMENTAL VERITIES EXIST-
ING IN THE EDUCATIONAL
SYSTEMS, RELIGIONS,
AND PHILOSOPHIES
OF ALL AGES

Vol. IV	AUGUST, 1927	No. 4

PUBLISHED EVERY MONTH BY

THE HALL PUBLISHING COMPANY

301 TRINITY AUDITORIUM BUILDING, TUcker 2603

NINTH AT GRAND AVENUE, LOS ANGELES, CALIFORNIA

MANLY P. HALL . . . . *Editor*
HARRY S. GERHART . . . . *Managing Editor*
MAUD F. GALIGHER . . . . *Associate Editor*
HOWARD W. WOOKEY . . . . *Art Director*

CONTENTS

Do You Know?

That the custom of casting a shoe after a bride grew out of the ancient practice of indicating the transfer of property by the delivery of a shoe, and in the case of a bride signified that the parents relinquished all right or dominion over their daughter.

That through the middle of the Church of the Holy Ghost in Heidelberg, Germany, a partition wall has been run, that services according to the Roman-Catholic and Protestant rituals may be held at the same time.

That pottery is the oldest, the longest, and the most widely diffused of human arts.

That in Algeria there is the strange phenomenon of a river of genuine ink formed by the junction of two streams, the waters of the first being strongly impregnated with iron and those of the second with gallic acid.

That on his deathbed Virgil wished to burn his epic poem, the Æneid, because after spending the last eleven years of his life in writing it he proposed to devote three years more to polish and complete the poem.

That while Latin ceased to be a spoken language A. D. 580, it remained the organ of general literature and diplomacy until the early part of the 17th century.

That upon hearing the story upon which Longfellow's poem, "Evangeline," is founded, Hawthorne first thought of making it the subject of a romance, but later turned it over to Longfellow as more suitable for an idyl.

That Titian's painting, "Christ with the Tribute Money," is considered by art critics to be the most perfect representation of the Godlike beauty and calm majesty of Christ.

The EDITOR'S BRIEFS

Mental Attitude as the Basis of Efficiency

Great corporations and industrial enterprises are beginning to realize more and more the part that mental attitude plays in business efficiency. They are realizing the value of the contented employe, and that the goodwill of their own servants plays no little part in the success of an enterprise. In days gone by the employe was looked upon as a necessary inconvenience, as a menial who must do as he was told or be fired. Those who were underlings forever stood with the sword of Damocles over their heads, living in awe of the boss and in momentary expectation of being fired, abject slaves of a commercial system which gave them no place. If they sought to rebel against this system, it meant unemployment, suffering and even starvation.

This day of tyranny, however, is over, for industry discovered that those who work through fear are only eye servants and that the sourness and hatred which was heaped upon industry by those who were as cogs in its wheels inhibited the output, diminished the efficiency, and left the officials of the corporation without friends or even the respect of their employes. In the days past the employer did not care what his help thought of him, but he is now beginning to realize that the attitude of his office force, and of his industrial workers, must be taken consideration and form one of the keynotes of an enterprise.

So today we find the cooperative plan—a plan in which the servant is consulted by his own master, in which he is given a living wage, and a voice in the running of the enterprise. Such a system increases the efficiency of the entire force and is now the only possible way to prevent a great industrial revolution.

The cheerful worker does three times the work of the overtaxed, underpaid, grumbling clerk. The smiling face of the employe sells the products of the corporation. It means that there will never be a shortage of labor in that corporation and that its workers, humanely treated and honestly considered, will give that touch of personal sympathy to the enterprise, which has a market value many times the amount of money expended in order to create it.

As this is true in the commercial world, so it is true in every walk of life. As man at the present time capitalizes the efficiency of his brother man and also realizes that his efficiency is his capital, both in the commercial world and in the world of letters, he is realizing more and more that the proper mental outlook on life is the basis of his ability to meet the problem of daily existence.

The ability to meet problems, to endure hardships, and to labor methodically are expressions of efficiency, and in this day and age of the world, not only must a product be sold but because of the keenness of competition it must literally sell itself, because of its economy and merits. And just as a product must sell itself, so the individual who wishes to be a success in world affairs must learn to sell himself to the world. Before a man can sell an automobile, he must sell himself to the purchaser; before a man will be promoted in the commercial world, he must sell himself to the employer.

Now let us briefly analyze what is meant when we say a person must sell himself. By this is simply meant that he must prove not only that he is necessary to the development of a certain thing but that he is the one best fitted to perform a certain work to attain a certain result or to demonstrate a certain quality. In other words, by selling oneself is meant that a person must convince another of his merits to the extent that the other comes to realize that the party in question is necessary to the success of the enterprise.

Efficiency sells a man in the commercial world more quickly than anything else and efficiency is 50 percent experience and 50 percent mental attitude. The drone may have experience but suffering from a diseased mental attitude and an unhealthy outlook on life he is of little value, while often an individual without experience but whose outlook upon life is healthy passes like a skyrocket through the heavens of industrialism, leaving far behind older and wiser heads who have become rutted or who suffer from an unhealthy or distorted mental outlook.

As we see it, there are three mental outlooks which at the present time are making failures out of people who would otherwise be successes. The first type who eliminates himself from the social order of things and in so doing loses his opportunity to sell himself to the world is the radical. Please do not think for a moment that there is no need for reforms or that man must not rise and see that the necessary steps are taken to correct the idiosyncrasies of our social system. But it is possible to be progressive without being bolshevistic, it is possible to assist materially in the mending of our social fabric without the attitude of the anarchist. The rabid mind which lives only to criticize, to tear down, and to abolitionize, destroys itself and at the same time removes itself from the field of useful labors. The radical has not a healthy outlook on life. His keynote is the critical mind. There is something the matter with everything he comes in contact —from the way his sausage is cooked to the way the country is run— and such an individual is seldom, if ever, a success in any walk of life. Such types finally mass themselves into a group of ragged, dirty, disheveled bolsheviks and soap box orators who can never wield a greater power than that of brute force. Their mental attitude has ostracized them from society and completely divided them from the very thing they sought to serve.

While the conformist is often forced to conform his will, the greatest good to the greatest number demands diplomacy in every walk of life. Diplomacy does not necessarily mean that the individual should sacrifice his personal viewpoint but it means that he will hold that viewpoint in abeyance until socially and economically he is successful or powerful enough in world affairs to make an intelligent use of that viewpoint. As a recognized leader in world affairs he will be capable of promulgating his viewpoint and, if necessary, of tearing down the social standard to rebuild it on a more solid foundation; but as a mere individual unhonored and unsung, the radical, instead of eliminating society and its evils, really eliminates himself from society.

Therefore, we say that the radical mind, the mind always set upon the unconventional and the unusual, is seldom desired by any enterprise wherein success plays an important function, because the radical mind succeeds in nothing except in making enemies. The healthy mental attitude is capable of taking the ideals of the radical and applying them to its life and unfoldment, but it does so in a big, broad, cheerful and constructive way, which surrounds it with friends and wellwishers. Often this cheerful mind will pass the new law and tear down the old subterfuge and sham without the world ever suspecting it, while the radical and the bolshevik, who is always tearing at the soul of sociology and economics, only lands himself in jail, in the law courts, and an untimely grave. One man cannot convert humanity by opposing it; he must convert humanity by gaining its confidence and have it moving with him instead of against him. By doing this, man sells his idea, while with the radical the plea merely destroys him. At the present time, there is a flood of radicalism in all walks of life. Radical government anarchists throw bombs of verbosity at each other, insipid parlor anarchists flay our social system, to replace the decaying ethics of the days gone by with still more rotten figments of their own imagination, and like most bolshevistic minds tear down eternally but have nothing better to offer to take the place of the thing they have destroyed. Therefore, we put first in the list of unhealthy mental attitudes the small-town bolshevik and half-baked "Red." He has an unhealthy outlook on life. Everything he sees is tinged with perversity. Regardless of his training or his education or his really spiritual ideals, his mental attitude debars him from society and leaves him helpless in his efforts to regenerate the plan of being.

The second undesirable mental attitude which we wish to discuss is the state of melancholia. We have not only the radical who wishes to blow up everything and get his fingers at the throat of something but we also have the individual who is just sour and lives entirely in a realm of failure, gloom, despondency and general dolefulness. These individuals are long-faced, sorrowful persons who spread gloom with their very presence. The world has no place for them because at this time everyone has more troubles than they know what to do with and few wish to discuss those of other people or be forced to shoulder the burdens of any save themselves. For this temperament there is but one remedy and that is the sunshine cure. They must realize that in spite of the fact that their mother-in-law cut them out of her will or that they had to pay brother's funeral expenses, the world cares little but hands the palm of the victor to the face with the smile. The attitude of indifference to responsibility and the lack of interest in the problem at hand is a poor recommendation in modern world affairs. A business takes an interest in the person who takes an interest in that business. The office manager today feels that he has really hired a man when he hires with personality the goodwill, and few succeed in enterprises which their hearts are not in. Where their treasure is there will their heart be also, the Scripture has stated, and the modern business world of today promotes and distinguishes those whose hearts are in their work. In spite of petty graft, the whole-hearted one seldom fails if he has energy and the proper mental outlook on life. Under the heading of melancholia we have the individual who lacks interest, who manifests incessantly those qualities which show that the blood moves slowly in his veins. The doors of enterprises, both spiritual and material, close upon the drone who does just what he has to and nothing more, who labors with his mind far away, or who is turned from the path of sunshine by every reverse. In this way, you see how the mental attitude and not the skill with the fingers makes and breaks us in the world of affairs.

The third division we will mention under the heading of mental attitude is the egotist. In the modern world, be it political, sociological, philosophical, or religious, the employer and the fellow-worker throws up his hands and turns away in despair when he finds blooming in a soul the flower of egotism. The great sorrow of the egotist is that he seldom recognizes the fault in himself. He fights the whole world to prove his own position, is blind to his own faults, and has the most helpless mental attitude that is known. There are always a great number of people to fill positions of little importance but there has never been a surfeit of great men and great women. The world delegates authority to all who are capable of standing it and egotism is the proof of the lack of control of self. When the world bestows power upon an individual, upon a group of individuals, upon a government, or upon a scheme of things, it does so because that individual has demonstrated the qualities of worthiness or because that organization, government, or scheme of things, exhibited fitness to be entrusted with responsibility. There is an endless need of people who can carry responsibility without showing it. In this world the successful manager is the one whoe superiority is the least suspected. The idea of the great man on the pedestal is dying out and men today serve men more and more because they recognize in the one they serve the qualities they themselves do not possess. The successful leader in all walks of life is the one who leads through confidence and not one who demands to be leader because of the sceptre of authority. Therefore, we say that the third mental attitude which destroys efficiency of individuals in world affairs is egotism. It convinces those who do not know that they know almost everything and causes exhibitions of power which are ever obnoxious to the democratic minds of the twentieth century.

If individuals would trace their own characters carefully and study their own mental attitude on life—whether the world they live in is bright and cheery or whether it is dark and gloomy with the forebodings of their own souls, whether they accept responsibility or not, whether they exhibit the carelessness of mentality which does not give a rap and many similar things—they will find in their own natures and their outlook on life the reason for the position they occupy in society, whether it be successful or unsuccessful. And for those who are molding characters-to-be, the natural, human, intelligent, cheerful outlook, if cultivated, will give them precedence in the world of men over many older and wiser heads whose views are radical, whose minds are sour, or whose lives are rutted with the crystallization of their own thoughts.

The development of the paraffin and other hydrocarbon industries during the present generation may make us fancy that this is a modern discovery; but it is the fact that the fire on the Hebre altar, fed by the Jewish priests, was our familiar petroleum, and was called "naphthar" or "nephi," a Hebrew word signifying purification.—James Campbell Brown.

PHILOSOPHY
SCIENCE & RELIGION

The Delphian Oracles

The worship of Apollo included the establishment and maintenance of places of prophecy, by means of which the gods could communicate with man and reveal futurity to such as deserved the boon. The early history of Greece abounds with accounts of talking trees, rivers, statues, and caves within which nymphs, dryads or dæmons had taken up their abodes and from which they delivered oracles. While Christian authors have tried to prove that oracular revelations were delivered by the Devil for the purpose of misleading humanity, they have not dared to attack the theory of oracles because of the repeated reference to oracles in their own sacred writings. If the onyx stones on the shoulders of Israel's high priest made known by their flashings the will of Jehovah, then a black dove, temporarily endowed with the faculty of speech, could certainly pronounce oracles in the temple of Jupiter Ammon. If the witch of Endor could invoke the shade of Samuel, who then gave prophecies to Saul, could not a priestess of Apollo call up the specter of her liege to foretell the destiny of Greece?

The most famous oracles of antiquity were those of Delphi, Dodona, Trophonius, and Latona, of which the talking oak trees of Dodona were the oldest. Though it is impossible to trace the genesis of the theory of oracular prophecy, it is known that many of the caves and fissures set aside by the Greek as oracles were sacred long before the rise of Grecian culture.

The oracle of Apollo at Delphi remains one of the unsolved mysteries of the ancients. Alexander Wilder derives the word *Delphi* from *delphos,* the womb. This name was chosen by the Greeks because of the shape of the cavern of the earth. The original name of the oracle was *Pytho,* so-called because its chambers had been the abode of the great serpent *Python,* a fearful creature which had crept out of the slime left by the receding flood that had destroyed all human beings except Deucalion and Pyrrha. Climbing the side of Mount Parnassus, Apollo slew the serpent after a prolonged combat and threw the body of the reptile down the fissure of the oracle. From that time on, the Sun-God, surnamed the Pythian Apollo, gave oracles from the vent and lent himself as the patron god of Delphi. Dionysius shared this honor with him. After being vanquished by Apollo, the spirit of *Python* remained at Delphi as the representative of his conqueror, and with the aid of his effluvium the priestess was able to come *en rapport* with the god. The fumes, rising from the fissure of the oracle, were supposed to come from the decaying body of *Python.* The name *Pythoness,* or *Pythia,* given to the female hierophant of the oracle, literally means one who has been thrown into a religious frenzy by inhaling fumes rising from decomposition. It is of further interest to note that the Greeks believed the oracle of Delphi to be the navel, or umbilicus, of the world, thus proving that they considered the planet as an immense human being. The connection between the principle of oracular revelation and the occult significance of the navel is an important secret belonging to the ancient Mysteries.

The oracle is much older, however, than the story given above, which was probably formulated by the priests to explain the phenomena to those inquisitive persons whom they did not consider worthy to be enlightened regarding the true esoteric nature of the oracle. Some believe that the Delphic fissure was discovered by a Hyperborean priest, but as far back as recorded history goes the cave was sacred and persons came from all parts of Greece and nearby countries to question the dæmon who dwelt in its chimney-like vent. Priests and priestesses guarded it and served the spirit who dwelt therein and who illuminated humanity through the gift of prophecy.

The story of the original discovery of the oracle runs something as follows: Shepherds tending their flocks on the side of Mount Parnassus were amazed at the antics of goats that wandered close to a great chasm on the southwestern spur of the hill. The animals jumped about as though trying to dance, and emitted strange cries unlike anything ever heard before. At last one of the shepherds, curious to learn the cause of the phenomenon, approached the vent from which were rising noxious fumes. Immediately he was seized with a prophetic ecstacy, danced with wild abandon, sang, pronounced inarticulate sounds, and also foretold that which was to come to pass in the future. Others tried with the same result. The fame of the place spread and many came to discover the future by inhaling the mephitic fumes which exhilarated to a point resembling the state of epilepsy. Not a few of those who came, being unable to control themselves and having temporarily the strength of madmen, tore themselves from those seeking to restrain them and, jumping into the vent, perished. In order to prevent this a wall was erected around the fissure and a prophetess was appointed to act as a mediator between the oracle and those who came to question it. According to later authorities, a tripod of gold ornamented with carvings of Apollo in the form of Python, the great serpent, was placed over the cleft, and on this arranged a specially-prepared seat so constructed that a person would have difficulty in falling off while under the influence of the oracular fumes. Just prior to this time the story to the effect that the fumes of the oracle were from the decaying body of Python was circulated. It is possible that the oracle itself revealed its own origin.

For many centuries during its early history, virgin maidens were consecrated to the service of the oracle. They were called the *Phoebades,* or *Pythiæ,* and constituted that famous order now known as the Pythian priesthood. It is probable that women were chosen to receive the oracles because their sensitive and emotional natures responded more completely and quickly to "the fumes of enthusiasm."

Three days before the time set to receive the communications from Apollo the virgin priestess commenced the ceremony of purification. She bathed in the Castallian well, abstained from all food, drank only from the fountain of Cassotis, which was brought into the temple through concealed pipes, and just before mounting the tripod chewed a few leaves of the sacred bay tree. It has been suspected that the water was drugged to bring on distorted visions or that the priests of Delphi were able to manufacture an exhilarating and intoxicating gas which they conducted by subterranean ducts and released into the shaft of the oracle some feet below the surface. Neither of these theories has been proved, however, nor do they in any way explain the accuracy of the predictions.

When the young prophetess had completed the process of purification, she was clothed in sanctified raiment and led to the tripod, upon which she seated herself, surrounded by the noxious vapors rising from the yawning fissure. Gradually, as she inhaled the fumes, a change came over her. It was as if a different spirit had entered into her body. She struggled, tore her clothing, and uttered inarticulate cries until after a time her struggles ceased. She then became very calm and a great majesty seemed to possess her, and with eyes fixed in space and her body rigid she uttered the prophetic words. The predictions were usually in the form of hexameter verse but the words were often ambiguous and unintelligible. Every sound that was made and every movement of her body was carefully recorded by the five Hosii, or holy men, who were appointed as scribes to preserve the minutest details of each divination. (The Hosii were appointed for life and were chosen from the direct descendants of Deucalion.)

Upon the delivery of the oracle, the Pythia began to struggle again and the spirit released her. She was then carried or supported to a chamber of rest, where she remained until the nervous ecstasy passed away.

In his dissertation on *The Mysteries,* Iamblichus describes how the spirit of the oracle—a fiery dæmon, even Apollo himself—took control of the Pythoness and manifested through her: "But the prophetess in Delphi, whether she gives oracles to mankind through an attenuated and fiery spirit, bursting from the mouth of the cavern or whether being seated in the adytum on a brazen tripod, or on a stool with four feet, she becomes sacred to the God; whichsoever of these is the case, she entirely gives herself up to a divine spirit, and is illuminated with a ray of divine fire. And when, indeed, fire ascending from the mouth of the cavern circularly invests her in collected abundance, she becomes filled from it with a divine splendour. But when she places herself on the seat of the God, she becomes coadapted to his stable prophetic power: and from both of these preparatory operations she becomes wholly possessed by the God. And then, indeed, he is present with and illuminates her in a separate manner, and is different from the fire, the spirit, the proper seat, and, in short, from all the visible apparatus of the place, whether physical or sacred."

Among the celebrities who visited the oracle of Delphi were the immortal Apollonius of Tyana and his disciple Damsi. After making offerings and being crowned with a laurel wreath and given a branch of the same plant to carry on his hand, Apollonius passed behind the statue of Apollo that stood before the entrance to the cave and descended into the sacred place of the oracle. The priestess was also crowned with laurel and her head bound with a band of white wool. When Apollonius asked the oracle if his name would be remembered by future generations, the Pythoness answered in the affirmative but declared that it would always be calumniated. Apollonius left the cavern in anger but time has proved the accuracy of the prediction, for the early church fathers perpetuated the name of Apollonius as the Antichrist. (For details of the story see *Historie de la Magie.*)

[105]

The messages given by the virgin prophetess were turned over to the philosophers of the oracle, whose duty it was to interpret the same and apply them to the problems on hand. The philosophers, having completed their labors, delivered the results to the poets, who immediately transposed the prophecies into odes and lyrics, setting forth in exquisite form the statements presumably made by Apollo, and published them for the edification of the populace.

Serpents were much in evidence at the oracle of Delphi. The base of the tripod upon which the Pythia sat was composed of the twisted bodies of three large snakes. According to some authorities, one of the methods used to produce the prophetic ecstasy was to force the young priestess to gaze into the eyes of a serpent, when, fascinated and hypnotized, she spoke forth with the voice of the god.

While the early Pythian priestesses were always maidens, some still in their teens, a law was later passed that only women over fifty years of age should be the mouthpiece of the oracle. These older women dressed as young girls and went through the same ceremonial as the first Pythiæ. The change was probably the direct result of a series of assaults made upon the persons of the priestesses by the profane.

During the early history of the Delphian oracle the god only spoke every seven years and then upon the birthday of Apollo. But as time went on the demand so increased that the Pythia was forced to seat herself upon the tripod every month. The time selected for the consultation and the questions to be answered were determined either by lot or a vote of the inhabitants of Delphi.

It is generally admitted that the effect of the Delphian oracle upon the Greek culture was both constructive and profound. James Gardner sums up its influence in the following words: "Its reponses revealed many a tyrant and foretold his fate. Through its means many an unhappy being was saved from destruction and many a perplexed mortal guided in the right way. It encouraged useful institutions and promoted the progress of useful discoveries. Its moral influence was on the side of virtue, and its political influence in favor of the advancement of civil liberty."—(See Faiths of the World.)

(First Published in "The Philosopher")

PERCEPTION OF TRUTH

Wisdom, as a principle, is inconceivable unless it becomes manifest in the wise, and only the wise are capable to recognize it. A man without knowledge knows nothing. It is not man in his aspect as a being without any principle who can know any principle whatever; it is always the principle itself that recognizes itself in other forms. Thus, if a person wants to know the truth, the truth must be alive in him; if there is no truth in him, he can perceive no truth, neither within himself nor in external nature. For ever the truth is crucified between two "thieves" called "superstitition" and "scepticism," and if we see only one of the crucified thieves, we are liable to mistake him for the truth; but the two forms of the thieves are distorted, or, to express it more correctly, the truth is distorted in them. Only when we are capable to recognize the straight form of the Saviour hanging between the two distorted thieves, will we see the difference and know where to search for the Redeemer.—Franz Hartmann.

A Notable Reprint

The Platonic Philosopher's Creed

(Note: In his preface to the volume from which the following extract is taken, Thomas Taylor, the translator, says: "The Creed of the Platonic Philosopher is added for the purpose of presenting the *intelligent* reader with a synoptical view of that sublime theology which was first obscurely promulgated by Orpheus, Pythagoras and Plato, and was afterwards perspicuously unfolded by their legitimate disciples; a theology which, however, it may be involved in oblivion in *barbarous,* and derided in *impious* ages, will again flourish for very extended periods, through all the infinite revolutions of time.")

1. I believe in one first cause of all things, whose nature is so immensely transcendent, that it is even super-essential; and that in consequence of this it cannot properly either be named, or spoken of, or conceived by opinion, or be known, or perceived by any being.

2. I believe, however, that if it be lawful to give a name to that which is truly ineffable, the appellations of *The One* and *The Good* are of all others the most adapted to it; the former of these names indicating that it is the principle of all things, and the latter that it is the ultimate object of desire to all things.

3. I believe that this immense principle produced such things as are first and proximate to itself, most similar to itself; just as the heat *immediately* proceeding from fire is most similar to the heat in the fire; and the light *immediately* emanating from the sun, to that which the sun essentially contains. Hence, this principle produces many principles proximately from itself.

4. I likewise believe that since all things differ from each other, and are multiplied with their proper differences, each of these multitudes is suspended from its one proper principle. That, in consequence of this, all beautiful things, whether in souls or in bodies, are suspended from one fountain of beauty. That whatever possesses symmetry, and whatever is true, and all principles are in a certain respect connate with the first principle, so far as they are principles, with an appropriate subjection and analogy. That all other principles are comprehended in this first principle, not with interval and multitude, but as parts in the whole, and number in the monad. That it is not a certain principle like each of the rest; for of these, one is the principle of beauty, another of truth, and another of something else, but it is *simply principle.* Nor is it simply the *principle of beings,* but it is the *principle of principles;* it being necessary that the characteristic property of principle, after the same manner as other things, should not begin from multitude, but should be collected into one monad as a summit, and which is the principle of principles.

5. I believe, therefore, that such things as are produced by the first good in consequence of being connascent with it, do not recede from essential goodness, since they are immovable and unchanged, and are eternally estab-

lished in the same blessedness. All other natures, however, being produced by the one good, and many goodnesses, since they fall off from essential goodness, and are not immovably established in the nature of divine goodness, possess on this account the good according to participation.

6. I believe that as all things considered as subsisting *causally* in this immense principle, are transcendently more excellent than they are when considered as effects proceeding from him; this principle is very properly said to be all things, *prior* to all; *priority* denoting exempt transcendency. Just as number may be considered as subsisting occultly in the monad, and the circle in the centre; this *occult* being the same in each with *causal* subsistence.

7. I believe that the most proper mode of venerating this great principle of principles is to extend in silence the ineffable parturitions of the soul to its ineffable co-sensation; and that if it be at all lawful to celebrate it, it is to be celebrated as thrice unknown darkness, as the god of all gods, and the unity of all unities, as more ineffable than all silence, and more occult than all essence, as holy among the holies, and concealed in its first progeny, the intelligible gods.

8. I believe that self-subsistent natures are the immediate offspring of this principle, if it be lawful thus to denominate things which ought rather to be called ineffable unfoldings into light from the ineffable.

9. I believe that incorporeal forms or ideas resident in a divine intellect, are the paradigms or models of every thing which has a perpetual subsistence according to nature. That these ideas subsist primarily in the highest intellects, secondarily in souls, and ultimately in sensible natures; and that they subsist in each, characterized by the essential properties of the beings in which they are contained. That they possess a *paternal, producing, guardian, connecting, perfective,* and *uniting* power. That in *divine beings* they possess a power fabricative and gnostic, in *nature* a power fabricative but not gnostic; and in *human souls* in their present condition through a degradation of intellect, a power gnostic, but not fabricative.

10. I believe that this world, depending on its divine artificer, who is himself an intelligible world, replete with the archetypal ideas of all things, is perpetually flowing, and perpetually advancing to being, and, compared with its paradigm, has no stability, or reality of being. That considered, however, as animated by a divine soul, and as being the receptacle of divinities from whom bodies are suspended, it is justly called by Plato, a blessed god.

11. I believe that the great body of this world, which subsists in a perpetual dispersion of temporal extension, may be properly called a *whole, with a total subsistence,* or a *whole of wholes,* on account of the perpetuity of its duration, though this is nothing more than a flowing eternity. That the other wholes which it contains are the celestial spheres, the sphere of æther, the whole of air considered as one great orb; the whole earth, and the whole sea. That these spheres are *parts with a total subsistence,* and through this subsistence are perpetual.

12. I believe that all the parts of the universe are unable to participate of the providence of divinity in a similar manner, but some of its parts enjoy this eternally, and others temporally; some in a primary and others in a secondary degree; for the universe being a perfect whole, must have a first, a middle, and a last part. But its first parts, as having the most excellent subsistence, must always exist according to nature; and its last parts must sometimes exist according to, and sometimes contrary to, nature. Hence, the celestial bodies, which are the first parts of the universe, perpetually subsist

according to nature, both the whole spheres, and the multitude co-ordinate to these wholes; and the only alteration which they experience is a mutation of figure, and variation of light at different periods, but in the sublunary region, while the spheres of the elements remain on account of their subsistence, as wholes, always according to nature; the parts of the wholes have sometimes a natural, and sometimes an unnatural subsistence: for thus alone can the circle of generation unfold all the variety which it contains. I believe, therefore, that the different periods in which these mutations happen, are with great propriety called by Plato, periods of *fertility* and *sterility*: for in these periods a fertility or sterility of men, animals, and plants takes place; so that in fertile periods mankind will be both more numerous, and upon the whole superior in mental and bodily endowments to the men of a barren period. And that a similar reasoning must be extended to irrational animals and plants. I also believe that the most dreadful consequence attending a barren period with respect to mankind is this, that in such a period they have no scientific theology, and deny the existence of the immediate progeny of the ineffable cause of all things.

13. I believe that as the world considered as one great comprehending whole is a divine animal, so likewise every whole which it contains is a world, possessing in the first place a self-perfect unity proceeding from the ineffable by which it becomes a god; in the second place, a divine intellect; in the third place, a divine soul; and in the last place a deified body. That each of these wholes is the producing cause of all the multitude which it contains, and on this account is said to be a whole prior to parts; because considered as possessing an eternal form which holds all its parts together, and gives to the whole perpetuity of subsistence, it is not indigent of such parts to the perfection of its being. And that it follows by a geometrical necessity, that these wholes which rank thus high in the universe must be animated.

14. Hence I believe that after the immense principle of principles in which all things causally subsist absorbed in super-essential light, and involved in unfathomable depths, a beautiful series of principles proceeds, all largely partaking of the ineffable, all stamped with the occult characters of deity, all possessing an overflowing fulness of good. That from these dazzling summits, these ineffable blossoms, these divine propagations, being, life, intellect, soul, nature, and body depend; *monads* suspended from *unities,* deified natures proceeding from deities. That each of these monads is the leader of a series which extends to the last of things, and which, while it proceeds from, at the same time abides in, and returns to its leader. Thus all beings proceed from and are comprehended in the first being; all intellects emanate from one first intellect; all souls from one first soul; all natures blossom from one first nature; and all bodies proceed from the vital and luminous body of the world. That all these great monads are comprehended in the first one, from which both they and all their depending series are unfolded into light. And that hence this first one is truly the unity of unities, the monad of monads, the principle of principles, the god of gods, one and all things, and yet one prior to all.

15. I also believe that man is a microcosm, comprehending in himself *partially* every thing which the world contains divinely and *totally.* That hence he is endued with an intellect subsisting in energy, and a rational soul proceeding from the same causes as those from which the intellect and soul of the universe proceed. And that he has likewise an ethereal vehicle analog-

ous to the heavens, and a terrestrial body composed from the four elements, and with which also it is co-ordinate.

16. I believe that the rational part of man, in which his essence consists, is of a self-motive nature, and that it subsists between intellect, which is immovable both in essence and energy, and nature, which both moves and is moved.

17. I believe that the human as well as every mundane soul, uses periods and restitutions of its proper life. For in consequence of being measured by time, it energizes transitively, and possesses a proper motion. But every thing which is moved perpetually, and participates of time, revolves periodically, and proceeds from the same to the same.

18. I also believe that as the human soul ranks among the number of those souls that *sometimes* follow the mundane divinities, in consequence of subsisting immediately after dæmons and heroes the *perpetual* attendants of the gods, it possesses a power of descending infinitely into the sublunary region, and of ascending from thence to real being. That in consequence of this, the soul while an inhabitant of earth is in a fallen condition, an apostate from deity, an exile from the orb of light. That she can only be restored while on earth to the divine likeness, and be able after death to reascend to the intelligible world, by the exercise of the *cathartic* and *theoretic* virtues; the former purifying her from the defilements of a mortal nature, and the latter elevating her to the vision of true being. And that such a soul returns after death to her kindred star from which she fell, and enjoys a blessed life.

19. I believe that the human soul essentially contains all knowledge, and that whatever knowledge she acquires in the present life, is nothing more than a recovery of what she once possessed; and which discipline evocates from its dormant retreats.

20. I also believe that the soul is punished in a future for the crimes she has committed in the present life; but that this punishment is proportioned to the crimes, and is not perpetual; divinity punishing, not from anger or revenge, but in order to purify the guilty soul, and restore her to the proper perfection of her nature.

21. I also believe that the human soul on its departure from the present life, will, if not properly purified, pass into other terrene bodies; and that if it passes into a human body, it becomes the soul of that body; but if into the body of a brute, it does not become the soul of the brute, but is externally connected with the brutal soul in the same manner as presiding dæmons are connected in their beneficent operations with mankind; for the rational part never becomes the soul of the irrational nature.

22. Lastly, I believe that souls that live according to virtue, shall in other respects be happy; and when separated from the irrational nature, and purified from all body, shall be conjoined with the gods, and govern the whole world, together with the deities by whom it was produced.

Emerson is a citizen of the universe who has taken up his residence for a few days and nights in this traveling caravansary between the two inns that hang out the signs of Venus and Mars.—Ralph Waldo Emerson, by Holmes.

Mr. Hall's Most Recent Picture

The accompanying reproduction is from an oil painting of Mr. Hall by the eminent English artist, Mr. E. Hodgson Smart.

The portrait—which is life size—will be on exhibition at the Church of the People the first Sunday morning in August.

Mr. Smart began his art career at the age of fourteen, having gained at that time the certificates from South Kensington, London, which qualified him to teach art in any of the South Kensington art schools in England. At the age of twenty he passed into the head class at the Antwerp Academy, gaining first prize in an examination where over two thousand pupils competed. The painting which won the prize is now in the old museum at Antwerp. Mr. Smart afterwards studied at Julian's in Paris, and later with Sir Hubert Von Herkomer in London.

His first important picture, "Prayer in a Belgian Church," was specially invited to every important exhibition at the time in England. Afterwards when his portraits of "The Lady in Black" and "The Artist's Mother" were hung in the Royal Academy of London he received many important commissions including one from the Duke of Northumberland; he also painted King Edward, Queen Alexandria, Earl Carrington, Duke of San Martino, Prince Pigniatelli, Baron van der Capellen, head of the Dutch Cavalry, Baron van Sytzama, and many other distinguished people.

Mr. Smart's work has always been characterized by its nobility, strength, and refinement. He believes the artist should be forgotten in the presence of his own work, and that the better the portrait the more it reveals of the sitter and the less of the painter.

Among Mr. Smart's most recent pictures are three portraits of Marshal Foch, three of General Pershing, three of President Harding, one of Admiral Sims, one of Sir Arthur Currie, one of Hon. Newton D. Baker, one of Sir Robert Borden, and a full-length seated portrait of Dr. Annie Besant. The artist believes his portrait of Mr. Hall—which is his very latest work—to be also one of his best.

Art and Archaeology published the following comment on Mr. Smart's portrait of President Harding:

"The President is very seriously interpreted, with great dignity, and the picture, which is a standing three-quarter length, cannot fail to impress all by the splendid character depicted. It is one of the few great portraits of a President. One may find in the Library of Congress Print Division almost numberless portraits of noted Presidents. Washington was successfully painted by many, perhaps best by Gilbert Stuart, President Jackson by Sully, Lincoln and Roosevelt by several artists, and Woodrow Wilson by John Singer Sargent. It is not too much to say that in the years to come Hodgson Smart's 'President Harding' will rank with the very best of these, for Mr. Smart is a very wonderful painter."

A portrait in oil
of
Manly P. Hall

by E. Hodgeson Smart

Orientalism

The Ten Incarnations of Vishnu
By MANLY P. HALL

On a rocky island in the harbor of Bombay is a series of remarkable caverns carved from the living rock. In the first of these is to be seen the colossal figure of the Brahmanic Creator in His threefold aspect of Brahma, Vishnu, and Shiva. The image consists of only the head and shoulders, is over twenty feet high, and was originally concealed from the eyes of the profane by swinging doors composed of great blocks of native rock. The *Trimurti,* as it is commonly called, constitutes one of the most sacred and secret emblems of the Hindus, being equivalent to the triangle of the Freemasons and the three-headed Christ of the early Christian mystics.

The island upon which the caves are situated was explored by the Portugese, who named it *Elephanta* because of a beautifully carved figure of an elephant which they found in a conspicuous place. Before this very *Trimurti* the great Pythagoras was initiated into the Brahman Mysteries, and in these same caves one of the most exquisite examples of a pre-Christian crucifix was discovered. The carvings in the Elephanta caverns are world famous for their beauty and lifelike appearance. We remember one group in particular. It was a scene depicting the marriage of Shiva and Pavti. Brahma is present to bless the marriage and the coy expression on the face of the bride is only equalled by the look of sheepishness on the features of the groom. The figures are life size and in high relief, but have been subjected to considerable mutilation at the hands of Mohammedans, Christian missionaries, and thoughtless tourists.

The great figure of the *Trimurti* in its gloomy recess means little to the hosts of tourists who gaze upon it and then turn to other wonders. Students of philosophy and comparative religion, however, see in this image a magnificent exposition of the Secret Doctrine of the ancient Brahmans, a doctrine which, alas, is fast disappearing from the people to whom it was originally revealed.

It matters little what nation be considered. In almost every instance its religion is founded upon the doctrine of a Trinity. The chief triad of the Greeks was Uranus, Saturn, and Jupiter; of the Egyptians, Ammon, Ra, and Osiris; of the Persians, Ahura-Mazda, Mithras, and Ahriman; of the Qabbalistic Hebrews, Kether, Chokmah, and Binah; of the Christians, the Father, Son, and Holy Ghost; of the Pythagoreans, the monad, the duad, and the triad.

In his *Inquiry into the Trinity of the Ancients* Isaac Preston Cory lists the following triads which were accepted by the ancients as representing the fundamental expressions of divine power and energy:

"From the different Orphic fragments we find that the Orphic Trinity consisted of

| Metis, | Phanes, or Eros, | Ericapæus. |

which are interpreted

| Will, or Counsel, | Light, or Love, | Life, or Lifegiver. |

From Acusilaus,

Metis,	Eros,	Ether.

From Hesiod, according to Damascius,

Earth,	Eros,	Tartarus.

From Pherecydes Syrius,

Fire,	Water,	Spirit, or Air.

From the Sidonians,

Cronus,	Love,	Cloudy darkness.

From the Phœnicians,

Ulomus,	Chusorus,	The Egg.

From the Chaldæan and Persian Oracles of Zoroaster,

Fire,	Sun,	Ether.
Fire,	Light,	Ether.

From the later Platonists,

Power,	Intellect,	Father.
Power,	Intellect,	Soul, or Spirit.

By the ancient Theologists, according to Macrobius, the Sun was invoked in the Mysteries, as

Power of the world,   Light of the world,   Spirit of the world.

To which may perhaps be added, from Sanchoniatho, the three sons of Genus,

Fire,   Light,   Flame."

To the list given by Cory may be added a very fundamental geometrical illustration: the triad of primitive symbols consisting of the point, the line, and the circle. The point is the appropriate emblem of the One Creative Cause—the First or the Source. All lines are merely rows of dots and all bodies aggregations of dots. In the Christian system of theology the dot would be the appropriate emblem of God the Father, for it is the One of which all creatures are but parts. The line is the outpouring of the dot, the One coming into expression; it is, therefore, the second person of the Creative Triad. In the Hindu school this second person is called *Vishnu*, which corresponds to the *Christ* of the Christians. The line bears witness to the potentialities of the dot for it is the outpouring or welling up of that Eternal Life forever concealed within the profundity of the germinative dot. The circle marks the circumference of the dot and limits the outpouring of the line. Therefore, it is the *destroyer*, the yawning mouth that swallows up the life of the dot, the *hades* into which the line descends and where it remains until it has overcome the mystery of death, which mystery is part of the secret of the circle. In India the circle is called *Shiva*, the *Destroyer*, the Lord of the mundane sphere; to Christendom it is known as the *Holy Ghost*, or the third person of the Divine Triad.

The dot, the line, and the circle may also be considered as natural emblems of life, intelligence, and substance—the three unknown causes which Huxley declared could never be discovered: consciousness, intelligence, and force. It is interesting to note that the three major divisions of human thought—namely the scientific, the philosophic, and the theologic—should have respectively the circle, the line, and the dot as their natural symbols. The circle, representing force and matter, limits the achievements of science to those elements from which the material universe was fabricated. The task of science is to solve the mystery of the circle; beyond that mystery it cannot go. Where science leaves off, however, philosophy must begin and the labor to which philosophy is dedicated is to solve the enigma of that intermediate line (the radius) which connects the dot and the circle. The name of that line is intelligence and the highest form of intelligence is that capable of accurately estimating the relationship existing between spirit and matter. Beyond reason philosophy cannot go, for reason is the highest phase of philosophic attainment. To theology, therefore, is assigned the labor of discovering and analyzing the nature of the dot—that spiritual Cause which neither the mind nor the hand can reach but which is cognizable only by its own spiritual correlate within the constitution of the individual.

By theology, however, is meant the divine science of spiritual things not the mass of conflicting creeds and dogmas which parade under the name of theology today. True theology bears the same relation to the arts and sciences of the world that the spirit does to the parts and members of its physical constitution. Theology is that divinely-revealed code by which man is assisted in the unfoldment of his spiritual potentialities. In this sense— and this sense only—theology is that divine science dedicated to the task of revealing to an ever-awakening humanity the mystery of the Creative Seed— the dot in the midst of the cosmic circle.

Have you ever realized how seldom a shrine, temple or church is erected to the Father Principle in religion? The churches of Christianity are all built to honor the second person of the Triad—the Christ. The same holds true in India, where not more than one or two temples to Brahma can be found but literally tens of thousands to Vishnu and Shiva. In Egypt there was but one temple to the Father Principle but scores to Ra and Osiris. In that country a precedent was established which was later incorporated in the Christian doctrine, namely the worship of the first Principle through the nature of the second. Hence the sanctifying of temples to Ammon-Ra.

Thus the second phase of the Creative Triad—Cosmic Intelligence— with its symbol, light, has been the dominating factor in religion since earliest times. In India Vishnu is the personification of the Universal Mind. In Him the divine potentialities of the incomprehensible Brahma are objectified, becoming the foundation of the world. One of the greatest secrets in mystical lore is that of the triangle. It has been truly said that any problem can be solved if its triangular base be first discovered. Every element, condition, or substance in the universe is founded upon a triad. Hence the multiplicity of triads constituting the Platonic theology.

The triangle is a continual reminder that every structure is essentially threefold and every intelligence a trinity of divine, human, and animal constituents. When man is considered as a sevenfold creature—as he invariably was in the ancient Mystery Schools—his nature was divided into two parts, of which the superior was made up of three divine elements and the inferior of four natural elements. The three spiritual parts of man are called the *Silent Ones.* They are the Three Immortals who remain throughout the ages meditating upon the fourfold body which they have permitted to exist but of which they themselves have never become a part.

In this 20th century it is generally conceded that an individual without a mind—or, more correctly, one who does not make proper use of his mental faculties—cannot succeed. Intelligence is accepted as a necessary basis for the computation of value and the rationalist is quite convinced that the salvation of the soul depends upon the clarity and organization of the reasoning faculties. This is in perfect harmony with theology; for the Savior-Gods of various peoples are really only the personifications of the Divine Intellect. As these deities come to save humanity, so the mind in man must become the *savior* of his lower constitution. The higher nature of man, being incapable

First and Second Incarnations

of death, is without need of salvation, but the lower man must build of the mind a bridge to connect his irrational soul with his divinely rational *Anthropos,* or *Over-Nature.*

Vishnu, being the active creative principle of the universe, and forever seeking the preserve His creation from the ravages of the destroying Shiva, is, therefore, looked upon as the benevolent and beneficent spirit. Here again we find a parallel between Vishnu and the human mind, for from the beginning of human civilization man has been using his mind as a weapon against the surrounding destructive forces of Nature. Man has only survived because of his intelligence, and as this increases in power he struggles ever more intelligently to counteract the forces of disintegration constantly working against him. The infant mind of primitive man conceived crude means for self-protection from both the ravages of the elements and the strange monsters of the prehistoric world. Man discovered that he could overcome the animal with fire; fire with water; water with earth. He turned the irrational elements upon themselves and thus saved his own life. Later he realized that he could harness the elements and, because he had a mind, he could control the mindless. He made the water-wheel and the windmill, with fire he tempered the metals, and harnessed the mindless beasts to plow his fields and bear his burdens, thus forcing them unquestioningly to obey his superior will. As new epochs in the history of the world brought new conditions, new faculties were evolved with which to conquer them. Man has finally come to realize that there is no problem so great, no mystery so profound, no element so strong, no beast so ferocious but that intelligence has proved its master.

However, the mind which was given to man proved not only a blessing but also a curse. Man discovered that he could accomplish anything that he *willed* to accomplish, for Nature was no longer able to control him. So man took the mind that was predestined to be his *savior* and used it as a weapon against his fellow creatures. He brutally enslaved the mindless; he broke the bodies of the beasts and, turning upon Nature of which he was a part, prostituted his newly-found faculty by devastating the very earth that bore him. Still unsatisfied, he discovered that some of his own kind were weaker than he. Armed with primitive weapons, he, therefore, descended upon the more primitive tribes of humanity, slaying and enslaving the weaker and spattering the earth with the blood of her noblest products.

Man's ingratitude for the blessings given him out of the treasure-house of natural potentiality is beautifully expressed in the tragic legend of Prometheus. At the price not only of his own liberty but of ages of suffering, Prometheus, the friend of man, brought fire from the abode of the gods. Concealing the spark in a hollow reed, he flew down with it to the abode of men and thus revealed to mankind the mystery of the flame. For this deed he was chained to the brow of Mt. Caucasus with a vulture to feed eternally upon his liver. Man repaid the noble sacrifice of the Titian by taking fire and with it forging weapons and armor with which to slay his fellows.

Today we see thought-power—the most recent boon of the gods—crucified like the Saviors of old between the thieves of greed and passion. The mental energy given to man that he might acquire a knowledge not only of himself but of the divine plan of which he is a part is now employed principally for the accomplishment of petty worldly ends. Man has forgotten the noble stock from which he sprung and the great purpose for which he was created. As the Philistines blinded Samson so man has blinded the giant of intellect and chained it to a grindstone. This divine being, capable of soaring into the very presence of Reality, now like a degraded beast paces round and round in ever-deepening ruts, grinding the corn of modern Philistia. But intellect is a rebellious slave, for deep within it is a divine urge. The race will yet live to see blinded giant tear down the pillars of materialism, for the intellect which man has perverted will prove his final undoing.

Throughout Eastern philosophy the Universal Mind is personified and, in spite of the seeming failure of races and individuals, it finally accomplishes the redemption and perfection of the race. The average individual finds it difficult to consider forces as personalities or to look upon every energy in Nature as an individualized creature possessing intellect and power. Such, however, is the Oriental conception. Therefore, Vishnu—the personified principle of Divine Knowledge, the mind which controls the working of the whole—periodically manifests Himself, becoming temporarily involved in the processes of creation that He may bring to the world spiritual understanding necessary to cope with the drastic changes taking place in civilization at certain periods.

"When virtue fails upon the earth, then I come forth," says Vishnu in the Bhagavad-Gita, and according to the secret doctrine of the Hindus the Great Mind has come into objective manifestation nine times already that He might prevent the failure of civilization. These incarnations of the Lord of the World are called the *avataras* or the incarnations of the Great Savior. Vishnu appeared for one or more of three reasons: (1) to overcome some great evil in the world threatening the future of humanity, in the legends this evil being usually personified as a wicked king, or a great monster such as a dragon or ferocious demon; (2) to purify the faiths of men from that con-

Third and Fourth Incarnations

tamination which invariably creeps into religion after the lapse of thousands of years; (3) to found a new faith or doctrine or to sound the key word of a new period of world endeavor. Accompanying this article is a series of ten drawings from Picart's *Religious Ceremonials,* showing the purposes of the ten incarnations according to East Indian symbolism. The tenth incarnation of Vishnu has not yet taken place, but the peoples of the East are waiting for His coming as many Christian sects look forward expectantly to the second coming of Jesus Christ.

In our little brochure on *Occult Anatomy* we called attention to the curious correspondence existing between the forms which Vishnu assumed during his incarnations and the months of the prenatal epoch. The intelligence of the human embryo during those periods closely parallels the intelligence of the various creatures through which Vishnu is said to incarnate. Since Pythagoras was initiated into the Brahman Mysteries, he may have founded his numerical philosophy upon the theory of Vishnu's incarnations. The ten dots which constitute the Pythagorean *tetractys* may be interpreted, therefore, in the same manner as Vishnu's incarnations. The same is true of the ten spheres of the Qabbalists in which the Universal Spirit incarnates sequentially during both involutionary and evolutionary processes. According to the legends of His followers, Vishnu—like the Christian Christ—will come in the last day of the universe and judge the souls of all creatures.

The first *avatara* of Vishnu is termed the *Matsya,* or fish, incarnation. At a very early time in the history of the world so great a corruption blighted mankind that the gods determined to destroy the human race with a great flood. The prince who ruled at that time was a very pious man and he and the seven Rishis, or Wise Men, their wives, and pairs of all the animals and other forms of life entered an ark. The Lord Vishnu took upon Himself the

[119]

Fifth and Sixth Incarnations

body of a fish and fastened the ark to His own body by means of a cable fashioned out of a serpent. When the flood subsided, Vishnu slew an evil monster who had stolen the Vedas, or sacred books of the law. The books being returned, a new human race was formed who treasured the sacred writings and obeyed them implicitly. In the sacred books of the Hindus the story of the first *avatara* requires 14,000 verses for its recital.

The second *avatara* of Vishnu is termed the *Kurma*, or tortoise, incarnation. This incarnation is connected indirectly also with the flood, for in it Vishnu took upon Himself the body of a turtle, supporting with His shell the sacred mountain, Mandara. Using the great serpent for a rope and the mountain as an axis, the gods and demons churned the great ocean in order to regain the sacred Amrita, or the beverage of the gods. By this churning process fourteen sacred articles were discovered. These are shown in the picture grouped about the central mountain and in the hands of the deities.

The third *avatara* of Vishnu is termed the *Varaha*, or boar, incarnation. In this incarnation Vishnu is generally depicted upholding the earth with his tusks, the earth being deposited within the concave surface of a lunar crescent. According to the allegory, there was once a *Daitya* who desired to become the ruler of the earth. He ultimately grew so powerful that he stole the planet and carried it with him into the depths of the ocean. Vishnu, assuming the form of a boar, dived into the abyss and fought with this monster for one thousand years. Ultimately slaying the evil one, Vishnu restored the earth to its proper position by raising it upon his tusks.

The fourth *avatara* of Vishnu is termed the *Narasingha*, or man-lion, incarnation. This is the story of a holy man who for ten thousand years prayed and meditated for the boon of universal monarchy and that of ever

Seventh and Eighth Incarnations

lasting life. Having become very great, he also grew equally selfish and arrogant. The gods led him into debate with his own son concerning the omnipresence of Deity. When his son told him that God was everywhere, even in the pillar supporting the roof of the palace, the evil prince in anger and blasphemy struck the pillar with his sword. The pillar, splitting in half, revealed Vishnu with the head of a lion, who after fighting with the egoistic prince for an hour dragged him into the hollow pillar and destroyed him, thus delivering the world from his arrogance.

The fifth *avatara* of Vishnu is termed the *Vamana,* or dwarf, incarnation. In this case a great monarch, becoming proud of the fact that he ruled over three worlds—heaven, earth, and hell—neglected the performance of the proper ceremonials to the gods. In the form of a dwarf, Vishnu appeared before the king, requesting a boon—that is, as much land as he could pace off with three steps. The king granted the request and ratified his promise by pouring water on the hand of the dwarf. Immediately the tiny figure increased in size until it filled the entire universe and, taking its three paces, owned the world, but out of kindly consideration for the virtues of the king permitted him to retain the government of hell.

The sixth *avatara* of Vishnu is termed the *Parasu Rama* incarnation. This is the first of the series of true human incarnations of the god. *Parasu Rama* was the son of a very aged holy man to whom the god Indra had entrusted the sacred cow. One of the Rajahs, desiring to possess the cow, finally brought about the death of the holy man, whose wife then committed *sati,* or suicide, praying with her last words that the gods would avenge the murder of her husband. Vishnu, answering the call, assumed the personality of *Parasu Rama* and after twenty battles slew the evil Rajah.

The seventh *avatara* of Vishnu, termed the *Rama Chandra* incarnation, is contained within the great Indian epic, the *Ramayana*. *Ravana,* the evil king of Lanka, which is now Ceylon, stole *Sita,* the ideal of East Indian womanhood from her beloved husband, *Rama.* Assisted by *Hunaman,* the king of the apes, *Rama Chandra* won back *Sita* and, having tested her by fire, proved that she had remained true to him. The apes in a single night built a stone bridge between Lanka and the coast of India. *Ravana,* in order to torture *Hunaman,* king of the apes, set fire to his tail. *Hunaman,* running through the streets of Lanka, in turn set fire to the city, thus virtually destroying the power of *Ravana.*

The eighth *avatara* of Vishnu is termed the *Krishna* incarnation. The story of *Krishna* is so well known that it hardly requires any elaborate description. The illustration depicts the birth of *Krishna* and also the legend of his escape from death while an infant by being carried across the river in a basket. The water rose, threatening to destroy the bearer of the sacred child. To prevent this calamity, *Krishna* permitted one of his feet to hang over the edge of the basket, whereupon the water subsided. There are numerous instances in the life of *Krishna* which parallel the experiences of Jesus. These include the slaughter of the innocents, the transfiguration, the crucifixion, the resurrection, and the ascension. *Krishna* is considered as a personification of the sun, and his consort, Radha, is the embodiment of the earth.

The ninth *avatara* of Vishnu is generally termed the *Buddha* incarnation, although a great number of Hindus disagree with this. Some Orientalists have gone so far as to declare that the Christ of Christendom represents the ninth *avatara* or incarnation of Vishnu. The life of *Buddha* is beautifully set forth in Sir Edwin Arnold's *Light of Asia.* *Buddha* was an Indian prince who, inspired by the needs of humanity, renounced his kingdom and dedicated himself to the service of mankind. After many years of renunciation and prayer the two great laws of life were revealed to him—reincarnation and karma. He lifted the Buddhist faith from comparative obscurity to the dignity of the world's greatest religion, and at his death or translation a great number of Indian nobles were present. It was found impossible to light the funeral pyre until the body burst into flames by the release of spiritual energy from a great emerald which adorned the body of the dead sage.

The tenth *avatara* of Vishnu is termed the *Kalki,* or horse, incarnation and is the one which is yet to come. This incarnation is generally symbolized by a picture of a man leading a riderless white horse. The animal is sometimes shown with wings like the fabled Pegasus of the Greeks. Among many nations the horse is an emblem of the animal world or the lower sphere of being. In this sense it may infer that when Vishnu appears for the last time he will be mounted upon the world—that is, victorious over the substances of inferior Nature. The Brahmans believe that in his tenth *avatara* Vishnu will act as the true Savior of the world, redeeming the faithful from the sorrows and limitations of mortal existence. No man knows the day of his coming, but the Hindus are positive that when the great need arises he will be there to preserve and redeem those who have been faithful to his laws and tenets. Such, in brief, is the story of the ten immortal incarnations of the Lord of Light.

A careful consideration of the graduated series of ever nobler creatures through which the great Vishnu incarnates reveals an evolutionary doctrine

Ninth and Tenth Incarnations

subtly concealed behind these curious emblems. Of this Madam Blavatsky writes as follows:

"In this diagram of avatars we see traced the gradual evolution and transformation of all species out of the ante-Silburian mud of Darwin and the *ilus* of Sanchoniathon and Berosus. Beginning with the Azoic time, corresponding to the *ilus* in which Brahma implants the creative germ, we pass through the palæozoic and Mesozoic times, covered by the first and second incarnations as the fish and tortoise; and the Cenozoic, which is embraced by the incarnations in the animal and semi-human forms of the boar and man-lion; and we come to the fifth and crowning geological period, designated as the 'era of mind, or age of man,' whose symbol in the Hindu mythology is the dwarf—the first attempt of nature at the creature of man. * * * From a fish the progress of this dual transformation carries on the physical form though the shape of a tortoise, a boar, and a man-lion; and then, appearing in the dwarf of humanity, it shows Parasu Rama physically, a perfect, spiritually, an undeveloped entity, until it carries mankind personified by one god-like man, to the apex of physical and spiritual perfection—a god on earth." (See *Isis Unveiled*.)

In the *Vishnupuranam* it is written: "This universe hath sprung from Vishnu,—and in Him it is established. He is the cause of creation, maintenance and destruction thereof, and He is the universe." Vishnu is thus to be considered both the fabricator and the fabric of the world structure. He is the Deity in which men live and move and have their being. He is that objective power which manifests the eternally subjective condition of Brahma, the first creative person of the Divine Triad. He stands between

[123]

the superior heavens which are of the nature of Brahma and the inferior world which is of the nature of Shiva. Therefore, He is the sun which, according to the Mysteries, occupies the focal point between abstraction and concretion. As Lord of the sun He is the patron of all creatures and forms, the bestower of life and the giver of abundance. He is often represented with blue skin, the blue representing the heavens which are his body and also the subtle invisible ethers which form his magic horse. In Indian art Vishnu is often depicted sleeping through the night of cosmic darkness upon the coils of a great serpent. When thus represented a lotus stalk is shown growing out of his navel and upon the blossom of this lotus sits the great Brahma with four heads. It is very difficult to secure any satisfactory explanation of this symbol which pertains to the deepest principles of Eastern occultism. In one sense of the word, Vishnu—like the Greek Cronus—destroys the power of his father and usurps his authority as Lord of the world. When Vishnu fabricates the universe he absorbs into it the great Brahma, for in the last analysis Vishnu forms the universe out of the nature of Brahma, of whose constitution He also is a part. The lotus growing from the navel may be interpreted to signify that Brahma is the Cause which nourishes the world through a spiritual umbilicus symbolized by the lotus stalk. The symbol may also be interpreted to mean the gradual growth or ascension of Brahma out of the nature of Vishnu, for when the latter deity is asleep in the coils of the dragon of measureless time Brahma rises out of and exists superior to the sleeping Vishnu.

The ten incarnations of Vishnu may be said to represent those creative efforts made by the gods while they were attempting to establish various species of organized life upon the face of the world. From earliest times life struggled to manifest itself through adequate vehicles and in its effort to discover the proper type of body for its purpose experimented with many forms and cast them aside. From these rejected structures have descended many species of irrational creatures to whom it was found the divine nature could not be imparted. Certain members of the simian family represent one of the types of bodies into which the Lords of Reason could not descend. Therefore, in them the conscious mind is absent.

For thousands of years every civilization, remembering the promise of the Lord of Light—which promise has been given equally to all men—has believed the time to be at hand for the last *avatara* of the Lord of the world. Each generation believes that it needs him more than any other generation of the past or of the future. For nineteen centuries Christians have been daily awaiting the second coming of the Messiah and the consequent end of the world. Today there is undoubtedly a grave decline of virtue and a great spiritual need, but who knows whether tomorrow will not offer a still greater problem?

When the World Lord shall come no man knows, for humanity is not farsighted enough to realize the moment of its own greatest need. But according to the deepest concepts of mysticism, He is always here, riding upon the white horse of the world, guiding with sure hand the reins of the divine steed. The white horse may well symbolize the purified soul of the redeemed man, its wings the spiritualization of the material body. Every pure heart and enlightened mind becomes a vehicle of expression for he World Lord, who is ever speaking to mankind through the lips of purified human creatures.

As with His last coming the Lord of enlightened love redeems His world and accepts his creatures back again into the nature of Himself, so in the life of every individual there comes a time when the Lord of enlightened love within himself becomes the dominant factor in his life. Once this spiritual being is cognized and its power appreciated, it becomes the ruler of man's lower world and gradually absorbs the mortal man into its own immortal nature.

Every human being has within himself a Lord Vishnu, the objectification of the spiritual germ—Brahma. This Vishnu is the immortal spirit of understanding of accomplishment, of realization, and of divinity itself. When man purifies his body, opens the chambers of his heart, and disentangles the skein of his thoughts he becomes finally a living temple. And to this temple Lord Vishnu comes because the house has been made ready for Him. Until this Universal Spirit of Light first comes to the individual, it will never come to the world. Each human being in turn must experience the mystery of the second coming of his Lord and until such time as this takes place his spiritual redemption is not consummated. All the mysteries of the outer world must take place within the little world of man's consciousness before they can be of any benefit to him.

Questions & answers·

Q. I have always had a deep love of Shakespeare—I think his "Hamlet" above all. And yet I never read "Hamlet" that I do not feel a hidden symbolism behind the character that is elusive and yet persistently puzzling. What is your opinion of the symbolism of "Hamlet," for the usual literal interpretation never seems adequate?—D. M. C.

A. As you probably know, the author of the Shakespearian plays borrowed the plot of Hamlet from a very much earlier writing, making such changes as he saw fit. The conversational parts, of course, are the ones which contain the most subtle shades of meaning and were written with the needs of an acrostic and also a biliteral cipher in mind. There is little doubt that the Shakespearian plays, if not written by Sir Francis Bacon, were at least prepared under his supervision and with his assistance. The name "Hamlet," having "Ham" for the first syllable, is a daring play upon the name of Bacon himself and, as may be expected, a certain part of his own life is involved in the story. There were certain mysteries in the early life of Lord Bacon which may, in part at least, be paralleled by incidents in the youth of the "melancholy Dane." The entire Shakespearian collection of plays and sonnets contains Masonic and Rosicrucian philosophy. In some cases this is deeply concealed and in others it is more apparent. There are many allusions to the mystical sciences in Hamlet, also in Macbeth, The Tempest, and The Tragedy of Cymbeline. The mystery surrounding the Shakespearian plays has not yet been solved, but everything points to the conclusion that they represent a direct effort on the part of certain European secret societies to promulgate their doctrines among the learned of Europe. One author who has written extensively on the subject claims to have discovered part of the rituals of the modern Masonic order in certain of the Shakespearian plays. Of course, philosophically, Hamlet may be considered as an allegorical depiction of the struggle through which every individual must pass on the path to self-mastery. The entire play of Hamlet is a Rosicrucian enigma and time alone can completely disentangle the skein.

Q. Will you please clarify the subject of prayer. Does man pray to a personal God? Is prayer merely auto-suggestion?—V. F. V.

A. As the philosopher realizes that there can be no personal God, he considers prayer in a light very different from the orthodox churchgoer. To the philosopher, God is a Principle, a Power, and a Spiritual Reality. God is the universal life everywhere and in all things. Man is, therefore, part of the nature and substance of God, for man is a composite creature consisting of spirit, soul or mind, and body. All that is visible in the physical world is the body, but within it and controlling it is a divine life which is part of the very nature of God. The spiritual part of man is called the *Anthropos* or, in the words of Emerson, the *Over-Soul*. There is a law in Nature that we attract to ourselves that which we desire and also that which we hate. So if we love anything or hate anything sufficiently, it finally becomes an inseparable part of ourselves. Everything that we desire, we actually pray for, for prayer and desire are of a similar nature. A desire for that which is right is a continual offering to the Deity; a desire for that which is evil is, in like manner, a continual blasphemy against the Divine Power in Nature which is ever effecting the perpetuation of good. It is not what we pray for in the morning or evening which constitutes true prayer; prayer is that which we desire continuously throughout every minute and hour of the day.

Q. Based upon the purely physical aspects of evolution, the materialist has formulated as the basis of ethics the law of the survival of the physically fittest. From a similar observation of intellectual processes and accomplishments, the intellectualist has enunciated the doctrine of the survival of the intellectually fittest. Is it not a fact, however, that evolution represents essentially the survival of the morally fittest?—F. V. S.

A. The physical body and the intellectual nature are both vehicles for the expression of an indwelling divine nature, which is superior to, but is hampered in its expression by, its mental and material constitutions. If you consider the moral nature to be that part of man which intuitively recognizes right, virtue, and integrity, and attempts to govern its compound structure according to the laws of ethics, then you are no longer referring to a vehicle but to that spiritual nature of man which is the source of his bodies. From a purely materialistic standpoint, the ethical nature is the highest expression of mental evolution because it is the result of an estimation of actions and reactions and their relationship to the self. The reaction of the spiritual nature upon the material nature results in the creation of the soul, and the soul is—to a certain degree, at least—the ethical nature. Spirit and matter are divine elements, in fact phases of one element, but the soul is an artificial element created in man by the processes of mental and physical evolution. By projecting Redbeard's law of the survival of the fittest into the true philosophical aspect of man's evolution, we find that the body of man is gradually devoured by that which is stronger than itself—that is, it is absorbed into the nature of the soul, for the soul is, in the last analysis, the highest condition of the regenerated body. The soul, in turn, is devoured by the spirit. Ultimately there is but one thing capable of survival, and that is spirit, because spirit is the only substance or condition not subject to destruction. Evolution progresses from the least degree of spirituality to the greatest degree of spirituality; involution from the greatest degree of spirituality to the least degree of spirituality. Ultimately spirit—like Saturn—devours all its children and is itself an eternal condition. Evolution is only noticeable because through its mysterious process the activity of spirit becomes ever more tangible and the control of matter ever less complete. One writer has declared evolution to be merely the process of turning the internal constitution of the creature outward and the outward constitution inward. In its pilgrimage through the varying degrees of substance—or, more accurately, the various conditions of separateness from its source—the life principle in man gradually unfolds a type of consciousness that is capable of self-recognition. Accomplishment of this step completes the process of involution, for man is then an individual unit with an individual center of self-awareness. The process of evolution then begins, and by it the center of awareness is continually increased until it gradually absorbs into itself the shell or personality originally inclosing it. During the process of evolution the center of self-consciousness stores up experience, which experience itself becomes an immortal part of man's divine nature. This immortal body thus built from the reactions and experiences of life gradually becomes the spiritual cause of the ethical nature, and when the evolutionary process is finally completed man will consist of a radiant center of self-consciousness plus the fruitage of experience—the soul.

Q. I find in occult literature references of a seemingly contradictory nature respecting the "mind" and its legitimate office in the compound constitution of man. For example, one author solemnly adjures us to make every doctrinal belief pass the gauntlet of reason, declaring that reason's torch is the safest guide to wisdom. In other writings along occult lines, however, I find numerous allusions to the "mind" as being the deprecatory factor that separates us from God. On the other hand, does the "mind" not stand as the mediator between the lower self and the Higher Self—that familiar figure of the reconciler of the extremes found not only in the teachings of philosophies but also in the occult constitution of the universe?—Anon.

A. There are two distinct schools of religion and philosophy. In one the reason is made the final criterion; in the other the heart and its intuitional facilities are considered supreme. Technically, the mind is divisible into two parts, one of which we can call the *spiritual* mind and the other the *material* mind. The spiritual mind is part of the divine constitution of man and in this sphere of consciousness the human spirit itself has its abode. The material, or animal, mind is united to the personality and is the one so often referred to by the Christian Scientists as the "mortal mind." The functions of ·the mind, however, are so abstract and bewildering that only with the greatest difficulty can even an expert distinguish the spiritual from the material mind. Some have declared the key-word of the lower (material) mind to be *analysis;* that of the higher (spiritual) mind, *synthesis.* The higher mind we know to be creative because it partakes of the creative power of spirit. The lower mind, on the other hand, is not creative but mimics the mental attainments of other creatures. The products of the higher mind cannot be dissociated from the consciousness itself; therefore, what the higher mind thinks, the individual is. On the contrary, the individual who functions only through the lower mind may act in absolute discord with his intellectual concept. Above mind in both of its phases, however, is a plane of higher cognition which is purely spiritual. This sphere of spiritual cognition is termed by the

Eastern philosophers the "Buddhic" level of consciousness. The Eastern Schools teach that it is possible to transcend the intellectual faculties and reach a condition of spiritual illumination without the use of the mind, but this is not possible in the Western world because of the intense activity of the lower constitution. That which the Westerner must do in order to attain the highest spiritual good for himself and those about him is to lift his level of thinking from the animal, or material, mind to its higher octave—the spiritual mind. By accomplishing this he becomes a creative thinker as the highest plane from which man may create at the present time is the mental. Most of the so-called spiritual impulses recorded in the constitution of the individual are really products of the higher mental nature. Lofty altruistic tendencies and idealistic concepts, together with the highest and fullest grasp of the deeper realities of life, come through the higher mental nature. When the individual transfers his center of thinking from the lower mind—which is notion—to the higher mind—which is reason—he has accomplished much. True reason is a divine faculty, not to be confused, however, with its shadow of argument and dissension in the material world. Reason overshadows thought in the same way that a learned person transcends an educated one, for education is merely dependent upon memory while learning is dependent upon understanding. Those who would reach the summit of philosophical attainment must first learn to think true, and thinking is never true until it has its source in the spiritual mind of man. The material mind is involved in the illusion of existence; it is a slave to convention; it is bound around with concepts of space and time; it is often ensouled with the racial spirit; and, like the material nature of man, it is sloughed off after death. On the other hand, the divine mind is free from the illusion of personality; it has never come into birth or become part of that nature which is born and dies; and, dwelling in eternity, it is above the delusion of time. Whereas the mortal mind knows only what it wants, the immortal mind is fully acquainted with the needs of the personality that is evolving under its protection. The individual who raises the mind so that he thinks in harmony with its immortal part is himself immortal; rather, we should say, is aware of his own immortality and, having reached this condition, is incapable of death.

THE · ALL· SEEING EYE

Being a Monthly Magazine
which is published in Los-
Angeles on the Fifteen-
th day of every month
edited by
Manly P. Hall
and
devoted to the Search for the
Fundamental Verities Existing in the Educational
Systems·Religions
and Philosophies
of All Ages

SEPTEMBER
MCMXXVII

The ALL-SEEING EYE

DEVOTED TO THE SEARCH FOR THE FUNDAMENTAL VERITIES EXIST-ING IN THE EDUCATIONAL SYSTEMS, RELIGIONS, AND PHILOSOPHIES OF ALL AGES

VOL. IV	SEPTEMBER, 1927	No. 5

PUBLISHED EVERY MONTH BY
THE HALL PUBLISHING COMPANY
301 TRINITY AUDITORIUM BUILDING, TUcker 2603
NINTH AT GRAND AVENUE, LOS ANGELES, CALIFORNIA

MANLY P. HALL . . . . *Editor*
HARRY S. GERHART . . . . *Managing Editor*
MAUD F. GALIGHER . . . . *Associate Editor*
HOWARD W. WOOKEY . . . . *Art Director*

CONTENTS

o You Know?

That sea shells have been found upon the summit of Mount Blanc, as well as many other high mountains in different parts of the world?

That with the aid of very finely adjusted instruments a tree has at last been induced to sign its own name—or at least "make its mark?"

That during the first half of the last century a French alchemist offered to supply the French National Mint with gold?

That only a small part, if any, of the famous Raphael's *Madonna* was actually painted by Raphael?

That according to the Coptic Christians, the century plant was the first plant to be converted to Christianity?

That Camille Flammarion is supposed to have had in his library a book bound in human skin?

That the nose of the Sphinx was knocked off in the ninth century A. D. by a Mohammedan, who feared that unless he disfigured the image it would lead his people into idolatry?

That there is still a blot of ink on the wall to mark the spot where Martin Luther threw his ink well at the devil?

That the drinking vessels of several European sovereigns of the Middle Ages were believed to have been made from the horns of unicorns?

The EDITOR'S BRIEFS

Concerning the Nature of God

Realizing that a man's conception of God is his God, let us consider together the mystery of Deity. Remember that it is not really God whom we define—it is merely our own conception of the highest expression of Wisdom, Beauty, and Truth. Col. Robert Ingersoll did not realize the magnitude of his statement which he said, "an honest God is the noblest work of man." Our God must be the God of the 20th century, for we see It through the eyes of our generation. Our God must march with us, sharing our problems or we cannot know It. God is always our God, for we can never realize or understand the God of another man. The Deity is always an omnipresent, omniscient, omnipotent, and omniactive agent, expressing in full the ideals which we express in part, attaining in full that which we attain only in part, and understanding clearly that great mystery called *life* which we understand not at all.

Not so long ago a man said to me, "Do you believe in God?" What he really meant was, "Do you believe in my concept of God?" This man had attended some of our lectures and, hearing us discuss the various religions of the world but not especially emphasize the one with which he was most concerned, came to the conclusion that, like the benighted heathen of old, we were following "false gods" and worshipping "graven images." If this same friend had chanced to see our collection of Javanese gods, Hindu, Japanese, and Chinese Buddhas, Egyptian Osirises, and Chaldean deities, he would have been absolutely certain that we were outside the pale of salvation. This man was sincere, true, honest, and, according to his own light, consistent and well-meaning. But to us his concept of God seemed so pitifully small. It lacked the dignity and serenity of a noble conception; it was puny and hopelessly inadequate; it was the God of a race, a family or a clan; it was not the God of a great universe; it had both friends and enemies; it neglected some and favored others, and was even so small that it descended to the level of human wrangling and petty faultfinding; it didn't like the Chinese and had permitted two-thirds of the world to live in darkness while it fostered a small group of chosen people; it ordered suffering, permitted crime, advocated sacrifice, and fought with men against men upon the field of battle. Therefore we were forced to say to this man, "We do believe in God but not in your God!" And he went away as dissatisfied and fearful as before, firmly convinced that we were not only idolatrous but, since our last statement, pantheistic in that we had affirmed a plurality of Deity.

Meditating upon the question of this sincere individual, "Do you believe in God?", we organized our concepts of Divinity and, having had the same question put to us on another occasion, have decided to present for your consideration the God we have found. Please remember that this is only our God and foolish is that man who follows the Gods of others; each must find his own God for himself and, having found It, build upon that spot a tabernacle. In ancient days when man found his God, he carved an image of It in wood or stone or molded It in clay. This was a fatal mistake, for the God in clay or stone could not grow, and age after age while the image remained the same the minds of men had grown. Therefore the Gods of our forefathers seem crude to us, for we are not our forefathers. We are the past plus the present and our Gods are the Gods of the present. The Navajo Indian will not make images of his deities, lest he fall into idolatry. When he desires to represent his God, he does so with colored sand and as soon as the image has served his purpose destroys it with a sweep of his hand. Each day the God of the wise man changes as his own wisdom increases, for the wise man realizes that the Supreme One never changes and is always the sum of everything. The mind of man is growing and each day it learns a little more concerning the mystery of being, and as the mind grows the knowledge of God grows. But only the perfect man, complete in every way, full of understanding, unlimited by any shadow of ignorance, can behold the Deity in the full glory and splendor of Its Being. And that man does not live today, nor will he exist until the endless milleniums of time bring the human race back again into the living presence of its Divine Source.

We conceive God to be an eternally-existing Principle: unborn—therefore incapable of death; uncreated—therefore incapable of dissolution. The most appropriate designation of this Principle is the *Good*. The full and unconditioned state of *Good* is the *Absolute,* beside which there is nothing else and outside of which there is no existence. All things are created out of the substance of the one and eternal *Good;* therefore are themselves part of the *Good,* partaking of the immortality of the *Good,* subsisting upon the nature of the *Good,* and at dissolution returning again into the perfect nature of the *Good.* The *Good* is both the source and ultimate of all existence, and the highest form of *Good* is the knowledge and understanding of the true condition of *Good.* As the *Good* is eternal, so all creatures composed of It and subsisting upon It are, like itself, eternal, indestructible, and incorruptible. The only ignorance is the ignorance of the *Good,* and death can only exist in that mind which has not yet discovered its fundamental oneness with the eternal and never-changing *Good.*

We conceive God to be One and incapable of division, for although a multiplicity of manifestations apparently diversified are perpetually manifesting within Its nature, It remains the sum of all Its parts and members. To man the universe appears as *unity* in *diversity,* but to the One the universe is *diversity* in *unity.* God being the Only Cause of all manifestation and expression, it must naturally follow that all manifestation and expression is *Good.* Therefore equality is established by the common benignity of cause. Difference may, and does, exist in the material sphere, this difference being based upon the proximity of manifestation to its own cause. That which is closest to cause unconsciously is youngest; that which is closest to cause consciously is oldest. Youth is proximity to beginning; age, proximity to end. But as beginning and end are one, age excels youth only in terms of understanding.

We conceive God to be One manifesting through a multiplicity, the foundation of that multiplicity being the threefold nature of the One. All the attributes of power cognizable by man may be reduced to three. These three are therefore termed the Trinity, or three persons of the Godhead.

The three persons are not the One, for the One cannot be divided, but are rather expressions of the One. When the One expresses Will, it is termed the *Father,* because the Will is the first after the One. When the One expresses Wisdom, it is called the *Son,* for it is the second after the One. When the One expresses Activity, it is called the *Holy Spirit,* for it is the third after the One. All three are in the One, are potentialities of the One, and are called the faces, or attributes, of the eternal and unconditioned One. The One by Its Will created the heavens; by Its Activity, the lower worlds; and by Its Wisdom It bound them together that they should be one even as It is One. Therefore the height of wisdom is the recognition of the One, for wisdom binds the parts together and man calls heaven the *Father* God and the lower worlds Mother Nature. Man places himself between the above and the below, for the wisdom of God is in his soul and his duty is to reconcile the above and the below, uniting them within himself.

We conceive God to manifest Itself through a multiplicity of powers emanating from the three, and this multiplicity we denominate the *Gods.* Thus we establish pantheism in monotheism, with monotheism supreme. The parts of the One are the *Gods;* the One formed of the parts is the *God.* The Gods are an illustrious chain of graduated divinities, uniting cause with effect. These divinities are merely the intelligent attributes of the One Intelligence. Man himself is *a* God but not *the* God, for man is a part but God is the sum of the parts. The Divinity in man is God and therefore worthy of libation and offering. How much more so then the greater divinities who partake in greater degree of Divinity! God is all of man, but man is not all of God. Therefore the part is inferior to the whole to the same degree that it is less than the whole, yet all are ultimately One and ultimately inseparable.

We conceive God to exist in all creatures in accordance with the individual comprehension of the creature. In other words, Divinity is present to the degree that it is recognized. The more of God man finds, the more of God is present in him. All growth is the process of increasing capacity to cognize *Good* and to apply the newly-cognized power to the problem of existence. Therefore all creatures, animate and inanimate, are ensouled by the *Good* and their power is commensurate with the expression which they are capable of giving to the *Good.* The grain of sand contains the *Good,* for it is a unit of the Absolute Life. But man considers the grain of sand inferior to himself inasmuch as it manifests the *Good* in a lesser degree than he. The planets are individual intelligences, being unfoldments of the Divine Life on a level greatly superior to that of man. For this reason the planets are denominated *Gods,* they having so greatly unfolded the Divine Power within themselves that they are capable of controlling not only animate forms like those of man but also of furnishing environments for races and species inferior to themselves. These races and species then offer libations to the unit of power which gives them the opportunity for individual expression. The result is the worship of the planetary Gods. But while these tutelary deities are honored, the intelligent worshipper is in reality making offering to the Absolute and Eternal One, for it is the presence of this Absolute and Eternal Power in the constitution of the tutelary deity that is the true cause of its existence.

We conceive God to be absolutely impersonal, for being a universal and all-pervading essence It is within the nature of every creature and substance, regardless of whether we term that creature or substance *good* or *bad*. This point is well illustrated by an ancient Eastern fable. Once there was a Hindu mendicant who was told that God was in everything. So, walking down the street, he said to himself, "God is in the dog, God is in the tree, God is in all things. Therefore nothing can hurt me." A few moments later an elephant ambled down the street, but the Hindu mendicant made no effort to avoid the animal, because he believed that God was in the elephant and therefore it would not hurt him. The man on the elephant's head cried out a warning, but the holy man did not heed it. The elephant, reaching him, twisted his trunk around his body and threw the amazed devotee over a nearby fence. Returning to his Master, the sorely injured Hindu complained that although he had affirmed God to be in everything, the elephant had cruelly injured him. After hearing the details of the story, the aged sage replied, "You did well, my son, save in one particular: You failed to hear the voice of God in the warning of the elephant-driver!" We cannot conceive of a God less universal than the universe itself. You will remember the story of the flattered king who to silence the meaningless babbling of his courtiers ordered his throne to be set up on the sea shore, declaring that if he were—as his nobles affirmed—greater than God, he would order the tide not to come in and wet his feet. He quickly demonstrated, however, that the tide knew no master among men. The God we worship must be as great, at least, as the tide which through the ages follows its predestined course. We can worship no anthropomorphic deity controlling the universe as fretfully and inconsistently as King James ruled England. God is infinite power, grand enough to whirl uncounted universes through milleniums inconceivable yet minute enough to evolve with endless consistency the tiniest forms of microscopic life. This God has no time for religious wranglings and creedal dissensions. The immutable laws of Nature are Its ministers. He who serves the *Good* is rewarded by that harmony which must exist between the Principle and Its servant. He who departs from the way of the *Good* suffers not from the jealousy of God or the revenge of an irritated Deity, but rather his suffering is caused by the very act of departing from the way of the *Good*. What matters it the faith a man belongs to if he serve the *Good,* or what does it profit him if he serve the *evil?* When all substances and creatures are of the nature of God, then all words used to describe them are synonyms of God. Consequently, what matters it what God be called? It is the understanding of *Good*— and not the name applied to it—which constitutes true reverence and veneration.

We conceive the three primary attributes of God to be the three fundamental paths also by which Deity may be approached. Therefore man may know God by will, by wisdom or by action. For man, *action* means service, and he who serves God will realize that no one can long serve his master without gaining a knowledge of the one he serves. God is revealed to Its servants by their very services, and he who is in doubt as to what to do to glorify his Creator can never go wrong if he dedicates his life to constructive and humanitarian labor. By *wisdom* man is enabled to glimpse in part the Divinity of his Maker, for wisdom organizes effects until the cause of those effects is hypothetically estimated. The wise man knows God because he alone realizes how necessary God is. The world could get along very

(*Continued on Page 156*)

PHILOSOPHY SCIENCE & RELIGION

The Seven Days of Creation

By MANLY P. HALL

Science and theology are widely at variance on the subject of the Creation Myth. The scientist is surrounded by ample evidence that all things grow slowly and naturally from a seed or germ containing potentially all of the parts and members which issue forth from it. The scientist firmly maintains that "nothing from nothing comes," whereas the theologian as emphatically declares that in the beginning there was "nothing" and from it came "everything!" When the enthusiastic clergyman announces that God reached out His right hand and made the sun and, grasping a handful of space with His left hand, molded it into the moon, the scientist is on the verge of nervous prostration.

In the first place, the prosaic man of letters has not the same conception of God as that which Michelangelo visualized while ornamenting the Sistine Chapel. Science refuses to take seriously the theological concept that God is a man, being convinced that if there were such a gigantic being floating around in space juggling constellations, the Mt. Wilson telescope would have discovered him ere this. On the other hand the theologian is sorely distressed lest the soul of the savant earn for itself a brimstone pit as the retribution for its heresies. "God is spirit," announces the minister confidently. "What is spirit?" thunders back the scientist. "There is no use discussing it with you," replies the theologian, "you are not in the right frame of mind." "God is energy," proclaims the savant, a profoundly wise look upon his face. "What is energy?" retorts the minister. "That's a point that has been bothering us," answers the scientist complacently, "but we are making rapid progress towards the discovery of its constituents."

After carefully measuring the whale's throat, science announces that it was physically impossible for Jonah to have passed through it, and further investigation also has demonstrated that no whales are to be found in that part of the world. Experts in hygiene, after due consideration, announce that sanitary conditions on the Ark left much to be desired and that to ventilate a structure containing from two to seven of every known creature with one window less than two feet square was setting a very bad example for the younger generation. The natural history expert then proclaims that if the Ark landed on Mt. Ararat, the original snails haven't reached home yet.

While such statements may seem utterly ridiculous, they are the greatest single cause why hundreds of thousands of persons are leaving the Christian churches annually. They explain the vast number of agnostics and atheists among the younger people, for the juvenile mind, if not mature, is at least too logical in its function to ignore such religious absurdities. We still occasionally hear the term "old-time religion," and desperate efforts have been made to convince the modern world that this form of faith has a practical value. Such efforts have proved decidedly unsuccessful. In olden times it was possible to force people to declare allegiance to something they did not believe or accept. Possibly the "persuasive" measures used at that time had something to do with the alarcity with which people saw the error of their ways. We no longer live, however, in those good old days when people were converted with the thumbscrew and the fires of their zeal kept brightly burning by visions of a torture chamber.

With the passing of physical torture as a method of demonstrating the love of God, there followed a period of mental torture. The thumbscrew gave place to the bogey of hell and the individual who for one reason or another was late to prayer meeting or missed communion was paralyzed with fear for the safety of is immortal soul. The day of the hell-fire and damnation sermonizing, when little children left church with ashen faces and trembling lips and strong men feared the dark, has also passed away except in a few outlying districts. These are the elements of the old-time religion: God was an autocrat, a tyrant, a despot; man a serf, who must enter the presence of His Maker groveling and dissembling piety.

The day that man fears His God is over. It may be true that now he fears nothing and consequently goes to excess in evil. Yet fear and love cannot exist together in the same heart. He who fears God does not love Him; he who loves God cannot fear Him. So there is coming into the world a new-time religion, which is nothing more nor less than a DEFENSE OF THE DEITY. Righteous men and women are rising up, declaring, "We know not who God is but something within our own souls tells us that He or It is God, impartial, just, true, and filled with mercy. Whereas in the past man's God was handed to him, man is now going forth in quest of a God, in search of a Deity noble and exalted enough to be a true ideal and an eternal inspiration. Thus, while the old-time religion may be defined as an acceptance of a man-made God, the new-time religion is a search for an eternally-existing Deity in no way subject to the limitations of human consciousness.

Where shall man search for a knowledge of His God? There are three places he may look: in his own heart, in his world, and in his sacred books. There was once a man who entered a temple to pray to his God and the priest of the temple came forward to receive his homage. And the man said to the priest, "Whose house is this?" and the priest answered, "This is the house of God." And the man who had come to pray turned to the priest, saying in a stern voice, "Then out of my way, MAN!"

God's dwelling is the heart of man; God's dwelling is His world. This is the doom of the church, for the wise man knows that every house is a church, every home an altar, every creature a shrine, and he himself a priest ordained since the beginning of the world.

The 20th century man and woman has reached a point in mental unfoldment which enables him or her to consider, with at least reasonable intelligence, the problem of individual salvation. The ever-increasing knowledge possessed by the race as a mass is also a great factor in man's growth. Excavations are bringing to light more complete records of the ancient world and gradually it is dawning upon the individual that the faith which he is serving is not properly understood—that he has been following vain superstitions and soulless illusions. He discovers that his Christianity is not the Christianity of the first century of the Christian Era. He realizes that he has been the victim of a great deceit; that the doctrines he has received were not those which would liberate him from the bondage of ignorance but rather false dogmas which would involve him ever more deeply in dependence.

Some day the religions of the world will be separated from the excrescences of superstition and their true purport revealed to humanity. The Scriptures are far greater than the interpretations given to them. They are ancient things, these Holy Books, and they have been preserved from generation to generation for uncounted thousands of years. Each nation has bequeathed to its successor a legacy of sacred writings and philosophic lore. The Scriptures constituting the King James' Bible have been gathered from every part of the world, from the very pagan nations to which it is shipped back in carloads for purposes of their "conversion." Do you realize that in nine cases out of ten the missionary who converts a pagan to the Bible is merely teaching him his own pagan cult under a new name? The missionary in India does not realize that his own Bible contains much Hindu mysticism. If he did, his mortification would know no bounds.

One of the most curious doctrines set forth in the Old Testment is that of the seven creative days described in the opening chapter of Genesis. It has been a never-failing source of amazement to me how it is possible for Christian ministers to discourse upon the opening verses of Genesis year after year, generation after generation, and never discover that they have misinterpreted and mistranslated the entire volume. Yet probably within the radius of a few miles may be found Hebrew scholars belonging to the Jewish faith who could in a very few moments show the Christian minister that he hadn't the faintest idea of the Creation Myth in the true light of Judaism. Jewish scholars know that the Christians have little or no comprehension whatsoever of the philosophical profundity of the Old Testment. Yet for centuries eminent divines have waxed eloquent on this most important subject, of which they nothing know.

In the same category with the Creation Myth is that endless source of ecclesiastical uneasiness—the Adam and Eve episode. For several hundred million years according to science and about four thousand years according to theology, this old planet has been struggling along attempting "to live down" the fatal mistake of our first and common parents who chanced to partake of a certain piece of fruit which all modern dietitians declare to be a most nutritious product especially if eaten in the forenoon. For this offense all humanity is supposed to pass through its mortal span with a hangdog look ever mindful that the sins of its ancestors were grievous indeed!

While we cannot blame the agnostic for shunning a cult which seriously affirms that the salvation of billions of human beings can be endangered by an apple, we believe that a sincere investigation of the meaning of these ancient allegories as preserved in their original tongues would prove both profitable and inspiring and also supply material for the most profound reflection. There is a meaning to these ancient stories, a meaning unconsidered, yes unsuspected, by the great masses who year after year have accepted the inane explanations advanced by minds wholly disqualified to interpret their hidden meanings.

If we would interpret aright the allegories and parables of our Scriptures, we must turn to the source of those allegories and parables, namely the Jewish faith. But here again we are confronted with an almost insurmountable difficulty, for the Jew of today has forgotten his own philosophy and his race. Having mingled itself with all the peoples of the earth, he has lost its sublime heritage of spiritual ethics. Most Jews today are satisfied with the Talmud and the scholars among their people are chiefly concerned with interpreting the religious code therein contained. While the Rabbis may understand in part the *Tora,* or the body of the law, they have ceased to consider those more mystical writings that reveal the true spirit of Judaism. Ignorant of the profundity of the subject, all too many of the younger Rabbis find it easier to ridicule than to learn. Therefore concerning himself with modern psychology, he seeks to supplant the secret doctrine of Israel with modernism—an almost meaningless and totally inadequate spiritual code.

Centuries of intercourse with adherents of other creeds and doctrines have had their effect upon the Jew. Especially does this appear to be true today, for it is very apparent that the Jew is assuming much of the culture and philosophy of Christendom. We lament this tendency, for while undobtedly an ever-increasing understanding between these two great religions will result in good, we fear that it may cause the Jewish scholar to interpret his own archaic lore more and more in the light of the absurdities advanced by Christian divines, thus making it ever more difficult to discover the true meaning of these ancient doctrines.

The *Mishna* and the *Qabbalah* are the keys to true Jewish mysticism, and the *Sepher Yetzirah* and the *Sepher ha Zohar* when properly interpreted reveal the very essence of the original Rabbinical knowledge. Like all other great faiths, Judaism is twofold, its lesser part to be revealed to the many and its greater part concealed from all but the few. The same is true in Christianity. That part which we have so long revered is really chaff, for we have not learned as yet to thresh our doctrines as we do our grain. Remembering that Scriptures have always been written to conceal rather than to reveal, let us briefly sketch over the Creation Myth of the ancients in the light of the Qabbalistic teachings of the Hebrews and the secret doctrine of the Brahmins and the Greeks. Before doing so let me warn you that the order of the verses in the first chapter of Genesis is incorrect and not according to the original meaning; that many of the words are improperly translated and consequently must not be accepted as having any meaning like that now assigned to them. A few examples will clarify the subject. The first chapter of Genesis in Hebrew reads: ALEIM BRA BRAChIT AT EChIM UAT EARTz. This has been interpreted to mean "In the beginning God created the heaven and the earth," but from it may be extracted the following more amplified description: "The Forces, or Makers, of the world carved, or sculptured, as a beginning of existence the substances of the celestial firmament and the starry heaven and the substances of the lower, or arid, earth." Again where it is written that the ALEIM made man in their own image, it should be interpreted "in their shadow." Of course, the gravest error by far is that of interpreting ALEIM as meaning "God." In fact, the word "God" itself is a poorly chosen term with which to designate Divinity. The ALEIM are the ancient "Builders," the "Fabricators" of the world. They are not one but many, and they move or "brood" upon the face of unfinished being. Again where it is written that "the earth was without form and void," the word "void" should be translated "an egg, or ovoid," for it signifies the Egg of Kosmos which the Egyptian deities are so often shown turning upon a potter's wheel.

According to the ancient Hebrews, in the beginning there was a complete and unconditioned state of eternal existence which stretched throughout and permeated the entire area of Being. This first and unconditioned potentiality they denominated AIN, or the Boundless. This Boundless and Limitless Existence, while actually indescribable, was hypothetically divided into three parts: AIN, the ALL; AIN SOPH, the Limitless One; and AIN SOPH AUR, the Limitless Light. These three together as one constituted THE ABSOLUTE. To define it was to defile it. It was the sure foundation of all existence and the universe was an inverted tree with its roots in the ALL and its branches descending through the different gradations of existence. To AIN SOPH the ancient Qabbalists gave many names in an effort to dignify it and exalt it above all creatures and forms. Its symbol was a closed eye, and it in no way partook of existence other than to contribute its eternal life to be the spirit of existing things.

Qabbalism is a doctrine of emanations and according to its exponents there emanated from the Eternal Condition, AIN SOPH, a bright and shining point—the Open Eye, the first of the Gods, the Ancient of Days, the Eternal Crown, the One from whom comes forth the many. This was denominated *Kether,* or the most ancient of the Fathers. In *Kether,* the Universal Seed, was contained the Universal Tree, which evolved out of it according to a fixed and immutable law. *Kether* corresponds to the "Father" in the Christian Triad who not only gives birth out of Himself to the Great Mother, *Aima,* which is called *Understanding,* but also to the Great Father, *Abba,* called *Wisdom.* Through the union of the Great Father and Great Mother is produced the Child—*Creation.*

The various schools of Qabbalism have different methods of evolving the first triad out of AIN SOPH. To some, *Kether* is the Father and *Binah* the Mother, with *Chochmah,* or Wisdom, as the Son. To others, *Chochmah* is the Father,, *Binah* the Mother, and *Tiphereth* the Son. To still a third group, *Chochmah* is the Father, *Binah* the Mother, and a mysterious hypothetical point called *Daath* is the Son. However the division may be effected, there is always a triune foundation consisting of Three revealing the One, thus establishing the triangular foundation of the world. At this point please consider the accompanying diagram which sets forth the principles of Creation according to what the Qabbalists call "The Universal Tree," or "The Tree of the Sephiroth." This Tree consists of ten globes joined together by 22 lines, or paths. The ten globes represent the ten numbers from 1 to 10 as shown and the 22 paths are the letters of the Hebrew alphabet. Taken together, these constitute the 32 paths of wisdom, the 32 degrees of Freemasonry, and the 32 teeth in the Divine Head.

The Tree consists of three vertical columns, those on the right and left being the pillars of *Jachin* and *Boaz* respectively, and the one in the center the sacred column of *Equilibrium,* which is dedicated to the Deity Himself. Thus positive and negative are revealed with equilibrium in the midst, and the true order of the universe is made manifest. Like the Pythagoreans, the Hebrews depict the universe as issuing in ten stages from the Absolute, these stages being shown as globes upon the branches of the Sephirothic Tree. This great Tree descends through four worlds and finally in the lowest consists of the ten divisions of the sidereal system in the following order:

No.	The Sephiroth		The Universe
1	Kether—The Crown		Primum Mobile
2	Chochmah—Wisdom	*han...d nitu*	The Zodiac
3	Binah—Understanding	*haui...*	Saturn
4	Chesed—Mercy	*agsi... sh...*	Jupiter
5	Geburah—Severity	*ha...cq*	Mars
6	Tiphereth—Beauty		Sun
7	Netsah—Victory		Venus
8	Hod—Glory		Mercury
9	Jesod—The Foundation		Moon
10	Malchuth—The Kingdom		Elements

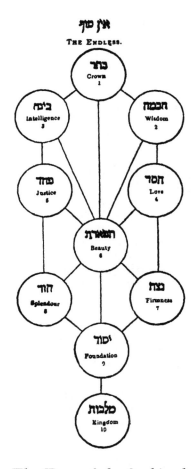

The Tree of the Sephiroth

To each of these spheres or globes the Hebrews assigned one of the ten great Names of God, one of the ten archangels, one of the ten angelic powers, one of the ten parts of the sidereal world, and one of the ten demons of the underworld. They also divided the Ten Commandments, assigning a Commandment to each of the Sephiroth, and later the Christian Qabbalists assigned a tenth part of the Lord's Prayer to each of these globes. At this time it is important to make clear the true meaning of the Sephirothic globes. They are to be considered as planes of Nature, of which each includes all less than itself and is included in all greater than itself. Thus, Kether, the first globe, actually contains within itself potentially the energies of the nine inferior spheres emanating from it. For this reason the Sephiroth are often shown as a series of concentric rings, with Kether at the outer edge of the circle and Malchuth in the center. The first three Sephiroth constitute the Triad, which is the foundation of the world. The remaining seven parts are divided into the six "Days" of Creation and the "Sabbath" of rest. Thus, Creation is the process of the Divine Life descending according to the order of the numbers from *Kether* to *Malchuth*.

The accompanying diagram shows the ten parts of Creation—the Sephiroth—assigned to the various sections of a great human body. The human figure is the Celestial Adam—the Great Man—in whose "image" the human man was created. Here we see *Kether,* the Crown, representing the spiritual center of the upper brain, possibly the pineal gland. *Chochmah* and *Binah*—the Father and Mother—are the two hemispheres of the cerebrum. *Chesed* and *Geburah* are the arms—the active parts of the Great Man. *Tiphereth* is the heart and, more generally, the entire trunk of the great body. *Netsah* and *Hod* are the two legs, or the supports of the universe. *Jesod* is the male generative power, and *Malchuth* both the feet and the female generative power. Thus the Cosmic Androgyne is in reality the Grand Man of Nebuchadnezzar's dream, with head of gold and feet of clay. In his *History of Magic,* Eliphas Levi thus describes the Creation of the world according to the ancient Jewish concept as embodied in the *Sepher ha Zohar:*

"That synthesis of the world, formulated by the human figure, ascended slowly and emerged from the water, like the sun in its rising. When the eyes appeared, light was made; when the mouth was manifested, there was the creation of spirits and the word passed into expression. The entire head was revealed, and this completed the first day of creation. The shoulders, the arms, the breast arose, and thereupon work began. With one hand the Divine Image put back the sea, while with the other it raised up continents and mountains. The Image grew and grew; the generative organs appeared, and all beings began to increase and multiply. The form stood at length erect, having one foot upon the earth and one upon the waters. Beholding itself at full length in the ocean of creation, it breathed on its own reflection and called its likeness into life. It said: Let us make man—and thus man was made. There is nothing so beautiful in the masterpiece of any poet as this vision of creation accomplished by the prototype of humanity. Hereby is man but the shadow of a shadow, and yet he is the image of divine power. He also can stretch forth his hands from East to West; to him is the earth given as a dominion. Such is Adam Kadmon, the primordial Adam of the Kabalists. Such is the sense in which he is depicted as a giant; and this is why Swedenborg, haunted in his dreams by reminiscences of the Kabalah, says that entire creation is only a titanic man and that we are made in the image of the universe."

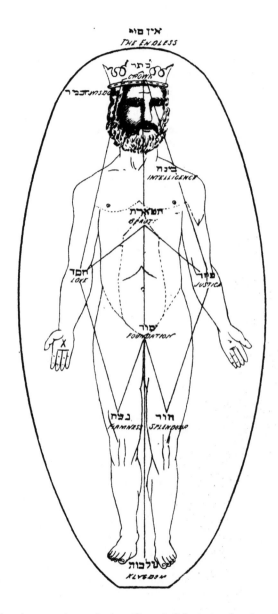

Thus the incarnation of the Grand Man results in the creation of environments suitable for the unfoldment of the multitudes of life potencies which in their sum constitute the Universal Being. In the secret teachings of the Zohar the Sephirothic Tree is divided into five distinct parts. The terms applied to these parts are quite familiar to students of philosophy and comparative religion, but few understand their exact meaning. In the Zohar, *Kether,* the Crown, which is literally the objectification of AIN SOPH, the Limitless and Eternal Being, is called *Macroprosophus*— the Great Face, the Long Face, or the Immense Countenance. Many chapters are devoted to a minute description of the parts of the Great Face. It is described as having no eyelids, for the "God of Israel neither slumbers nor sleeps." Its hair and beard are divided into a vast number of parts and its brain is filled with the divine dew. From its mouth issue the sacred letters and numbers by which the universe is established, and its power is without limit. The second of the five primary divisions is *Chochmah, Abba,* the Father, the term applied in the Qabbalah to the principle of Wisdom, a positive emanating power, flowing forth into the third division, *Binah,* or *Aima,* the Mother, termed in the *Zohar* Understanding. The fourth division is *Microprosophus,* the Short Face, the Lesser Face, the Smaller Countenance. This is the composed of the six Sephiroth—*Chesed, Geburah, Tiphereth, Netsah, Hod* and *Jesod*—and is commonly called *Zauir Anpin,* or the Lesser Adam, whereas *Macroprosophus* is designed *Arikh Anpin,* or the Superior Adam. The Lesser Face, consisting of six parts, is appropriately symbolized by a cub, which body consists of six surfaces. It is also the double interlaced triangles of Zion, the signet seal of Solomon. It represents the cardinal directions, north, east, south, west, up, and down, and the evolution of life through its globes constitutes the six Days of Creation. The tenth sphere—*Malchuth*—constitutes the fifth division and its designation is "The Bride of *Microprosophus.*" *Malchuth* is composed of the four elements, and being the physical sphere, is an epitome of all the divine planes which are involved in its existence. It is the foundation, or the feet, of the world and is the sphere alluded to in the Lord's Prayer where it is written, "For thine is the kingdom, the power, and the glory."

According to both the Greek and Hermetic schools as well as that of the Hebrew Qabbalists, the spirit of man, entering into the mystery of birth, descended through the supermundane spheres from the birthplace of souls—the Milky Way, or the sphere of the fixed stars. The ladder used in the Mithraic initiations signifies by its seven rungs the spheres of the seven planets which, according to the ancients, constituted the sidereal world. In coming into physical manifestation, the soul first reached the sphere of Saturn. Here the Governor of the Saturnian ring gave man a divine principle, in fact a certain part of the power of Saturn actually entered into the composition of man. From the ring of Saturn the soul descended to that of Jupiter, where it was further clothed. From the sphere of Jupiter it descended into that of Mars, where a third garment or veil was given to it. From Mars it descended into the sun, where the light and intelligence of the divine globe was imparted to the descending soul. From the sphere of the sun the soul descended to that of Venus, where the fifth veil was cast over it. From here it descended to the sphere of Mercury, where it was invested with the sixth veil. From Mercury it descended to the sphere of the moon, where the seventh veil was added, and from there it descended into the earth, bringing with it the septenary constitution imparted to it by the Governors of the supermundane spheres.

In the various schools the order of the planets differs somewhat, but in every case the principle involved is the same. The seven Days of Creation are not "days" or "years," but are the seven stages through which the soul must pass in order to reach perfection. The spirit of man, stripped of its vehicles and the bequests of the Governors, is a radiant spiritual center of power and force. The Lord of the first ring imparts its power and the spirit of man becomes limited by the vestments with which it is enswathed. These vestments become its invisible bodies and when it assumes material form they are the causal forces which result in certain peculiarities in the physical constitution and nature.

In the evolution of this physical globe the Lord of the first ring gave to the spirits of the earth chain the bodies of stones, and this constituted "the first Day." Then the Lord of the second ring gave the mineral the power of growth and it became a plant, and this constituted "the second Day." Then the Lord of the third ring gave to the plant the power of motion and emotion, and it became an animal, and this constituted "the third Day." Then the Lord of the fourth ring—the golden globe of the sun—gave to the animal the power of thought and the animal became a man, and this constituted "the fourth Day." In the fifth "Day" the fifth Lord will give to man a new and spiritualized faculty which will make him a superman, a true *Ben-Aleim,* and on the sixth "Day" the Lord of the sixth ring will also bestow his gift, and the superman will then become what to us must appear a demigod. Upon the seventh "Day" the seventh power will be added, but it is called a "Day of rest," because the power is not a new faculty but rather the gift of coordination, wherein all the parts are brought under the control of one divine power—the spiritual Ego.

One of the subtlest shades of meaning concealed within the above description of the involving soul is that the nature of man serves as a point for the incarnation of the Lords of the rings of the various planets. In other words, the powers and faculties with which man expresses himself are in reality the energies or hierarchies constituting the septenary body of the Solar Lord. Therefore man is not one but seven in one. Of this seven three are primary and four secondary. The three primary are the invisible or causal nature and the four secondary are the visible or reflective nature. The seven powers represented by the lower seven Sephiroth are the colors of the spectrum, the three primary being the superior and the four secondary the inferior. The three primary powers have their musical analogy in the first, third and fifth notes, and the four secondary powers in the remaining notes of the octave.

From the above a glimpse may be obtained of the real involvements to be met with in a study of the Old Testment: Thousands of pages of Qabbalistical writings must be culled, and the legends and allegories of a score of nations must be fitted together if the Biblical student is really to gain an understanding of the documents given to him out of antiquity.

The Discipline and Doctrine of Pythagoras

From "The History of Philosophy," Thomas Stanley, London, 1687

The great Authority and Esteem of Pythagoras amongst his Disciples

Pythagoras, to render his Disciples capable of Philosophy, prepared them by a Discipline so strict and severe, as might seem incredible to have been undergone by free persons, were it not founded upon the great authority and reputation which he had amongst them.

The Credit of their Opinions they conceived to be this, That he who first communicated them was no ordinary Person, but a God; and one of these Acousmata is, Who Pythagoras was: for they say, He was *Hyperborean Apollo*. In confirmation hereof, they instance those Wonders related in his Life, and the like, which being acknowledged to be true, and it being impossible they should all be performed by one Man, they conceive it manifest, that these relations are to be ascribed not to a Human Person but to something above Mankind. This they acknowledge; for amongst them there is a saying, That,

> *Two-footed Man, and Bird*
> *Is, and another Third.*

by which Third they meant Pythagoras. And Aristotle, in his Book of Pythagorick Philosophy, relates, That such a Division as this was preserved by the Pythagoreans amongst their ineffable secrets. Of Rational Animals, one kind is God; another, Man; a third between both these, Pythagoras.

They esteemed Pythagoras in the next place to the Gods, as some good Genius indulgent to Mankind: some affirming that he was *Pythian;* others, *Hyperborean Apollo;* some, one of those *Genii* which dwell in the Moon; others, one of the Celestial Deities, appearing at that time in a human shape, for the benefit and direction of Mortal Life, that he might communicate the wholesome illuminations of Beatitude and Philosophy to Mortal Nature; than which, a greater good can never come, nor shall ever come, which is given by the Gods through the means of this Pythagoras. Whence to this day the Proverb of the fair-haired *Samian* is used for a most reverend person.

Porphyry saith, They reckoned him amongst the Gods; and, therefore, whensoever they went to deliver to others any excellent thing, out of the secrets of his Philosophy, whence many Physical Conclusions might be deduced, then they swore by the *Tetractys,* and calling Pythagoras, as some God, to witness, said,

> *Who the Tetractys to our Souls expressed,*
> *Eternal Nature's Fountain I attest.*

Which Oath they used, as forbearing, through Reverence, to name him; for they were very sparing in using the Name of any God.

So great indeed was the respect they bare him, That it was not lawful for any one to doubt of what he said, nor to question him further concerning it; but they did acquiesce in all things that he delivered, as if they were

Oracles. And when he went abroad to cities, it was reported, He went not to teach, but to cure.

Hence it came to pass, That when they asserted anything in dispute, if they were questioned why it was so, they used to answer, He said it, which *He* was Pythagoras. This Hero himself was amongst them the first and greatest of Doctrines, his Judgment being a Reason free from, and above all Examination and Censure.

The Two Sorts of Auditors: and first of the Exoteric, how he Explored them

The Auditors of Pythagoras (such, I mean, as belonged to the family) were of two sorts, *Exoteric* and *Esoteric*: The *Exoterics* were those who were under probation, which if they well performed, they were admitted to be *Esoterics*. For, of those who came to Pythagoras, he admitted not every one, but only those whom he liked: first, upon choice; and next, by trial.

The Pythagoreans are said to have been averse from those who sell learning, and open their souls like the gates of an Inn, to every one that comes to them; and if they find not a vent or sale in this manner, then they run into Cities, and ransack the Gymnasia, and exact a reward from dishonourable persons: Whereas Pythagoras hid much of his speeches; so as they who were purely initiated might plainly understand them. But the rest, as Homer said of Tantalus, grieve, for that being in the midst of learning, they cannot taste of it. Moreover, they said, That they who for hire teach such as come to them, are meaner than Statuaries and Chariot-makers; for, a Statuary, when he would make a Mercury, seeks out some piece of wood fit to receive that form; but these, of every disposition endeavour to make that of Virtue.

When (therefore) any friends came to him, and desired to learn of him, he admitted them not, till he had made trial and judgment of them. First, he enquired, how they did heretofore converse with their parents and friends; next, he observed their unseasonable laughters, and unnecessary silence or discourse. Moreover, what their inclinations were, whether possessed with passion and intemperance, whether prone to anger or unchaste desires, or contentious or ambitious, and how they behaved themselves in contention and friendship. As likewise what friends those were, with whom they were intimate, and their conversation with them, and in whose society they spent the greatest part of the day; likewise upon what occasions they joyed and grieved.

Moreover he considered their presence and their gait, and the whole motion of their body: and, physiognomizing them by the symptoms, he discovered by manifest signs the occult dispositions of their souls. For, he first studied that Science concerning men, thereby discovering of what disposition every one was; neither did he admit any into his friendship and acquaintance, before he had physiognomized the man what he were. This word (saith *Agellius,* upon the same occasion) signifieth to make enquiry into the manners of some, by some kind of conjecture of the wit by the face and countenance, and by the air and habit of the whole body.

If upon exact observation of all these particulars, he found them to be of good dispositions, then he examined whether they had good manners, and were docile; first, whether they could readily and ingeniously follow that which he told them; next, whether they had any love to those things which they heard. For he considered what disposition they were of as to being made gentle; for he accounted roughness an enemy to his way of teaching,

Pythagoras

because it is attended by impatience, intemperance, anger, obtuseness, confusion, dishumour, and the like; but mildness and gentleness by their contraries.

Likewise in making the first trial of them, he considered, whether if they could learn that which they heard, they were able to be silent, and to keep it to themselves.

Purificative Institution by Sufferings

The chiefest scope which Pythagoras proposed was to deliver and free the mind from the engagements and fetters, in which it is confined from her first infancy; without which freedom, none can learn any thing sound or true, nor can perceive by what that which is unsound in sense operates. For, the mind (according to him) seeth all, and heareth all, the rest are deaf and blind.

This he performed by many exercises which he appointed for purification of the mind, and for the probation of such as came to him, which endured five years before they were admitted.

If upon this examination (which we declared) he judged any person capable, he then remitted him three years to be despised, making a test of his constancy and true love to learning, and whether he were sufficiently instructed as to despise glory, to contemn honour, and the like.

He conceived it in general requisite, that they should take much labour and pains, for the acquisition of Arts and Sciences; and to that end he appointed for them some torments of cauterizing and incision to be performed by fire and steel, which none that were of an ill inclination would undergo.

Silence

Moreover, he enjoined those that came to him Silence for five years, making trial how firmly they would behave themselves in the most difficult of all continencies; for such is the government of the tongue, as is manifest from those who have divulged mysteries.

The reason of this Silence was, That the soul might be converted into herself from external things, and from the irrational passions in her, and from the body even unto her own life, which is to live forever. Or, as Clemens Alexandrinus expresseth it, That his disciples, being diverted from sensible things, might seek God with a pure mind. Hence Lucian to the demand, how Pythagoras could reduce men to the remembrance of the things which they had formerly known, (for he held Science to be only Reminiscence) makes him answer, First, by long quiet and silence, speaking nothing for five whole years.

Yet *Agellius* affirms, That he appointed not the same length of silence to all, but several to several persons, according to their particular capacities. And Apuleius, That for the graver sort of persons, this taciturnity was moderated by a shorter space; but the more talkative were punished, as it were, by exile from speech five years.

He who kept silence, heard what was said by others, but was not allowed either to question, if he understood not, or to write down what he heard. None kept silence less than two years. *Agellius* adds, That these within the time of silence and hearing, were called *Acoustici*. But when they had learned these things the most difficult of all, to hold their peace, and to hear, and were now grown learned in silence, then they were allowed to speak, and to question, and to write what they heard, and what they conceived. At this time they were called *Mathematici*, from those Arts which they then began to learn and to meditate. Thus *Agellius*, how rightly, I question; for *Mathematici* and *Acousmatici* were distinctive appellations of the Pythagoreans, not in probation, but after admission, as we shall see hereafter.

Thus Apuleius saith, He taught nothing to his disciples before silence; And with him, the first meditation, for one that meant to be a wise man, was wholly to restrain the tongue of words, those words which the Poets call Winged, to pluck off the fears, and to confine them within the walls of our teeth. This, I say, was the first rudiment of wisdom, to learn to meditate, and to unlearn to talk.

Abstinence, Temperance, and Other Ways of Purification

Moreover, he commanded them to abstain from all things that had life, and from certain other meats also which obstruct the clearness of the under-standing, and for the same end (viz. in order to the inquisition and the apprehension of the most difficult Theorems) he likewise commanded them to abstain from wine, to eat little, to sleep little; a careless contempt of honour, riches, and the like; an unfeigned respect towards kindred, sincere equality and kindness towards such as were of the same age, and a propensity to further the younger without envy.

In fine, he procured to his Disciples a conversation with the gods by visions and dreams, which never happen to a soul disturbed with anger or pleasure, or any other unbefitting transportation, or with impurity and a rigid ignorance of all these. He cleansed, and purified the soul divinely from all these, and inkindled the divine part in her, and preserved her, and directed in her that intellectual divine eye which is better, (as *Plato* saith) then a thousand eyes of flesh, for by the help of this only, Truth is apprehended; After this manner he procured purification of the Intellect: And such was his form of Institution as to those things.

Diodorus saith, they had an exercise of temperance after this manner: There being prepared and set before them all sorts of delicate food, they looked upon it a good while, and after that their appetites were fully pro-voked by the sight thereof, they commanded it to be taken off and given to the servants, they themselves going away without dining; (this they did, saith *Iamblichus*) to punish their appetite.

Community of Estates

In this time, all that they had (that is their whole estate) was made common (put together and made one). They brought forth, saith *Agellius,* whatsoever they had of stock or money, and constituted an inseparable Society, as being that ancient way of association, which truly is termed *Koinobion.* This was given up to such of the Disciples, as were appointed for that pur-pose, and were called *Politici* and *Oeconomici,* as being persons fit to govern a family, and to give Laws.

This was conformable to the precepts of Pythagoras (as *Timeus* affirms) first, All common amongst friends; and, friendship, equality; and, esteem nothing your own. By this means he exterminated all propriety, and increased community even to their last possessions, as being causes of dissension and trouble; for all things were common amongst them, no man had a propriety to any thing.

But what *Agellius* terms *an inseparable Society,* is to be understood only conditionally, provided that they misliked not at any time this com-munity: for, whosoever did so, *took again his own estate, and more than that which he brought into the community, and departed.*

Admission or Rejection

They who appeared worthy to participate of his doctrines, judging by their lives and moderation, after their five years' silence, were made *Esoterics,* and were admitted to hear Pythagoras within the Screen, and to see him; but before that time they heard him discourse, being on the outside of the Screen, and not seeing him, giving a long time experiment of their proper manners by Hearing only. But if they were rejected, they received their estate double, and a tomb was made by the Disciples, as if they had been dead; for so all that were about Pythagoras spoke of them, and when they met them, behaved themselves towards them, as if they had been some other persons, but the men themselves they said were dead.

Distinction

Whatsoever he discoursed to those that came to him, he declared either plainly or symbolically (for he had a two-fold form of teaching): and of those who came to him, some were called *Mathematici,* others *Acousmatici.* The *Mathematici* were those who learnt the fuller and more exactly-elaborate reason of Science. The *Acousmatici* they, who heard only the chief heads of learning, without more exact explication.

Thus as there were two kinds of Philosophy, so were there two sorts of those who studied Philosophy. The *Acousmatici* did confess that the *Mathematici* were Pythagoreans; but the *Mathematici* did not acknowledge that the *Acousmatici* were Pythagoreans; for they had their learning, not from Pythagoras, but from *Hippasus;* who, some say, was of *Crotona,* others of *Metapontium.*

The Philosophy of the *Acousmatici* consists of Doctrines without demonstrations and reasons, but that, So it must be done, and the like, which they were to observe as so many Divine Doctrines, and they did esteem those amongst them the wisest, who had most of these *Acousmata.* Now all these *Acousmata* were divided into three kinds; some tell, *what something is;* others tell, *what is most such a thing;* the third sort tell, *what is to be done, and what not.* Those that tell *what a thing is,* are of this kind, *as* What is the Island of the Blessed? The Sun? The Moon? What is the Oracle at *Delphi?* The Tetractys? What is the Music of the Sirens?

Those which tell *what is most,* as, *What is most just?* To sacrifice. *What is the wisest? Number; and in the next place that which gave names to things. What is the wisest amongst us? Medicine. What the most beautiful? Harmony. What the most powerful? Reason. What the best? Beatitude. What the truest? That men are wicked.* For which (they say) he commended *Hippodamus,* a Poet of *Salamis,* who said,

O Gods! whence are you? How so good? so blest?
O Men! whence are you? How with ill possest?

These and such like are the *Acousmata* of this kind; for every one of these telleth, What is most. The same it is with that which is called the wisdom of the Seven Sages, for they enquired not what is good, but what is most good; not what is difficult, but what is most difficult, which is to know ourselves; not what is facile, but what is most facile, which is the custom of Nations; Those *Acousmata* seem to follow this kind of wisdom, for those Sages were before Pythagoras. The *Acousmata* which tell *what is to be done, or what is not to be done, are thus, As that we ought to beget children, for we must leave behind us such as may serve the Gods in our room; or, that we ought to put off the right shoe first; or, that we ought not to go in the common Road,* and the like. Such were the *Acousmata;* but those which have most said upon them, are *concerning sacrifices,* at what times, and after what manner they are to be performed, and *concerning removal* from our place of habitation, and concerning *Sepulture,* how we must bury the Dead, for some whereof there is a *reason* given. As, that *we ought to get children, that we may leave in our room another servant of the Gods.* But of others there is no reason; and, in some, that which follows the precept seems to be allied to the words, but in others is wholly distant, as, *that we ought not to break bread, because it conduceth to judgment in Hell.* But the reasons that are applied to these, are not Pythagorean, but given by some other who studied Pythagorean Learning, endeavouring to apply some probable conjecture to them; As of the last mentioned, That Bread is not to be broken; some say, He who gathers together, ought not to dissolve. For anciently all Friends used after a barbarous manner to meet at one Loaf; others, That you must not give so bad an omen, as, when you are going about any thing, to break it off.

But there was one *Hippomedon,* an *Agrimean,* a Pythagorean of the Acousmatic rank, who said, That Pythagoras gave reasons and demonstrations of all these things; but because they were delivered by Tradition through many, and those still growing more idle, that the Reasons were taken away, and the Problems only left. Now the Mathematical Pythagoreans grant all this to be true, but the occasion of the difference they say was this: Pythagoras went from Iona, and Samus, in the time of Policrates' reign, to Italy, which was then in a flourishing condition, where the chiefest persons of the cities became conversant with him. To the most ancient of these, and such as had least leisure, (because they were taken up with public employments, so that it would be very hard for them to learn Mathematics and Demonstrations) he discoursed barely, conceiving it did nothing less advantage them, even without the causes, to know what they had to do: as Patients, not enquiring why such things are prescribed them, nevertheless obtain health. But to the younger, who were able to act and learn, he imparted by Demonstrations and Mathematics. The *Mathematici* professed that they came from these; the *Acousmatici,* from the others, chiefly from *Hippasus,* who was one of the Pythagoreans. But because he published (their doctrine) and first wrote of the Sphere of twelve Pentagons, he died in the Sea as an impious person, not obtaining the fame at which he aimed.

How They Disposed the Day

We shall next speak concerning those things which he taught them in the day; for, according to his directions, thus did they who were taught by him. These men performed their morning walks by themselves, and in such places where they might be exceeding quiet and retired, where were Temples, and Groves, and other delightful places; for they thought it was not fit they should speak with any one, till they had first composed their Souls, and fitted their intellect, and that such quiet was requisite for the composure of their intellect; for, as soon as they arose, to intrude among the people, they thought a tumultuous thing. Therefore, all the Pythagoreans ever made choice of the most sacred places.

After their morning walk, they came to one another, chiefly in the Temples, or in some such places. They made use of these times for doctrines and disciplines, and rectification of their manners.

After they had studied a while, they went to their morning exercises; the greater part used to anoint themselves, and run races; the fewer, to wrestle in Orchards and in Groves; some, by throwing sledges, or by grappling hands, to make trial of their strength; choosing such exercises as they judged most convenient for them.

At Dinner they used Bread and Honey. Wine after meals they drunk not. The time after Dinner they employed in Political affairs, as well foreign as domestic, according to the injunction of their Laws; for they endeavoured to manage every thing in the afternoons. As soon as the evening came, they betook themselves again, not singly, as in their morning walks, but two or three walked together, repeating the Doctrines they had learnt, and exercising themselves in virtuous employments. After their walks, they used baths and washing; having washed, they met together to eat; but they did not eat together more than ten persons. As soon as they who were to come together were met, they used libations, and sacrifices of meal and frankincense. Then they went to supper, that they might end it before the Sun were set. They used Wine, and Maza, and Bread, and Broth, and Herbs, both raw and boiled: they likewise set before them the flesh of such beasts as used to be sacrificed. They seldom eat broths of fish, because some of them are, in some respects, very hurtful; likewise (seldom) the flesh of such creatures as use not to hurt mankind. After Supper, they offered libations, then had lectures. Their custom was, that the youngest amongst them should read, and the eldest should, as President, order what and how he should read. When they were to depart, he who filled the Wine poured forth to them in libation; and during the libation, the eldest of them declared these things: That none should hurt or kill a domestic plant or fruit; besides, that they should speak well, and think reverently of the gods, dæmons, and heroes; likewise to think well of Parents and Benefactors; to assist Law, and oppose Rebellion. This said, every one departed to his house.

They wore a white and clean garment; they had also coverlets white and clean of linen, for they used not any of skins, because they approved not the exercise of Hunting.

These were the Traditions that were delivered to that society of men, partly concerning diet, (of which hereafter more particularly) partly concerning the course of life.

How They Examined Their Actions Morning and Evening

These and all other actions of the day, they contrived in the morning before they rose, and examined at night before they slept; thus, by a twofold act, exercising the memory. *They conceived that it was requisite to retain and preserve in memory all which they learnt, and that lessons and doctrines should be so far, acquired, as until they are able to remember what they have learnt; for that is it which they ought to know, and bear in mind. For this reason they cherished memory much, and exercised it, and took great care of it; and in learning they gave not over, until they had gotten their lesson perfectly by heart. A Pythagorean rose not out of bed, before he had called to mind the actions of the day past, which recollection he performed in this manner: He endeavoured to call to mind what he first, as soon as he rose, either had heard, or given in charge to his servants; and what in the second place, and what in the third, and so on in the same order. And then for his going forth, whom he met first, whom next; and what discourses he had with the first, what with the second, what with the third, and so of the rest; for he endeavoured to repeat in memory all that happened throughout the whole day, in order as it happened: And if at their uprising they had more leisure, then after the same manner they endeavoured to recollect all that happened to them for three days before. Thus they chiefly exercised the memory; for they conceived that nothing conduceth more to science, experience, and prudence, than to remember many things.*

This was comfortable to the institution of *Pythagoras; for, He advised to have regard chiefly to two times, that when we went to sleep, and that when we rose from sleep; at each of these we ought to consider, what actions are past, and what to come. Of the past, we ought to require an account of ourselves; of the future, we ought to have a providential care. Wherefore he advised every one to repeat to himself these verses (so soon as he came home, or) before he slept.*

> Nor suffer sleep at night to close thine eyes,
> Till thrice thy acts that day thou hast o'er-run,
> How slipt? what deeds? what duty left undone?

And before they arose, these:

> As soon as ere thou wakest, in order lay
> The actions to be done that following day.

To this effect *Ausonius* hath a *Pythagorical Acroasis,* as he terms it.

> *A good wise person, such as hardly one*
> *Of many thousands to Apollo known,*
> *He his own judge strictly himself surveys,*
> *Nor minds the Noble's or the Common's ways:*
> *But, like the world itself, is smooth and round,*
> *In all his polisht frame no blemish found.*
> *He thinks how long Cancer the day extends,*
> *And Capricorn the night: Himself perpends*
> *In a just balance, that no flaw there be,*
> *Nothing exuberant, but that all agree;*
> *Within that all be solid, nothing by*
> *A hollow sound betray vacuity.*
> *Nor suffer sleep to seize his eyes, before*
> *All acts of that long day he hath run o'er;*
> *What things were missed, what done in time, what not;*
> *Why here respect, or reason there forgot;*
> *Why kept the worse opinion? when relieved*
> *A beggar; why with broken passion grieved;*
> *What wished which had been better not desired;*
> *Why profit before honesty required?*
> *If any by some speech or look offended,*
> *Why nature more than discipline attended?*
> *All words and deeds thus searcht from morn to night,*
> *He sorrows for the ill, rewards the right.*

Secrecy

Besides the five-year silence of the *Pythagoreans,* whilst they were Exoterics, there was another, termed perpetual or compleat silence, (or secrecy) proper to the Esoterics, not amongst one another, but towards all such as were not of their society.

The principal and most efficacious of their Doctrines they all kept ever amongst themselves, as not to be spoken, with exact *Echemythia* (silence) towards extraneous persons, continuing them unwritten and preserved only by memory to their successors, to whom they delivered them as mysteries of the gods; by which means, nothing of any moment came abroad from them. What had been taught and learnt a long time, was only known within the walls; and if at any time there were any extraneous, and as I may say, profane persons amongst them, the Men (so commonly were the *Pythagoreans* termed) signified their meaning to one another by Symbols.

Hence *Lysis* reproving *Hipparchus*, for communicating the discourse to uninitiated persons, void of Mathematics and Theory, saith, They report, that you teach Philosophy in public to all that come, which *Pythagoras* would not do, as you, *Hipparchus*, learnt with much pains. But you took no heed after you had tasted (O noble person) the *Sicilian* delicacies, which you ought not to have tasted a second time. If you are changed, I shall rejoice; if not, you are dead to me; for he said, We ought to remember, that it is impious, according to the direction of divine and human exhortations, that the goods of wisdom ought not to be communicated to those, whose soul is not purified so much as in dream. For it is not lawful to bestow on every one that which was acquired with so much labour, nor to reveal the mysteries of the *Eleusian* Goddesses to profane persons; for they who do both these, are alike unjust and irreligious. It is good to consider within ourselves, how much time was employed in taking away the spots that were in our breasts, that after five years we might be made capable of his discourses. For as Dyers first wash and wring out the clothes they intend to dye, that they may take the dye so, as that it can never be washed out, or taken away; in like manner the Divine prepared those who were inclined to Philosophy, lest he might be deceived by those, of whom he hoped that they would prove good and honest. For he used no adulterate learning, nor the nets wherewith many of the Sophists entangle the young men; but he was skilful in things divine and human: whereas they, under the pretence of his Doctrine, do many strange things, inveigling the young men unbeseemingly, and as they meet them, whereby they render their Auditors rough and rash. For they infuse free Theorems and Discourses, into manners that are not free but disordered. As if into a deep Well full of dirt and mire, we should put clear transparent water, it troubles the dirt, and spoils the water: the same is it, as to those who teach and are taught; for, about the minds and hearts of such as are not initiated, there grows thick and tall coverts, which darken all modesty and meekness, and reason, hindering it from increasing there. Hence spring all kinds of ills, growing up, and hindering the reason, and not suffering it to look out. I will first name their mothers, Intemperance and Avarice, both exceeding fruitful. From Intemperance spring up unlawful marriages, lust, and drunkenness, and perdition, and unnatural pleasures, and certain vehement appetites leading to death and ruin; for some have been so violently carried away with pleasures, that they have not refrained from their own mothers and daughters; but violating the Commonwealth, and the Laws, tyrannically imprison men, and carrying about their Stocks violently hurry them to destruction. From Avarice proceed rapines, thefts, parricides, sacrileges, poisonings, and whatsoever is allied to these. It behooves, therefore, first, to cut away the matter wherein these vices are bred, with fire and sword, and all arts of discipline, purifying and freeing the reason from these evils; and then to plant something that is good in it. Thus *Lysis*, Neither is that expression, (If you are not changed, you are dead to me) to be understood simply: for this *Hipparchus*, because he communicated, and publicly set forth by writing, the *Pythagoric* Doctrines, was expelled the School, and a Tomb was made for him, as if he were dead, (according to the custom formerly mentioned). So strict were the *Pythagoreans* in observance of this Secrecy.

rientalism

Japan

If you were to ask me what nation most perfectly embodies the quality of appreciation, I would answer, Japan. In all the world there is no more appreciative an individual than a Japanese, nor is there a more cultured, gracious, or comprehending person than the Japanese gentlemen. There is a certain quaintness in his nature which is a charming contrast to the brusqueness of the average American. Within the last few months several occurrences have come to my notice which make me feel that the average individual should appreciate more fully the finer qualities of the Japanese people, for we are too prone merely to consider them as rivals for Asiatic trade or as a menace to the white man's supremacy. From all the evidence which we have been able to gather, we find the Japanese a very human as well as a very kindly person. Our first example of this pertains to gratitude. A certain white man took into his home in America a Japanese boy in serious difficulties, assisting this boy to find his way and establish himself in the Western world. Sometime later this white gentleman with his wife visited Japan. In some way the Japanese youth sent word to his own country, and when the benevolent American arrived he was not only treated as a friend but as an honored friend, who for his service to a single member of their race was entitled to the deepest and most profound respect from the entire nation. A banquet was spread in his honor and when the meal was finished a Japanese dignitary arose, holding in his hand a little box of lacquered wood tied with a silken cord. This dignitary made a short speech in which he said that for the kindness which the American had shown to the people of the Japanese race the Mikado of Japan was sincerely grateful and appreciative, and in recognition of his kindly act to the lonely Japanese boy the Mikado took the greatest pleasure in presenting to him the fourth degree of the Order of the Rising Sun and to his wife a solid golden bowl bearing upon its concave surface the royal arms of Japan. The jewel was duly presented.

It seems to me that a nation so thoughtful, so grateful for services rendered, so willing to acknowledge and respect the friendly member of another race must have within it much that is commendable and worthy; that where such a feeling exists it should not be difficult to solve international problems with kindness and friendship.

The second incident was told me by a friend who had lived for many years in Japan and taught in the Japanese schools. There was in Japan a certain American school teacher, an excellent woman with a fine understanding of the Japanese soul. Through her labors a number of Japanese youth had been converted to the Christian faith, and as she had lived many years in the empire numbers of her students had grown to manhood and established themselves in various lines of business. At last after many years

—in fact nearly a lifetime of teaching—the American woman decided to take a vacation in the States, her plans from the time on being somewhat indefinite. Just before her departure one of her pupils, who had long since graduated and entered business, visited her, the substance of his errand being as follows:

"The great service which you rendered me and my fellow countrymen in matters pertaining to education cannot be lightly overlooked. I owe much to you and am very desirous of showing my appreciation for your many favors and great goodness. I am a fairly wealthy man and when you return from your visit to the States, it is my most earnest desire that you will permit me to adopt you as my mother. I will then build for you a home in American style and you shall be the mistress of that home. I shall support you all the rest of your life and shall consider you in exactly the same light and with the same reverence and love that I would my own mother."

This might seem an isolated incident, for it would certainly be very rare that any American school child would feel so deep a regard of his instructor that they would want to support her for the rest of their lives. My friend assures me, however—and he is a man of absolute integrity—that this school teacher received several such offers from different students on the eve of her departure and that this practice is not uncommon among the Japanese people, who seemingly can never completely repay a favor, if that favor be done without ulterior motive.

A third incident which I would like to relate is an effort recently made by the Japanese to assist a certain American city to secure a better understanding of Japanese life and Japanese problems. In order to improve the understanding between the two countries, a certain Japanese corporation is sending each year two of the public school teachers of the American city to Japan, paying the entire expense of their trip and sojourn there. By such courtesies they hope to bring home to the people of the American city the nearness and friendliness of the Japanese nation.—M. P. H.

Editorial

(*Continued from Page 134*)
well without the God that most men worship, but the wise man's God is the very mechanism of the universe. The wise man's God is the fuel, the machine, and the product all in one. By *will* the Mysteries accomplish the union of man with his Divine Source, for will is the divine urge to accomplishment, and once that urge is awakened the ultimate result is certain, though untold ages may intervene.

We conceive God to be without the human concept of revenge. We believe in no vengeful God, for upon what can It wreak vengeance but upon Itself? If there be a hell, it also must be part of God, and what true man or woman can conceive a Deity within whose nature an Inferno can exist? Hell is the condition of ignorance and can only exist in the soul that has never found the *Universal Good*. Heaven is light and he who dwells in the light dwells in the consciousness of *Good* and is immortal. There is no mortality except for those who believe in death. There is no immortality save that which man discovers when he recognizes his unity with his Creator. The universe is life. Life thrills through every part of it. Life pulsates through every atom of it. Life stretches out boundlessly before everything.

Yet in the midst of all this pulsating life, man believes that he can die. There is no death but ignorance; there is no life but wisdom. But wisdom is supreme; therefore life is supreme. Among the ancient peoples there were some who believed that *good* and *evil* were eternally-existing principles which should combat themselves forever. This conception is founded upon man's limitations of sense perception. Seeing what he believes to be evil, man therefore assumes that which he believes to be true, failing to realize that his narrow-sightedness has caused him to perceive only an infinitesimal part of a plan which, could he comprehend it all, would reveal its absolute goodness.

We conceive God to be the inward parts of all beings and things and that, having this divine all-powerful potentiality within, each one may accomplish any worthy motive which inspires him. The Divinity within man means infinite capacity, but only through ages of growth and development may he bring to flower these divine potentialities within himself. The Divinity within man is a seed that is sown in the ground of his material nature. Whether this seed shall blossom forth depends upon the quality of the soil (his body) and the presence of sunlight (his mind), for without water (the body) and fire (the mind) the seed of the spirit cannot grow. Therefore it must remain through the ages awaiting an environment suitable for its expression. You will remember the grains of wheat found clasped in the mummified hand of an Egyptian Pharaoh. After 5,000 years they were planted and produced a harvest. Like these grains of wheat is the spiritual Self in man which, though it lies long in the tomb, will bring forth its kind in abundant harvest when planted in the proper soil.

So we believe in a God of infinite power, unlimited by mortal concept, unimpeded by the limitations of human fancy; a God in all, of all, through all; a common parent, a common father, and a common urge to accomplishment. We believe ourselves to be part of that Supreme One, sharing a common birthright of immortality and omnipotence. We believe all temples to be Its house, all hearts Its shrine, all hands Its hands, all ideals Its ideals, all dreams Its dreams, and all accomplishment unity with Itself.

Man

To the eye of vulgar Logic, says he, what is man? An omnivorous Biped that wears Breeches.

To the eye of Pure Reason what is he? A Soul, a Spirit, and divine Apparition. Round his mysterious ME, there lies, under all those wool-rags, a Garment of Flesh (or of Senses), contextured in the Loom of Heaven; whereby he is revealed to his like, and dwells with them in UNION and DIVISION; and sees and fashions for himself a Universe, with azure Starry Spaces, and long Thousands of Years. Deep-hidden is he under that strange Garment; amid Sounds and Colors and Forms, as it were, swathed-in, and inextricably overshrouded: yet it is sky-woven, and worthy of a God. Stands he not thereby in the centre of Immensities, in the conflux of Eternities?—Sartor Resartus.

Questions & answers·

Q. Where is the line of demarkation between knowledge which may be sold and knowledge which must be given? H. S.

A. Webster defines knowledge as "familiarity gained by actual experience." Accepting this definition, it becomes evident that knowledge cannot be sold but must be acquired first-hand by actual intimacy or association with the subject concerning which knowledge is desired. In the last analysis, all arts and crafts are divine and any knowledge an individual may secure concerning them is divine knowledge. We are, for fortunately or unfortunately, living in a material civilization in which the dollar is supreme. Monetary reward is the only incentive left to man for excellence and man now struggles to acquire the almighty dollar with all the zeal with which he once labored to attain a worthy name. In Greece and Rome philosophers were crowned with laurel wreath and their writings were upon every man's tongue, whereas in America in the 20th century philosophers are few and the laurel wreaths are reserved for prizefighters and football players. The question sometimes arises whether we would have more philosophers if we encouraged them a little more heartily with financial support. Why should a great thinker with a message needed by the whole world be forced, Homer-like, to wander from town to town, begging his bread and reciting his poems for a pittance to pay for shelter? When Homer died all Greece laid claim to him and erected monuments to his honor. If the money expended to do him post-mortem homage had been lavished upon him during life, it would have contributed much to his material comfort. Nations are taxed for roads and various improvements to the community. Each individual land owner also contributes to the support of his public schools, his penal institutions, his orphanages, and his homes for the decrepit. In this way he shares with others the common responsibilities of the state and enjoys thereby the common conveniences thus secured. Is not a great mind, however, the most precious possession of the state? Is a philosopher not a school wherein education is dispensed? Is a great philosopher not a public park contributing to the health and beauty of the community? Therefore, should not the poet, the musician, the artist, the philosopher, and the writer, who all contribute so vastly to the finer side of human nature, be maintained by the state in a position of dignity befitting the excellence of their intellect? Certain Central European countries have established national funds for the furtherance of scientific and artistic pursuits. Thus the poor inventor may secure the facilities necessary to perfect his idea, and the impoverished musician maintain himself in food and clothing while he pursues the study of his art.

Generally speaking, the creative thinker or idealist is a failure in the commercial world. Therefore, there is a general belief that to think is to be impractical. An inventor seldom profits by his invention; the poet receives little remuneration for his efforts; and composers like Franz Schubert secure but a few cents for masterpieces. If genius will prostitute itself and descend to the level of a "jazz" crazed age, it may become financially successful. If not, it goes threadbare and lives in hall bedrooms.

From earliest times it has been considered sacrilegious to sell religion or to place a price upon those sacred arts and sciences which the gods have given to mankind that it might regain its lost estate. Sacred knowledge is the highest form of knowledge and no one capable of commercializing it is capable of possessing it. Therefore, in the last analysis, it is never sold, because the seller cannot deliver the goods. To tell something to a man is not to give him knowledge. Knowledge cannot be communicated from one person to another. All that one man can reveal to another is the existence of knowledge, for each one discovering that knowledge does exist must search for it in his own way and discover it at the cost of individual labor. As well say "For a $1.25 I will digest your dinner" as to say "I will sell you knowledge." You may sell a man food but he must digest it for himself. You may sell a man facts but he does not *know* them until through a gradual process requiring the active agency of his own reason he incorporates, through repeated experimentation and experience, these facts into his own nature.

The world is filled with people who have nothing and desire to share it with somebody. It also contains a great number who, knowing nothing, deal out their ignorance at so much per measure. The only reason why the business is successful is that the intellience of the buyer is on a par with that of the merchant. It has been my own experience that the majority of so-called eminent teachers of things spiritual have no knowledge of any kind concerning the subjects they profess to teach. Many of them have come to me and admitted frankly that they were absolutely without a foundation, that they did not know which way to turn and were themselves in the very midst of an apparently hopeless religious, philosophical, and ethical dilemma. Yet these same individuals go forth into the world, posing as teachers and charging anywhere from a few dollars to several hundred for their precious information. Such misrepresentatives as these are the outstanding cause for the disrepute into which the so-called superphysical doctrines have fallen. From a purely commercial standpoint, such individuals masquerading under the guise of teachers of philosophy, psychology, and metaphysics are as guilty of fraud as the man who circulates bogus oil stock or holds up a bank late at night.

Religion is the single hope of the race and to the extent it becomes commercialized, the world's greatest ethical influence is weakened. Yet the churches are gradually transforming themselves into vaudeville shows with county fairs in the basement. The majority of people, being unable to differentiate between the church and the religion for which it stands, have come to the conclusion that religion encourages commercialization. This viewpoint is incorrect and he who attempts to sell salvation is establishing a dangerous precedent. Knowledge and integrity must be achieved and he who attempts to impart them for any consideration other than that of individual virtue and integrity prostitutes the sacred sciences. If salvation could be bought and sold, all the rich would be in heaven and the poor in hell, but fortunately there is a coin of the realm superior to gold. Spiritual merchandise must be bought with a spiritual coin and the name of that coin is INDIVIDUAL WORTH.

Q.   Does Cervantes' *Don Quioxote* contain any philosophical or mystical symbolism? If so, please give an outline of it. Anon.

A.   *Don Quioxote* is now one of the books included in those ascribed to Sir Francis Bacon or at least the Secret Society which he represented. If this link be established, the volume may very possibly contain profound and occult material, especially relating to the Rosicrucian controversy. *Don Quioxote* has long been considered as a volume written for the purpose of ridiculing the knight-errantry of the Middle Ages. It is one of the great masterpieces of literature and contains a vast amount of good common sense concealed in the ludicrous situations in which *Don Quioxote* and his faithful *Sancho Panza* are so often involved. The simplest and most direct lesson that the volume contains, in my estimation, is that of the hopelessness of attempting to live in any generation other than one's own.

Mr. Manly P. Hall is presenting the following series of lectures in San Francisco, from September 8th to 30th inclusive, 8:00 P.M.:

Hidden Chapters of History

Sept. 8th—The King of Kings.
" 9th—Pages from the Unwritten History of the United States.
" 10th—Comte de St. Germain.

The Secret Doctrine of Israel

Sept. 11th—The Keynote of Ancient Jewish Philosophy.
" 12th—The Mystery of the Ten Commandments.
" 13th—The Grand Man of the Zohar.

Greek Superphysics

Sept. 14th—The Platonic Solution to the Mystery of Life.
" 15th—The "Musical Medicine" of Pythagoras.
" 16th—Three Keys to the Riddle of Existence.

The Philosophies of India

Sept. 17th—The Ten Incarnations of Vishnu.
" 18th—The Four Ages of the World.
" 19th—The Jewels of Buddhism.

Christian Mysticism

Sept. 20th—The Creative Trinity.
" 21st—The Myth of the Dying God.
" 22nd—Pagan Origins of Christian Symbolism.

Egyptian Esotericism

Sept. 23rd—The Vision of Hermes—the Problem of Universal Mind.
" 25th—A New Lecture on the Great Pyramid.
" 26th—The Theory of Universal Education.

Concerning the Nature of Man

Sept. 27th—The Lotus Lords.
" 28th—Turning the Wheel of the Law.
" 29th—Opening the Gate of the Gods.
Sept. 30th—An Arabian Nights Entertainment.

Scottish Rite Auditorium
Sutter at Van Ness

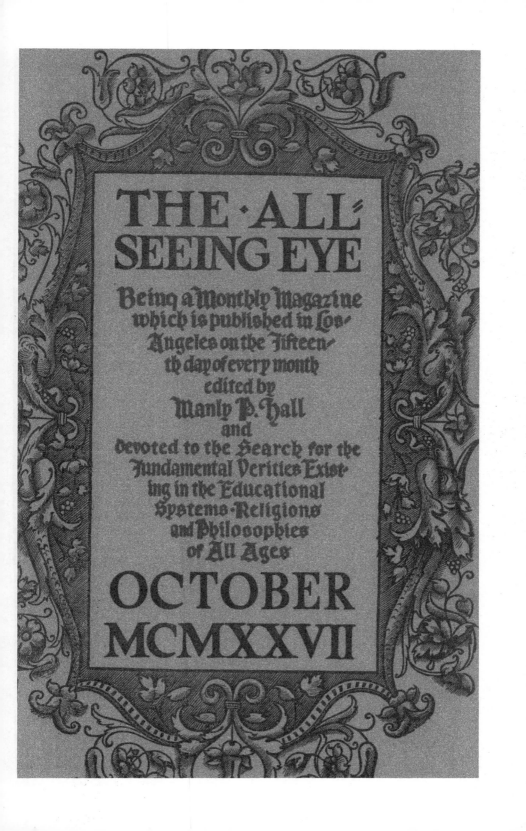

THE·ALL·SEEING EYE

Being a Monthly Magazine
which is published in Los-
Angeles on the Fifteen-
th day of every month
edited by
Manly P. Hall
and
devoted to the Search for the
Fundamental Verities Existing in the Educational
Systems·Religions
and Philosophies
of All Ages

OCTOBER
MCMXXVII

The ALL-SEEING EYE

DEVOTED TO THE SEARCH FOR THE
FUNDAMENTAL VERITIES EXIST-
ING IN THE EDUCATIONAL
SYSTEMS, RELIGIONS,
AND PHILOSOPHIES
OF ALL AGES

VOL. IV	OCTOBER, 1927	No. 6

PUBLISHED EVERY MONTH BY

THE HALL PUBLISHING COMPANY
301 TRINITY AUDITORIUM BUILDING, TUcker 2603
NINTH AT GRAND AVENUE, LOS ANGELES, CALIFORNIA

MANLY P. HALL . . . . *Editor*
HARRY S. GERHART . . . . *Managing Editor*
MAUD F. GALIGHER . . . . *Associate Editor*
HOWARD W. WOOKEY . . . . *Art Director*

CONTENTS

Change of address must be in this office not later than the first of the month preceding issue. Please give both old and new addresses.

*Entered as second-class matter February 11, 1927, at the post office at Los Angeles,
California, under the act of March 3, 1879*

PER COPY, 25c—SIX MONTHS $1.00—ONE YEAR $2.00
FOREIGN, SIX MONTHS $1.15—ONE YEAR $2.25

Do You Know?

That Napoleon Bonaparte turned down as impractical the plans for the first submarine boat?

That the ruler of the East Indian State of Baroda has the finest collection of pearls in the world?

That the fashion of ornamenting the upper ends of gateposts with knobs is a survival of the ancient savage custom of mounting the skulls of enemies on either side of the doorway?

That the ancient Britons, being unable to temper the metal used in the making of swords, were forced to stop every little while and straighten out their bent sword blades before continuing their fighting?

That one of Sarah Bernhardt's friends presented her with a coffin, which she always carried about with her lest, in her own words, she should die suddenly without sufficient cash to supply one?

That the Gypsies are in all probability the descendants of the priests of the Egyptian temple of Serapis at Alexandria, driven into exile by the destruction of that edifice by Theodosius, the Christian Emperor?

That the Hindu Emperor, Akbar the Great, one of the most illustrious of the Mogul rulers, used to play chess with the native princes in the courtyard of the palace? All the pieces were living men dressed in varicolored costumes.

That the ancient Egyptian women bobbed their hair, rouged their lips, painted their faces, wore short skirts, high heels, thus possessing nearly all the traits of the modern flapper?

That while the ancient Romans did not possess spectacles, they were able to aid failing eyesight by constructing rings in which was set an upright transparent, or partly transparent, gem polished in the shape of a magnifying glass? By squinting with one eye, they were thus able to read through their rings.

The EDITOR'S BRIEFS

Building Statelier Mansions

In its final analysis, the entire composite constitution of man is composed of gradations of a single substance or condition—namely, that of spirit. The ultimate *energy* of the physicist is synonymous with the *spirit* of the theologian and philosopher. That which the scientist chooses to term *matter* is really but a condition of this *energy* or *spirit,* for when reduced to its ultimate form substance is but a unit of potential energy. While the materialist flounders in a maze of little-understood elements in the effort to substantiate his theory that intelligence is the result of friction, fermentation or the chemical product of a peculiar atomic compound, the philosopher realizes that mind is actually spirit manifesting through a certain level, which for convenience may be called the mental plane. The ultimate atom of this plane is the *mentoid* of Herbert Spencer.

Only when the student attempts to reconcile the theories of modern science with the deductions of the early philosophers does he realize that the ancient world was conversant with many doctrines which the modern world claims as its own discoveries. The *heaven* and *hell* of theology are merely the graduated planes of energy familiar to modern science, and it makes little difference whether the 20th century savant calls the ultimate energy of the universe *force,* or, like the Brahmin, he names it *Brahma.* Science and theology are divided not by their doctrines but rather by their systems of terminology. Stripped of misleading verbiage, both are advancing the same explanation to the "mystery" of life.

Science moves cautiously, believing only that which can be demonstrated in the laboratory or rendered visible by powerful instruments. For this reason the materialistic scientist is limited in his explorations to the elements of physical substance. Only within the last few years have attempts been made to explore what Longfellow so beautifully termed "the universe of thought."

Notice to Subscribers

This number completes Vol. IV of The All-Seeing Eye. As it is necessary for Mr. Hall to prepare for an extensive period of public work on the lecture platform, including a prospective national tour, it will be impossible for him to prepare the necessary material for a monthly magazine at this time. Therefore the publication of The All-Seeing Eye will be suspended until such time as it is possible for Mr. Hall to continue the preparation of the necessary articles. You will be notified in due time concerning Vol. V.

NOTE: Be sure to secure either a bound copy of Vol IV or else send in your file of magazines and we will have them bound for you as per notice on inside front cover.

We thank you.

Even Huxley, the grand patron of science, was forced to admit that there were three questions for which he could find no answer. He even went so far as to declare that in his estimation they would never be answered. The first queston was "What is life?", the second, "What is intelligence?", and the third, "What is force?" Did Huxley realize that his *life, intelligence,* and *force* constitute the fundamental Trinity of all religious doctrines and that long before modern civilization was dreamed of the sages of the prehistoric world had affirmed this Trinity to be the Unknowable Source of the manifested universe?

But let us take these three "unknowables" of science and study them in the light of the Ancient Wisdom, keeping in mind the olden adage that the universe is erected upon a triangular base and that everywhere in Nature are to be found examples of these fundamental triads.

The subject of the triad is magnificently set forth in the famous Bembine Table of Isis, in which 45 main figures are grouped into 15 triads representing the fundamental manifestations of all the varied natural laws. In the Chaldean oracles the Deity is repeatedly referred to as a triad or a triple flame. By the famous Hermetic *law of analogy* we see that in the last analysis man consists of a fundamental trinity of *life, intelligence,* and *force.* The center of life is the spirit, the center of intelligence the mind, and the center of force the body. If modern science but knew, the Father, Son, and Holy Ghost of Christian theology are merely the personifications of these unknown but universal principles.

Life is the *Universal Creator,* intelligence the *Universal Preserver,* and force the *Universal Destroyer.* While a definite description of these principles is impossible, their manifestations are everywhere discernible. Integration is continually taking place. It is followed by a period of manifestation that, in turn, is succeeded by a process of disintegration which analogically must result in subsequent reintegration. If the ancient Greeks chose to call universal force *Jupiter* and its disintegrative quality *Pluto,* then the modern scientific world should feel less inclined to regard the Hellenic philosophers as uncouth barbarians. Nor would we, if we exemplified the true spirit of religious tolerance, call the Hindus idolaters because they personify universal intelligence in the form of Vishnu.

As the life of the individual naturally divides itself into a series of periods—called in the Shakesperian plays the "seven ages of man"—so the history of the human race may be divided into a number of epochs. These epochs the Greeks designated as the *golden age,* the *silver age,* the *bronze age,* and the *iron age.* Recognizing that the life of a race—like the life of man—has but one period of adolescence, one great author has termed the civilization of ancient Greece the adolescent period in the life of philosophy.

It is difficult for us to visualize a civilization in which everyone was well educated according to the standards of the times. We assuredly cannot claim such a condition even here in America, which probably enjoys the most-liberal educational facilities of the modern world. Yet in Greece there was a *golden age* of culture when the poorest man understood the divine sciences of geometry and trigonometry, and the lowliest laborer could stand up and recite the poetic masterpieces of Hesiod and Homer.

We therefore must not be amazed by the assertion that ancient Greece did the world's heavy thinking, for she produced more philosophers and educators than any other nation of antiquity. In Greek culture we find the most perfect expression of symmetry, the most tangible proof of this perfect balance being the surpassing physical beauty of the Greek people. That ideal which either an individual or a nation strives for over an extended period of time at last becomes a material reality. The Greeks assiduously cultivated the æsthetic arts. They emphasized rhythmic thinking and harmonious living, built graceful and inspiring buildngs, and gradually the beauty with which they surrounded themselves thus became the dominant keyword of their entire civilization.

Certain localities are peculiarly adapted to certain undertakings. For example, there is a small area near Stuttgart, in Germany, where it is easier to write books of a philosophical nature than any other spot on the face of the earth. This is the answer to the reason for Greek supremacy in philosophy and ethics. A foreigner with only a mediocre mind who came and settled in Greece would find that there he could think clearer and his thoughts be more logical. Philosophy and logic were in the air and so permeated the entire fabric of Greek life that it was impossible not to express them. To some degree, at least, the spirit of commercialism has a similar hold upon modern civilization. Our so-called "captains of industry" are as truly the products of an attitude common to the race as were Plato and Aristotle the products of their ethical environment.

It is therefore a mistake to assume that knowledge is either primitive or obsolete because it is old. Even in our day we have made no marked advance over the standards of ancient Greece and Egypt in those arts and sciences dependent upon abstract thinking, for from the time of the Roman Empire philosophy began to deteriorate, commerce and conquest obsessed the mind of man, and for over 2,000 years we have labored to erect a civilization which is practically devoid of the true elements of culture.

Today we are confronted with a vast number of problems, most of them requiring a far greater knowledge of the fundamental principles of life than that possessed by the average individual. The mind of man is groping through a world of selfishness and materiality in the vain search for an intelligible solution to the riddle of human existence.

For thousands of years theology has advanced dogmatic and arbitrary explanations but has failed to convince that something in the soul of man which persists in recognizing those rational elements ignored by religion. Atheism is rampant in the land; every day creedal theology is losing more of its devotees; materialism augmented by the findings of science is spreading like wildfire through the world. Man has lost faith in the God of the church and, knowing no other God, is attempting to maintain a universe without a Creator and to prove that the wisdom of the universe is based upon a thought which is not the product of a Thinker.

By way of contrasting ancient ideals with our own, let us imagine that one of the great minds of antiquity has been transplanted from his civilization to ours. He is totally unaware of modern methods of thought or systems of culture, but seeing about him conditions and problems similar to those of his own civilization, he attempts to solve them by the culture and ethics of his time. As country roads are no longer available, we seat ourselves on a curbstone and thus discuss the vital issues of this generation:

"O illustrious sage, does this civilization with all its turmoil and excitement, with its endless rushing hither and thither amaze you, or did you foresee it in your dreams when you lived in Athens 2,500 years ago?"

"My son, all these strange sights, while of great interest, do not amaze me, for I recognize in each of your strange inventions and curious practices the projection of some principle or law first taught by us in our ancient schools. The world in which you live is merely an objectification of the mind with which you think. This confusion which I see about me is but the natural offspring of that confusion within yourselves. The bustling crowds and noisy clatter of your streets tells me that the calm and peace of ancient days no longer abides within your souls. Your ugly, angular buildings piled together represent the heaped-up and disorganized state of your thoughts; your narrow, gloomy streets reflect the rutted channels of your thoughts. The absence of flowers, trees, and birds warns me that you have lost the mystic touch and love of Nature; therefore your entire cultural system is unnatural. You are able to see as much of God as you can of the tiny patch of blue sky hemmed in by your mighty skyscrapers. You are able to see as much of the broad vistas of truth as you can of the hills, the sight of which is shut off by the structures of your hands. I fear that this civilization is not to my liking and that I shall not thrive here. I see too much blasphemy about, for it is blasphemy for man with his puny hands and mind to strive to surpass the works of God by building an unnatural world in the midst of a divine world."

As we sat together on the curbstone a strange sound was wafted to our ears. Someone had just tuned the radio in on a "jazz" band. The venerable philosopher listened for a few moments. A strange look passed over his features.

"By Zeus, what strange discords affect mine ears? This is no Dorian or Phrygian mode! Is it music or is it a battle?" My efforts to explain that it was 20th century dance music caused the sage to nod his head two or three times reflectively. "I might have known it would come, for the ever-increasing acuteness of the nervous system would finally demand such stimuli! But I warn you such sounds as these I hear are sufficient to overthrow a nation. Now I remember that once in Athens a poet composed a lyric such as this and a gathering of the Elders decided that for the good of the community he should be banished from the state and deprived of his rights as a citizen, for the entire ethical structure of a civilization can be overturned by the character of its music and poetry. This very discord which I hear is sufficient in itself to breed war, hate, savagery, discontent, rebellion, revenge, lust, greed, passion, and avarice in the souls of men. I fear we had best move on, lest I myself become contaminated, for already my mental faculties are perturbed."

We walked together for a short time and finally stopped on a busy corner to watch the surging sea of pedestrians of which we were a part. The seer stroked his long beard as he watched the sight. "Is this a normal concourse of the populace or is some great philosopher in the city?" he asked. "Oh," I answered, "it is only Monday with the usual white goods sales in the downtown store basements." "It is, indeed, a rare opportunity," he replied, "to be alive at this day and behold so much confusion over matters of so little moment. If I should have told this in the lyceum at Sparta they would have ridiculed me from my seat. But the day is very warm and the crowd oppresses me. Let us go where we may sit and rest and where it will be more cool."

We immediately suggested a local theater and, accompanied by the seer, secured reasonably good seats for the matinee. After watching the performance for a short time with a very bored air, the philosopher finally turned to me and asked the question, "Which poet is going to recite this afternoon?" We assured him that no one would attend a theater to hear poetry in the 20th century, and—what was more—there were very few good poets! "It seems incredible," he murmured, "to conceive of a great civilization that does not love poetry. But we must be resigned to the will of the gods. Of course there will be a speech on some important subject. I trust it will be mathematics or astronomy."

It required a lengthy explanation on our part to convince the sage that modern audiences never attend the theater to be educated but solely to be amused. "But," he continued incredulously, "how can intelligent men and women be amused except by education and why should so vast a number gather in a place of worship only to laugh?" "But," we interposed, "this is not a place of worship." "A barbaric people," murmured the philosopher, "that they should divorce the drama from the temple. I fear that I shall never become reconciled to your culture. Let us go hence. Why should I remain and waste my time if no one is going to recite the classics, discourse on the arts and sciences or present a pageantry from the Mysteries?"

We took a taxi and drove out several miles into the country, and finally coming to a secluded and wooded spot which seemed to the liking of the great sage, we dismissed the cab and seated ourselves under some spreading trees. A sigh of relief escaped my companion's lips as he found himself again in an environment more congenial. "In Athens," he began, "it was always customary to gather a short distance from the city and there discourse on the verities of Nature, for it is only when you are close to the earth, the birds, the flowers, and the trees that your heart and soul can comprehend the beauties of the universe. The congestion of the city fills the mind with a false concept of reality. It makes man feel that bustle and confusion are God-ordained when in reality the peace and harmony of the hills represent the true spirit of the Creator. Your world does not seem to realize that man can learn little from man but much from Nature."

"Why is it," we asked, "that man is forced to struggle through all the ages building empires and deserting them, building bodies and dying, dreaming dreams and having them shattered, lifting up only to have all torn down again?" Gazing out into space for a few seconds, the seer replied, "Only the foolish build with those constituents that are perishable, only the ignorant die, and only the foolish dreamer dreams such dreams as can be shattered. It is this way: Man is really two beings—one a divine and perfect creature partaking of the nature and substance of the immortals; the other a human and imperfect creature partaking of the nature and substance of the mortal. These two natures are bound together in one constitution where, by the foolish, they are mistaken for a single individual. The true is that which forever is; the false that which exists only for a time. The divine creature in man is eternal, permanent, and undying. It is unaware of the illusion of birth and death, for it partakes of the immortal nature of the gods. It is a Mt. Olympus far above the clouds and divided from the cognition of the world below by the mist and fog of ignorance. The first step which man must take if he would become wise is to distinguish the real man from the false, the divine nature from the human, the eternal constitution from the temporal. When he has accomplished this, the true and divine part becomes the master and the human and temporal part the disciple.

"When the sage has torn away the veil that hides the truth from mortal gaze, he is instructed to go forth and teach it to all men. But the first one whom he must convince is his own lower nature—his mortal self. If he can convince his own animal soul that he has found Divinity, has come into a realization of Reality, then he has made his first convert and that first convert will change the beliefs of the entire world. Every man proves that he recognizes the duality of his own nature when he attempts to deceive himself, as many are wont to do, for there are times when the lower nature says, 'I desire to do an ignoble thing, but first of all I must convince myself that there is a reason why I should do it.' So the animal soul argues with the spiritual soul and as the spiritual man manifests but slightly in the lower world, the animal soul usually silences the protests of conscience and does the ignoble deed to gratify its baser nature.

"Since man is composed of both a spiritual and a material nature, it .is also necessary that you should realize that these two natures are not evenly distributed. As little of the material constitution is capable of functioning in the spiritual world, so little of the spiritual constitution is capable of manifesting in the material world. At the present stage of man's evolution, the lower nature is nearly five times stronger than the spiritual nature in the material world. For that reason evil apparently flourishes and those who strive to do that which is right are crushed by the preponderance of materiality against them. Time, however, will eventually reverse the situation. Down through the ages the human soul is slowly but surely accumulating an increment of power. It is gradually acquiring a more direct control over its various vehicles, which will result in an increase of virtue and integrity in the world and the ultimate victory and survival of right.

"In ancient Greece we taught that the spiritual development of man depends wholly upon the *quality* of his vehicles. We realized that refinement was merely the process of spiritualizing the body; that gradually the spiritual nature came to dominate the personality, a truth carefully concealed under the allegory of Perseus and Andromeda. Do you realize that as ages pass the nervous system of man becomes more sensitive, that each individual part of the body is being more closely connected with the center of thought and consciousness? Man's sense-perceptions are in their infancy at present. The oldest of them—feeling—is the most highly developed. Therefore we are controlled by our desires rather than by our reason. How few realize that every nerve terminus is not only a potential eye, but also a potential ear, mouth, and olfactory bulb!

"How proud man would be if he fully appreciated his own inherent greatness and, again, how hopelessly insolent and egotistic would he become, for all the powers of the universe lie dormant within him, waiting like tiny seeds for the time to germinate and grow into the mighty monarchs of the forest. But century after century, like some blind mole, humanity burrows into its hills or it raises gloomy cities and battles with the segments of itself, alternately playing the roles of conqueror and conquered. Yet with all its progress and achievement humanity still remains pitifully ignorant of its own inherent divinity. The years of earthly existence so graciously bestowed by the gods for the attainment of immortality, men and women daily squander in the vain struggle to accumulate *unreal* and *impermanent* treasures such as temporal power and fleeting fame. Twenty-five hundred years ago there were a few who grasped in part, at least, the plan of the gods. Today in your generation I presume the same is true. Nay, it must be so, for truth can never entirely die. But it seems the voices of the wise are not heard in the 20th century as loudly as they were in the days of Alexander.

"But I am weary. For a little while I have assumed the *illusion* of your civilization and these few hours have tired me more than my hundred years in Greece. So I will go back again into my realization of eternal life and there await a generation more kindly disposed towards poets and mathematicians, for I live for but two things: either I must teach or I must learn. All other endeavors and pursuits are useless. Your music frightens me, your civilization oppresses me. As for teaching, a few weeks in your bustling confusion I fear would cause me to forget what little I already know. Therefore I beg to take my leave at this time, for we are in a pleasant spot and I fear if I become enmeshed again in the discords of your civilization I shall go mad before I can escape. Farewell."

The Greek philosopher, having thus disposed of himself, permits us to make a few remarks behind his back. It will take thousands of years for our civilization to reach the ethical pinnacle of the ancient Greeks. It is not improbable that in the centuries to come minds such as Plato and Pythagoras will be honored in their true dignity as the two greatest teachers produced by the Aryan race. The infantile state of man's intelligence today is unable either to appraise the superlative qualities of their intellects or to sound the depths of their erudition. But as the world continues to acquire a broader mental outlook, it will recognize more and more the profound integrity of these illumined souls. Until then we must work patiently, unfolding as sequentially and fully as possible the divine faculties and attributes latent within our own individual natures.

The human mind has a multiplicity of channels for expression. It is capable of interesting itself in a vast number of issues. In some cases it can actually accomplish several separate and distinct labors at one time. Julius Caesar did ten things at once and did them well, and the Comte de St. Germain wrote simultaneously ten verses of poetry with his right hand and ten verses with his left. Not only did he possess the ambidextrous ability to write with both hands but he composed the poetry for both sets of verses while writing them. A young Japanese boy is now giving public demonstrations in this country of his ability to copy articles from a newspaper on the blackboard behind him, writing the words upside down and backwards and at the same time conversing with a number of people, answering such questions as possible methods of squaring the circle and the mathematical establishment of the fourth dimension.

The foregoing illustrations demonstrate the versatility of the human mind and also provoke the question whether the average individual exercises the numerous faculties of his brain in such manner that they will serve him most intelligently. The brain has forty-three different ways of looking at every problem and likewise is capable of handling forty-three separate and distinct subjects at one time. With this vast equipment behind ·

him, the ordinary man employs only one or two faculties with any degree of success. Too often the average mind of today is the "single track" variety. So limited, however, is man's ability to direct and control his mental processes that concentration upon but a *single* subject is an individual feat rarely met with. The mental vehicle of man is now only in the swaddling clothes stage of its unfoldment. Like the infant, it is powerless to visualize its own latent possibilities.

Those who find thinking an effort and therefore seek to evade mental exercise have a very dismal future to face. It is now being scientifically demonstrated that day by day more involuntary functions are coming under the control of the individual will. This means that some day it will be necessary to digest our food by a conscious mental process; that assimilation will work only when it is ordered to work; and that an absent-minded person may drop dead because he forgot to keep his heart beating! This will be a hard world then for that vast percentage of humanity who just can't keep their minds on the details.

In spite of its persistent efforts to stay "young," the human race, however, is growing up. And with maturity comes responsibility. As time goes on this responsibility will become heavier and heavier. Man is predestined to become an agency of executive power. He was created to rule and the first step in his coming of age is to become ruler of himself.

By the brain the body is controlled and by the spirit the brain is manipulated. Consciousness—the resultant phenomena from this action of spirit upon brain matter—manifests itself as intelligence, and intelligence is that organizing power which not only maintains the structure of Nature but also supplies that inextinguishable urge in every creature for self-completion. The mind is far greater than the brain through which it manifests; the mind contains a storehouse of potentialities which can only become active potencies when given expression through a highly organized and cultured brain.

When a school child has studied arithmetic for forty-five minutes, a certain faculty of the brain has become "tired" and is no longer capable of concentrating successfully upon that particular subject. But this same scholar is actually rested by passing into another schoolroom and studying geography for a similar period of time. A new faculty of the mind is thus brought into action and the change constitutes a rest. In its last analysis, there is really no rest for man. The thing which he calls rest is merely a change, for both mind and body are rejuvenated by variety. The thing we have to do is *work;* the think we love to do is *play.* It is monotony—not labor—that tears tears down the nervous system and leaves the individual on the proverbial "ragged edge."

As you get out the sandpaper to polish up your golf clubs or send your tennis racket down town to be restrung how thankful you are for a little rest—a change—and then ask yourself if it would not be wise to give certain brain centers an occasional vacation.

For example, take John Doe No. 1. He is a botanist and his life has been given to the study and cataloging of the earth's variegated flora. But as time goes on, botany ceases to become a study—it becomes an obsession. Flowers become the Alpha and the Omega of existence. In a world of a thousand beauties, John Doe No. 1 can see but a single wonder—his flowers.

(Continued on Page 186)

PHILOSOPHY SCIENCE & RELIGION

Zoroaster and the Worship of Fire

By MANLY P. HALL

The Prophet of the Parsis is *Zarathustra,* more commonly known as *Zoroaster,* concerning whose life practically nothing is known to the modern member of that faith. It is generally believed that Zoroaster lived between three and four thousand years ago and the religion founded by him exercised a most profound influence over the people of Persia up to the time of the Greek conquest of that country. It then began to wane, but in the first centuries of Christianity it was reestablished and continued a power in the religious world for nearly five hundred years. From that time on the number of its followers steadily decreased, until today it is listed with the minor cults. In various parts of India there are still a number of Parsis, many of them occupying positions of dignity and power. They are particularly numerous in and about Bombay. The Mohammedans destroyed most of their early sacred books and the faith of Islam has to a great extent superseded the Persian cult even in the land of its own genesis.

The original Zoroastrian doctrines were somewhat modified during the first centuries of the Christian Era and a simplified form of the faith under the name of the *Mithraic Mysteries* secured a very strong foothold in the then all-powerful Roman Empire. The *Mithraic* doctrines became extremely popular with the Roman soldiery, great numbers of whom were converted to its principles. The Roman soldiers carried the *Mithraic* faith with them in their wars of conquest and as a result a great part of Europe accepted the teachings expounded by the *Mithraic* priests. Even today remnants of *Mithraic* carvings may be found in England, France, Germany, and Italy.

While the *Mysteries of Mithras* did not contain the full philosophy of the Zoroastrians, its power lay in its simplicity. The initiation rituals were given in the catacombs and subterranean chapels under the City of Rome, which in a few years came to serve as the first meeting-places of the persecuted Christians. So influential did the rite of *Mithras* become that at least one Emperor of Rome was initiated into it.

It is impossible in the 20th century A. D. to form any adequate comprehension of the original Zoroastrian belief. It is not even possible to describe the founder of that cult. There is one picture supposedly of Zoroaster, a copy of which is reproduced herewith. The original is a rock carving, the face mutilated beyond recognition. Although this is generally accepted as a likeness of the Magus, there is a reasonable doubt as to its authenticity and those best equipped to pass an opinion on the subject hazard the guess that the sculpturing was intended as a representation of *Ahura-Mazda,* the Persian *Principle of Good...* The face may have been destroyed either by a zealous Zoroastrian, for the members of this faith are strongly

Zoroaster

opposed to idolatry, or it may have been mutilated by the Mohammedans.

Most accounts agree that Zoroaster was born of an immaculate conception. His father in performing his religious ceremonial drank the sacred *Homa* juice, which is the same as the *Soma* of the Hindus. As a result, his wife conceived a child. The occurrence was accompanied by supernatural manifestations and other strong experiences. The king of the country, becoming alarmed lest the celestially-conceived child should ultimately usurp his throne, made several efforts to kill the infant, but these were frustrated by the intercession of Divine Being. According to some accounts, the father of Zoroaster was in reality a supernatural being, a great Fire Spirit. Those affirming this theory regard the sacred Zoroastrian fire as a symbol of the father of the Magus. The king's jealousy and the attempts of that monarch to destroy the infant prophet parallel the account of the Nativities of both Jesus and Krishna. Like Jesus, Zoroaster began his public ministry at his thirtieth year. He first converted the king to his faith, the courtiers naturally followed their monarch, and in a comparatively short time the entire nation had accepted the creed. One of the legends concerning the life of Zoroaster asserts that he spent 20 years in fasting and meditation in the Persian deserts, practically his only food during that time being a certain sacred cheese which never grew old or moldy. At one time he is supposed to have lived upon a sacred mountain, which was surrounded always by a ring of flames. Through these flames the Prophet could pass without danger of being burned, but if others attempted to follow him they were immediately consumed. The sacred Scriptures of the Parsis mention three sons and three daughters of Zoroaster, but whether these were actually historical personages or merely allegorical figures cannot be ascertained.

The manner of the Prophet's death is also a great mystery. According to one account, he was killed by a weapon hurled at him while at prayer by an envious and wicked noble. This allegory further relates that before dying the mortally wounded Magus threw his rosary at the noble, who was killed by the string of beads as though they had been a bolt from heaven. The most popular story concerning the death of Zoroaster is to the effect that he was destroyed by a bolt of lighting descending from the constellation of Orion. Some believe the sheet of flame which descended and consumed him was the fiery body of his father who, gathering up the mortal remains of his illustrious son, bore them into the heavens.

The Zoroastrian theology is dualism in monotheism. It was established to combat the prevailing pantheism which Zoroaster believed was endangering the spiritual well-being of his people. Zoroaster taught that the one Supreme Nature was divisible into two parts. The first of these parts was the Spirit of Good, popularly termed *Ahura-Mazda*. The second was the Spirit of Evil, designated *Ahriman*. In the beginning both *Ahriman* and *Ahura-Mazda* were radiant spiritual beings, partaking equally of the effulgency of their common Father—the One Eternal Light. But *Ahriman,* being possessed of pride and jealousy, rebelled against his brother and, hurling himself downward from the mouth of light, created for himself a great darkness in which he dwelt with his angels, who became the spirits of darkness. In the darkness which he had created the perverse spirit, or *adversary,* brooded moodily for many ages. Here he set up his kingdom of dark spirits. In the meantime *Ahura-Mazda,* who had remained true and beautiful and was consequently a glorious light being, proceeded to establish a beautiful universe according to the will of the Infinite Creator. As soon as the light appeared in the sphere of darkness, *Ahriman* and his legions attacked it, attempting to thwart the plan of divine progress. *Ahriman* realized that ultimately the light of *Ahura-Mazda* would destroy all the darkness he had created and then the perverted genius, being unable to dwell in the light, would be compelled to submit himself to the radiant will of his brother.

Whenever *Ahura-Mazda* created a beautiful sphere or a perfect creature, *Ahriman* incorporated into the creation the spirit of negation and perverseness. For every good thing which *Ahura-Mazda* did *Ahriman* fashioned an evil shadow. So an eternal warfare existed between the light and the darkness. As long as shadow existed, *Ahriman* could remain a rebellious spirit, but when the last shadow was dispersed by the light, then *Ahriman* must admit himself defeated and acknowledge the light to be stronger than the darkness. There is no doubt that the Persian concept of the anthropomorphic deity was accepted by the early Christians and incorporated by them into their faith, for the *devil* of Christianity is the perverse spirit of the Persian *Ahriman*. *Ahriman* is that something of darkness which resides in the nature of everything and which led the disciple to declare that when he would do good, evil was ever near him. The theory of God and the devil contending for the soul of man is nowhere more clearly brought out than in the ancient Persian Mysteries. Yet though the war waged, it was always evident that *Ahura-Mazda* would finally conquer, for he was armed with the power and glory of the One Deity, by whose orders he was establishing creation.

Thus when *Ahura-Mazda* created man, *Ahriman* also entered into the composite constitution of man, contributing his lower and irrational self. He who sins, therefore, increases the shadow and thereby lengthens the existence of *Ahriman*, while he who does virtuous acts radiates light and truth and hastens the day when *Ahura-Mazda* will redeem the entire world from darkness. In the *Mithraic* form of Zoroastrianism, a third element is introduced which serves as the *mediator* between *Ahura-Mazda* and *Ahriman*. This *mediator* is *Mithras*, the Persian Christ, who was brought into being to hasten the reconciliation of the light and the darkness. *Mithras*, likewise, is born of an immaculate conception and, even as Jesus, his place of birth was a grotto, or stable. The Christian God-man—the Christ—is a composite of *Mithras, Orpheus,* and *Serapis*. From *Mithras* comes the concept of the resurrected Lord, who after three days in the tomb rolls away the stone and redeems His world. From the sad-faced Serapis, with his long hair and curls upon his shoulders, the Christians borrowed their *Man of Sorrows,* and from the radiant *Orpheus,* their concept of the *Son of God.*

Mithras, the *mediator,* became the most powerful deity of the Zoroastrian faith. Unlike the strict monotheism of the first followers of Zoroaster, the devotees of *Mithras* made many and varied reproductions of their deity and also of *Kronos,* the lion-headed god of time. *Mithras* evidently signifies the human mind, *Ahura-Mazda* the human spirit, and *Ahriman* the human body. The light of the mind dispels the darkness of ignorance, and mankind thus illumined recognizes and adores its divine Creator.

The Zoroastrians are generally termed "fire-worshippers," for under this symbol they revere the Deity. Fire is the origin of light and heat. It is a cleansing element. It is an element eternally alive and eternally active, therefore naturally appropriate as a symbol of that divine fire which burns within the heart and soul of every creature. The ancient Parsis had many peculiar beliefs concerning the sanctity of the elements. For example, earth was sacred. To bury a dead thing in it was to pollute the earth. Water was sacred and to stop its flow was a grievous sin. Air was sacred and should not be polluted with evil odors. Fire was sacred and nothing which was unclean should be burned, lest the first itself become polluted. It was a most grievous sin to pollute any of the elements. These beliefs rather complicated the problem of sanitation, especially in connection with the last offices to the dead. To care for this situation, the *Towers of Silence* were erected. These towers are very highly revered and it is most difficult to secure even a photograph of them. None but the proper representatives of the faith are permitted to enter them. For the sake of tourists, however, there is a model of the *Tower of Silence* a short distance from the actual tower in Bombay. These towers are the Parsi repositories of the dead, and are usually circular in shape and not very high, varying from ten to twenty feet in height. In these towers the dead bodies are laid and the ever-present buzzards and vultures speedily dispose of the remains. Thus the elements are not polluted and death itself is made to serve the purposes of life.

There is a curious myth concerning the Zoroastrian fires to the effect that many of them burn for centuries without ever going out. The oldest of the Zoroastrian fires has burned continuously for over 3,000 years and from it have been lighted fires unnumbered. There is a tradition to the effect that at the present time this ancient fire is in America, but we have been unable to discover any tangible evidence in support of this belief.

The religion of the Persians has produced a profound effect upon its followers, who are noted for their honesty, integrity, devotion, and sincerity. There is practically no crime among them and they live together in friendliness and understanding. They preserve with great care the doctrines of their people and are models that might well be imitated in matters pertaining to religious tolerance. They are sympathetic with the Christians and will gladly work hand in hand with the members of any faith as long as those members are honest and sincere. In India the Parsis are noted contributors to charities and public institutions. They have succeeded greatly in various commercial pursuits, especially banking and brokerage lines. They are most generous with their possessions, considering it a sin to refuse aid to the needy, and their kindliness and gentleness are recognized wherever they have established themselves. Thy are never aggressive and will only defend their own rights, never assailing the rights of others. They are interested in educational institutions and evidence a high degree of culture. The Parsi is an excellent demonstration of the fact that the religious codes of ancient times were both noble and exalted. The faith of the Parsi is very old but the attitude which that faith creates in its followers is one much needed by the modern world.

Men in great place are thrice servants, servants to the sovereign or state, servants of fame and servants of business; so as they have no freedom, neither in their person, nor in their actions, nor in their times.—Bacon.

Vocabulary of Occult Terms

Written for the Purpose of Mitigating the Confusion Created by the Building of the Tower of Babylon.

From *The Secret Symbols of The Rosicrucians*, by Franz Hartmann, M. D.

"*Omnia ab Uno*" is one of the mottoes of the Rosicrucians. It expresses the idea that the All has been evolved from One; or, in other words, that God is one and indivisible, and that the multifarious activities of life which we see in the universe are merely various forms of manifestations of God; or, to express it more correctly, of the *creative Power*, the *Light* and *substance of Life*, which emanated from the eternal cause of all existence in the beginning of our day of creation, and which has been called the *Logos*, the *Verbum* or *Word*, the *Christ*.

As the Universal One manifested itself, it assumed various aspects. and it therefore appears as a great variety of powers and as innumerable forms of various substances, although all powers and substances are essentially and fundamentally one. The various terms used in occult science are consequently not intended to describe powers and principles radically different from each other, but merely the various aspects of the one universal principle; and as the aspect of things changes according to the point of view from which they are considered, consequently a name applied to a power, if considered from one point of view, may not be applicable if the same principle is considered from another point of view. Likewise, the four sides of a pyramid originate in one point and end in one, each side appearing to have a distinct individuality of its own. The higher we rise towards the summit, the more does this differentiation disappear, and the more does the Unity of all things and their identity with each other become apparent, until all difference is again absolved in the ultimate *One*. He who knows the *One* knows All; he who believes to know many things knows nothing. The One is the starting-point for all occult science.

ALPHA AND OMEGA.—The Beginning and End of all things; i. e., the beginning and end of all manifestation of activity and life in the Cosmos; the *Logos* or *Christ*. See *Logos*.

ADAM.—Primal man in his aspect as a spiritual power, containing the male and female elements. The spiritual principle, constituting humanity, before it became differentiated in matter and assumed gross material forms.

THE CELESTIAL ADAM.—The divine man-forming power in its original state of purity as an image of the Creator.

THE TERRESTRIAL ADAM.—Adam after his "fall;" i. e. the original man having become the *distorted* image of God by having lost his original purity in consequence of disobedience to the law and desertion of the straight line of the universal divine will. This disobedience is illustrated by the allegory of the "eating of the apple in paradise;" the "snake" which tempted Adam and Eve is the illusion of self, causing man to imagine to be something different from the universal God, and thus creating within him personal desires.

ADONAI.—God in his aspect as the *Summum Bonum* in nature; i. e. the Light of the Logos having become manifested in nature.

AER.—Air, *Pneuma*, Soul, a universal and invisible principle. See *Elements*.

ALCHEMY.—The science of guiding the invisible processes of Life for the purpose of attaining certain results on the material, astral or spiritual plane. Alchemy is not only a science, but an *art*, for the power to exercise it must be acquired; a man must first come into possession of certain powers before he can be taught to employ them; he must know what "Life" is, and learn to control the life-processes within his own organism before he can guide and control such processes in other organisms. *Chemistry* is not *Alchemy*. The former deals with so-called dead substances, the latter with the principle of life. The composition or decomposition of a chemical substance is a *chemical* process; the growth of a tree or an animal, an alchemical process. The highest *Alchemy* is the evolution of a divine and immortal being out of a mortal semi-animal man.

Note:—The Song of Solomon describes alchemical processes.

ANGELS.—Conscious spiritual powers acting within the realm of the Soul, i. e. certain individualized spiritual states of the universal consciousness.

[176]

ANIMA.—See *Soul*.

ANIMATO.—Animation. (Alch.) The act of infusing life into a thing or of causing its own latent life-principle to become active. See *Life*.

ANTIMONY.—(Alch.) A symbol representing the element of the *Earth* in its gross material aspect; primordial matter, also represented as the insatiable *Wulf*, the destroyer of forms.

AQUA.—(Alch.) Water. See *Elements*.

AQUILA.—(Alch.) *Eagle*, the emblem of *Jupiter;* the symbol of the Spiritual Soul.

ARCANUM.—(Alch.) Secret. A mystery which is not within everybody's grasp; a certain knowledge which requires a certain amount of development to be comprehended. It also means certain secrets which are not to be divulged to the vulgar, who would be likely to misuse that knowledge.

ARCHÆUS.—The great invisible storehouse of Nature, wherein the characters of all things are contained and preserved. To one aspect it represents the *Astral Light;* in another, *Primordial Matter*.

ARGENTUM.—(Alch.) Silver. Symbolized by the *Moon*.

ASTRAL BODY.—A semi-material substance, forming—so to say—the denser parts of the soul, which connect the latter with the physical body. Each thing in which the principle of life exists, from minerals up to man, has an astral body, being the ethereal counterpart of the external visible form.

ASTRAL LIGHT.—The *Light of Nature*. The *Memory,* or universal storehouse of nature, in which the characters of all things that ever existed are preserved. He who can see the images existing in the Astral Light can read the history of all past events. and prophesy the future.

AZOTH.—(Alch.) The universal creative principle of life.

BABYLON.—Humanity in her unregenerated state, the world of fashion, superficiality, animality and intellectuality without spirituality. The world of superficial Knowledge, self-conceit, and ignorance, living in externals, and being attached to illusions.

BEAST.—(False prophet, Babylonian whore, etc.) Animality, sensuality, and selfishness; but especially *intellectuality without spirituality,* Knowledge without love, scientific ignorance, skepticism, arrogance, materialism, brutality. The *Antichrist,* i. e. false prophets, who are putting man's authority in the place of the universal truth, who degrade religion into sectarianism, and prostitute divine things for selfish purposes,—idolatry, bigotry, superstition, priestcraft, cunning, false logic, etc.

BIBLE.—The "sacred books" of the "Christians," containing a great deal of ancient wisdom clothed in fables and allegories, and describing many occult processes in the shape of personifications of powers and historical events believed to have taken place among the Jews. Some of the events described in these books seem to have actually taken place on the external plane, while other are merely figurative; and it appears to be at present impossible to determine in the Bible the exact line between fiction and history.

BLOOD.—(Alch.) The vehicle for the principle of Life; the seat of the Will.

BODY.—Matter in a certain state of density, exhibiting a form. A body may be visible or invisible, corporeal or ethereal.

CABALA.—The science which teaches the relations existing between the visible and invisible side of nature; i. e. the character of things and their forms in regard to *weight, number,* and *measure*. It is the knowledge of the laws of harmony which exist in the universe.

CAPUT MORTUUM.—(Alch.) Refuse. Dead matter.

CARITAS.—Spiritual Love, benevolence, charity.

CELESTIAL.—A spiritual, divine state; a state of perfection.

CHAOS.—The universal *matrix* or storehouse of nature. See *Archæus*.

CHIMIA.—Chemistry. Sometimes the term refers to the Chemistry of Life, Alchemy.

CHRIST.—Spiritual consciousness, Life and Light. The divine element in humanity, which if it manifests itself in man, becomes the personal Christ in individual man. "Christ" means therefore an internal spiritual living and conscious power or principle, identical in its nature with the *Logos,* with which the highest spiritual attributes of each human being will become ultimately united, if that human being has developed any such Christlike attributes. This principle is in itself of a threefold nature, but it appears to be useless to speculate about its attributes, as they will be comprehensible only to him who realizes its presence within himself. See *Logos*.

Note:—The misconception of the original meaning of the term *"Christ"* (Kristos) has been the cause of many bloody wars and of the most cruel religious persecutions. Upon such a misconception are still based the claims of certain "Christian" sects. "Christ" originally signifies a universal spiritual principle, the "Crown of the Astral-Light," coexistent from all eternity with the "Father," i. e. the Divine source from which it emanated in the beginning. This principle is said to have on many occasions penetrated with its light certain human beings, incarnated itself in them, and thus produced great heroes, reformers, or *Avatars*. Those who cannot rise up to the sublimity of this conception look upon "Christ" as being merely a historical person, who in some incomprehensible manner took upon himself the sins of the world. There have been so many clerical dogmas and misconceptions heaped around this term, that it appears to be impossible to throw any light upon this matter, unless we call to our aid the sacred books of the Hindus and compare the doctrines of *Krishna* with those of Christ.

COAGULATIO.—(Alch.) Coagulation. The act of some fluid or ethereal substance assuming a state of corporeal density.

COMBINATIO.—(Alch.) Combination. The act of combining certain visible or invisible things.

CONJUNCTO.—(Alch.) Conjunction. The act of two or more things joining together or coming into harmonious relationship with each other.

CORPUS.—(Alch.) Body. Matter is a state of corporeal density. The vehicle of a power.

CREATION.—The external, visible manifestation of an internal, invisible power. The production of a visible form out of invisible, formless substance. The calling into existence of a form.

Note:—The term "creation" has often been misrepresented as meaning a creation of something out of nothing; but we know of no passage in the Bible which might justify such an irrational definition. The only persons who believe that something can come from nothing are certain self-styled "scientists," who imagine that life and consciousness are products of the mechanical activity of the body; which is identical with saying that something superior can be produced by something inferior; in other words, by something which according to all known laws of nature is not able to produce it.

CROSS.—A symbol expressing various ideas, but especially the creative power of *Life* in a spiritual aspect, acting within the Macrocosm of nature and within the Microcosm of man. It also represents Spirit and Matter ascending and descending. The perpendicular beam represents Spirit, the horizontal bar the animal or earthly principle, being penetrated by the divine Spirit. Universal as well as individual man may be symbolized by a Cross. Man's animal body is a Cross, or instrument of torture for the soul. By means of his battle with the lower elements of his constitution, his divine nature becomes developed. By means of his physical body, man is *nailed* to the plane of suffering appertaining to terrestrial existence. The animal elements are to die upon that Cross, and the spiritual man is to be resurrected to become united with the Christ. "Death upon the Cross" represents the giving up of one's own personality and the entering into eternal and universal life. The *inscription* sometimes found at the top of the Cross, consisting of the letters I, N, R, I, means, in its esoteric sense, *Igne Natura Renovatus Integra;* that is to say: By the (divine) Fire (of Love) all Nature becomes renewed. The *golden Cross* represents spiritual Life, illuminated by Wisdom. It is the symbol of immortality.

DEUS.—God.

DEVIL.—The principle of Evil, the antithesis of the principle or cause of Good, in the same sense as *Darkness* is the antithesis of Light. *God,* being the cause of all powers and principles, is also the cause of the "Devil," but not its direct cause; for as *evil* is nothing else but perverted *good,* likewise the power called *Devil* is, so to say, the reaction of *God,* or the cause which perverts good into evil. The devil may be said to be the dark, and consequently inferior counterpart of God; consequently, like God, a *Trinity of thought, word,* and its *manifestation.*

EARTH.—See *Elements.*

EAGLE.—(Alch.) The spiritual Soul. *"The Gluten of the White Eagle."*— pure spiritual love, the fiery substance of the spiritual Soul.

ELEMENTA.—(Alch.) Elements. Universal and (to us) invisible principles, the causes of all visible phenomena, whether they are an *earthly* (material), *watery* (liquid), *airy* (gaseous), or *fiery* (ethereal) nature.

There are consequently four "Elements," namely:—

1. *Earth,* representing primordial matter, an invisible ethereal substance, forming the basis of all external corporeal appearances.

2. *Water,* referring to the realm of the Soul, the connecting link between spirit and matter. It also represents Thought.

3. *Fire,* representing the realm of the Spirit or *Life.*

4. *Air,* alluding to Space or Form. It is not. strictly speaking, an "Element."

There is a *fifth element,* which is the spiritual *Quint-essence* (the *Mercury*) of all things. Each element may be considered from a variety of aspects. Each element constitutes, so to say, a world of its own, with its own inhabitants, the "elementary spirits of nature;" and by a combination of those elements under various conditions, an endless variety of forms is produced.

ELOHIM.—The light of the Logos in its aspect as a spiritual power or influence, whose presence may be felt as it penetrates the soul and body of the worshipper in his moments of spiritual exaltation. This Light, having been the cause and beginning of creation, the term *Elohim* also expresses its aspect as the creative power of the universe.

EVA.—*Eve.* The female or generative power in nature; the eternal mother of all, an ever-immaculate virgin; because she has no connection with any external god, but contains the fructifying spiritual principal (the *Holy Ghost*) within her own self.

The celestial Eve represents *Theo-Sophia,* divine Wisdom, or Nature in her spiritual aspect.

The terrestrial Eve represent Nature in a more material aspect, as the womb or matrix out of which forms are continually evolved, and into which they are reabsorbed.

Note:—Primordial man was a bisexual spiritual being; the separation of sex took place in consequence of the differentiation of spirit in matter. Man is still to a certain extent bisexual; because each male human being contains female, and each female being male elements. Sex is merely an attribute of the external form; the spiritual man who inhabits the outward form has no particular sex.

EVIL.—The antithesis of *Good,* i. e. the reaction of good against itself, or good perverted. There can be no absolute Evil, because such a thing would destroy itself.

EX CENTRO IN CENTRUM.—Everything originates from one centre and returns to that centre.

FAITH.—Spiritual knowledge. A power by which the spirit may feel the existence of truths which transcend external sensual perception. *"Faith"* should never be confounded with "Belief;" the latter being merely a controvertible opinion about something of which nothing is known. *Faith* rests upon direct perception; *Belief,* upon intellectual speculation.

FATHER.—(Trinity.) The divine and incomprehensible *Fire,* from which emanated the *Light* (the *Son*). We cannot conceive of *"the Father"* except as the incomprehensible *Absolute,* the Cause of all existence, the Centre of Life, becoming comprehensible only when he manifests himself as the "Son." In the same sense a geometrical point is merely an abstraction and incomprehensible, and must expand into a circle before it can become an object of our imagination.

FIAT—The active expression of the Will and Thought of the *Great First Cause* by which *God* manifested himself in the act of creation; in other words, the energy by which he threw the Light which created the universe into an objective existence. The *outbreathing of Brahm* at the beginning of a *Manvantara. Fiat Lux,*—Let there be Light!

FIDES.—See *Faith.*

FIRE.—An internal activity whose manifestations are heat and light. This activity differs in character according to the plane on which it manifests itself. "Fire" on the spiritual plane represents Love or Hate; on the astral plane it represents Desire and Passion; on the physical plane, Combustion. It is the purifying element, and in a certain aspect identical with *"Life."* See *Elements.*

FIRMAMENT.—Realm. Space in its various aspects. The physical and mental horizon. That which limits the physical or mental perception. The sky.

FIXATIO.—(Alch.) Fixation. The act of rendering a volatile substance (for instance a thought) fixed. The act of rendering the impermanent permanent.

FOUNDATION.—The Real. The basis or centre of things, in contradistinction to their phenomenal illusive and transient appearance. We may look upon all things as having a common basis, which in each manifests certain attributes. We may know the attributes of things, but not the thing itself.

GLUTEN.—Adhesion. Spiritual Substance. See *Eagle.*

GOD.—The eternal, omnipresent, self-existent Cause of all things. in its aspect as the Cause of all Good. The meaning of the term "God" differs according to the standpoint from which we view it; but in its highest meaning it is necessarily beyond the intellectual comprehension of imperfect man; because the imperfect cannot conceive the perfect; nor the finite the infinite. In one aspect everything that exists is God, and nothing can possibly exist which is not God; for it is the One Life, and in every being has its life and existence. God is the only eternal Reality, unknowable to man; all that we know of him are his manifestations. In one aspect God is looked upon as the spiritual central Sun of the Cosmos, Whose rays and substance penetrate the universe with life, light. and power. God being *the Absolute,* cannot have any conceivable relative attributes; because as nothing exists but himself, he stands in relation to no thing, and is therefore non-existent from a relative point of view. We cannot possibly form any conception of the unmanifested *Absolute;* but as soon as the latter becomes manifest, it appears as a Trinity of *Thought, Word,* and *Revelation,* i. e. as the *"Father,"* the *"Son,"* and the *"Holy Ghost."*

Note:—Innumerable people have been killed because they differed in regard to their opinions how the term "God" should be defined; but it is obvious that a Cause which is beyond all human conception is also beyond any possible correct definition, and that, therefore, all theological disputations about the nature of God are absurd and useless.

GOD.—A human being in whom divine powers have become active. An *Adept.*

GOOD.—Everything conducive to a purpose in view is *relatively* good; but only that which leads to permanent happiness is permanent Good. Everything, therefore, which ennobles and elevates mankind may be called good, while that which degrades is evil. Supreme Good is that which establishes real and permanent happiness.

GOLD.—(Alch.) An emblem of perfection upon the terrestrial plane, as the Sun is a symbol of perfection on the superterrestrial plane. There is a considerable amount of historical evidence that the ancient Rosicrucians possessed the power to transmute base metals into gold by alchemical means, by causing it to grow out of its own "seed," and it is claimed that persons possessing such powers exist even today.

GRACE.——A spiritual power emanating from the *Logos.* It should not be confounded with "favor" or "partiality." It is a spiritual influence comparable to the light of the sun, which shines everywhere, but for which not all things are equally receptive.

HEAVEN.—A state of happiness and contentment. Man can only be perfectly happy when he forgets his own self. "Heaven" refers to a spiritual state, free from the bonds of matter.

HELL.—The antithesis of Heaven; a state of misery and discontent. A person suffers when he is conscious of his own personality and its imperfections. Each being suffers when it is surrounded by conditions which are not adapted to its welfare; consequently, the soul of man surrounded by evil elements suffers until the elements of evil are expelled from his organization. The state in which the divine and consequently pure spirit is still connected with an impure soul, seeking to throw off the impurities of the latter is called *Purgatory* (Kama loca). When this has taken place, the consciousness of the disembodied entity will be centered in his spiritual organization, and he will be happy; but if the consciousness has been centred in the impure soul, and remains with the latter, the soul will be unhappy and in a state of Hell. The latter takes place especially in such cases where people of great intellectual powers, but with evil tendencies, perform knowingly and purposely evil acts.

HOLY GHOST.—(Trinity.) The Light of the manifested *Logos,* representing the body and substance of Christ. The Spirit of Truth, coming from the *Father* and *Son.*

HOMO.—Man.

HOPE.—Spiritual hope is a state of spiritual consciousness, resulting from the perception of a certain truth, and based upon a conviction that a certain desire will be realized This kind of hope should not be confused with the hope which rests merely upon opinion, formed by logical conclusions or caused by uncertain promises.

HYLE.—The universal primordial invisible principle of matter, containing the germs of everything that is to come into objective existence. See *Archæus.*

IGNIS.—*Fire.*

ILLUSION.—All that refers to *Form* and outward appearance. All that is of a *phenomenal* character, transient and impermanent; in contradistinction to the *Real* and Permanent.

JEHOVAH.—*Jod-He-Vah.*—God manifest, in his aspect as the creative, transforming, and regenerating power of the universe. The self-existent, universal God.

JERUSALEM.—Humanity in its spiritual condition. The soul in a state of purity.

JESUS.—The divine man. Each man's spiritual *Ego*. Each person's personal god or *Atman*. The redeeming principle in Man, with which man may hope to become united during his life.

Jesus of Nazareth is believed to have been an Adept; i. e. a pure and great man, teacher and reformer, in whom the Logos has taken form; in other words, a human being in whom the Christ-principle has incarnated itself.

JUPITER.—The supreme God. Jehovah.

KNOWLEDGE.—Science, based upon the perception and understanding of a truth. It should never be confounded with *"learning,"* which means the adoption of certain opinion or theory on the strength of some hearsay or logical speculation. We cannot really know anything except that which we are able to perceive with our external or internal senses.

LAPIS PHILOSOPHORUM.—(Alch.) A mystery, known only to the practical occultist who has experienced its power

LEAD.—(Alch.) symbolized by *Saturn;* the emblem of Matter; the element of Earth.

LEO.—(Alch.) *Lion.* The symbol of strength and fortitude; corresponding to *Mars. "The Blood of the Red Lion,"* the vehicle of the Life-principle.

LIFE.—A universal principle; a function of the universal Spirit.

Note:—Life is present everywhere, in a stone or plant as well as in an animal or man, and there is nothing in nature which is entirely destitute of life; because all things are a manifestation of the *One Life,* which fills the universe. In some bodies the activity of life acts very slow, so that it may be looked at as dormant or latent, in others it acts rapidly; but a form which is deserted by the life-principle ceases to exist as a form. Attraction, Cohesion, Gravitation. etc., are all manifestations of life, while in animals this activity enters a state of self-consciousness, which is perfected in man. To suppose that Life is a product of the mechanical or physiological activity of an organism is to mistake effects for causes, and causes for effects. See *Creation.*

LIGHT.—An external visible manifestation of an internal invisible power.

The *Divine Light of Grace* is a spiritual Light, the Light of the *Logos,* illuminating the mind of the *Adept.*

The *Light of Nature* in the *Astral Light.*

LIMBUS.—The universal *matrix* of all things. See *Archæus.*

LOGOS & LOGOI.—A centre or centres of spiritual activity, Life and light, existing from all eternity in the manifested GOD (the *Absolute*). The Christ-principle, which, shining into the heart of man, may produce an *Avatar* or *Christ.*

Note:—It is taught that at certain periods such an incarnation of the divine Light of the Logos takes place upon the Earth, and thus causes a new saviour, redeemer, and reformer to appear among mankind, teaching the old and half-forgotten truths again by word and example, and thus producing a new revival of the religious sentiment. The ancient religions speak of several such *Avatars* in which "the *Word* has become Flesh."

LOVE.—Spiritual Love is an all-penetrating spiritual power, uniting the higher elements of Humanity into one inseparable whole. It is not led by external sensuous attractions. It is the power by which man recognizes the unity of the All, and the product of that knowledge which springs into existence, when man recognizes the identity of his own spirit with the spirit of every other being. This spiritual Love should never be confounded with sexual desire, parental affection, etc., which are merely sentiments, subject to attraction and change.

LUCIFER.—The bearer of Light. An angel of Light, possessed of Wisdom. *Lucifer in his fallen state* is Intellectuality without Spirituality; knowledge without the light of wisdom.

LUMEN.—A power emitting Light.

LUNA.—See *Moon.*

LUX.—See *Light.*

MACROCOSM & MICROCOSM.—The great and the little world; the latter being an image or representation of the former, but on a smaller scale. The microcosm of Man resembles the macrocosm of the universe in all his aspects except in external form.

MATRIX.—(Alch.) Womb. The mother wherein a germ, seed, or principle is brought to ripening. Every germ requires a certain appropriate matrix for its development. Minerals, plants, or animals require a matrix in the incipient state of their growth.

MATTER.—An external manifestation of an internal power.

MERCURY.—(Alch.) One of the *Three Substances*. The Astral Light. The principle of Mind. The spiritual quintessence of all things.

METALS.—(Alch.) Certain occult powers. The "metals" of which a man is made and which produce his virtues or vices are more permanent and lasting than the body composed of flesh and blood.

MOON.—(Alch.) A reflection caused by the rays of the Sun. The Intellect, being a reflection of the divine light emanating from the Fire of the heart.

MORTIFICATIO.—(Alch.) Mortification. The art of rendering the lower elements passive, so that the higher ones can become active. The art of dissolving the body, so that the spirit may become free.

MULTIPLICATIO.—(Alch.) Multiplication. Increase. The character is the great multiplicator.

Note:—Not only is man thus an image of "God," but every part of our organism has the character of the whole impressed upon it, in the same sense as the qualities of a tree are latent in the seed. It is therefore possible for those who can read in the Light of Nature, to know the character, attributes, and history of a thing by examining one of its parts.

MAGIC.—The science and art of employing spiritual powers to obtain certain results. No one can exercise Magic unless he possesses magic powers, and to obtain such powers man must be spiritually developed. *"Magic"* should never be confounded with *"Sorcery."* The former deals with the *Real*, the latter deals with *Illusions.* Magic is the culmination of all sciences, and includes them all; but there can be no true science without wisdom, and no wisdom without sanctification.

Man.—The *real* man is an invisible internal and spiritual power which in its outward manifestation, appears as a human being.

Note:—Man may be looked upon as an individual ray emanating from the great spiritual Sun of the universe. having become polarized in the heart of an incipient human organism, endows the latter with life and stimulates its growth. At a certain state of its development that organism becomes conscious of its existence in the phenomenal world, and with this the illusion of self is created. There is nothing real and permanent about the being called *Man*, except this internal divine power which is called the *Spirit*. which is ultimately identical with the universal Spirit— the *Christ.*

MARS.—The power which endows beings with strength. See *Leo.*

MARIA.—The universal matrix of Nature. *Ceres, Tris,* etc. See *Eve.*

MATERIA PRIMA.—(Alch.) Primordial Matter. *A'Wasa.* A universal and invisible principle, the basic substance of which all things are formed. By reducing a thing into its *prima materia,* and clothing it with new attributes, it may be transformed into another thing by him who possesses spiritual power and knowledge. There are several states of matter, from primordial down to gross visible matter, and the Alchemists therefore distinguish between *Materia proxima, Materia remota,* and *Materia ultima.*

NATURAL, UNNATURAL. SUPERNATURAL.—Relative terms, referring to the relations existing between certain things and certain conditions. Everything in Nature is natural in the *absolute* meaning of this term; but not everything is surrounded by such conditions as according to the laws of its own nature it ought to be surrounded by. Air is natural, but to a fish it is not his natural element; a supernatural being is one who exists in a spiritual condition superior to that of lower beings, and in which gross material beings cannot exist.

NATURE.—The external manifestation of an internal creative power. The whole of nature can be nothing else but a *thought* of God, having been thrown into objectivity by the power of his *Word* and grown into forms according to the law of evolution. *"The nature of a thing"* means the summary of its attributes.

NOTHING.—The antithesis of something. The term nothing is sometimes applied to signify something which is inconceivable and therefore *no thing* to us. *Form* is no *thing;* it is merely a shape, and does not exist in the *Absolute.* If a thought becomes expressed in a form, that which was nothing *to us* becomes something.

OCCULTISM.—The science of things which transcend the ordinary powers of observation. The science of things whose perception requires extraordinary or superior faculties of perception. Everything is occult to us as long as we cannot see it, and with every enlargement of the field of our perception a new and heretofore "occult" world becomes open to our investigation. We may speculate about the Unseen; but we cannot actually know anything about it, unless we can mentally grasp its spirit. See *Knowledge.*

OCULUS.—Eye.

OCULUS DIVINUS.—The symbol of spiritual consciousness and knowledge.

OCULUS NATURÆ.—The Astral Light.

OMBIA AB UNO.—"Everything originates from the *One.*"

PATER.—Father.

PERFECTIO.—(Alch.) Perfection.

PERSON.—An individual, organized, self-conscious being or principle, capable to think and to will different from other beings or principles. An indivisible unity.

PERSONALITY.—Mask. The sum and substance of the attributes which go to distinguish one individual from others. As one and the same actor may appear in various costumes and masks; likewise one individual spiritual entity may appear successively on the stage of life as various personalities.

Note:—To comprehend the doctrine of *Reincarnation,* it should be remembered that at and after the transformation called "death" only those attributes of a person which have reached a certain degree of spirituality, and are therefore fit to survive, will remain with the individual spirit. When the latter again overshadows a new-born form, it develops a new set of attributes, which go to make up its new personality.

PHILOSOPHY.—True "Philosophy" is practical knowledge of causes and effects; but what is today called "Philosophy" is a system of speculation based upon logical deductions, or *opinions* arrived at by reasoning from that which we *imagine to know* to the unknown.

Note:—The fundamental basis upon which our modern philosophy rests is erroneous and illusive, because it rests upon the assumption that man could know something without knowing himself; while, in truth, man can possess no positive knowledge of anything whatever except that which exists within his own self, and he can know nothing about divine things as long as the divinity within himself has not become alive and self-conscious. *Philosophy* without *Theosophy* is, therefore, mere speculation, and frequently leads to error.

PHŒNIX.——(Alch.) A fabulous bird: the symbol of death and regeneration.

PRAYER.—An effort of the will to obtain that which one desires. Prayer on the physical plane consists in acts; prayer on the plane of thought consists in thoughts; prayer on the spiritual plane consists in the act of rising in thought up to the highest, and to become united with it.

PRIMUM.—(Alch.) Primordial Motion. The first Life-impulse.

PRINCIPIUM.—Principle, Cause, Beginning of Acitivity.

PRIMA MATERIA.—See *Materia Prima.*

PROJECTIO.—(Alch.) Projection. The act of endowing a thing with a certain power or quality by means of an occult power whose root is the Will.

PUREFACTIO.—(Alch.) Purification.

PUTREFACTIO.—(Alch.) Putrification.

RAVEN.—(Alch.) A symbol for a certain occult power.

REBIS.—(Alch.) Refuse. Matter to be remodelled.

REGENERATIO.—(Alch.) Regeneration. The act of being reborn in the spirit. The penetration of the soul and body by the divine heat of love and the light of intelligence, emanating from the divine fire within the heart. The awakening and development of spiritual self-consciousness and self-knowledge.

RESURRECTIO.—(Alch.) Resurrection. Initiation into a higher states of existence. The new life into which the perfected elements of a being enters after the imperfect ones with which they have been amalgamated have been destroyed.

ROSE.—(Alch.) The symbol of evolution, and unfolding and beauty.

ROSICRUCIAN.—A person who by the process of spiritual awakening has attained a *practical* knowledge of the secret signification of the *Rose* and the *Cross.* A Hermetic philosopher. A real Theosophist or *Adept.* One who possesses spiritual knowledge and power.

Note:—Names have no true meaning if they do not express the true character of a thing. To call a person a Rosicurcian does not make him one, nor does the act of calling a person a Christian make him a Christ. The real Rosicrucian or Mason cannot be made; he must grow to be one by the expansion and unfoldment of the divine power within his own heart. The inattention to this truth is the cause that many churches and secret societies are far from being that which their names express.

SAL.—(Alch.) Salt. Substance. One of the three substances. The Will. Wisdom.

SATURN.—(Alch) The symbol of the universal principle of matter; the producer and destroyer of forms.

SEED.—(Alch.) A germ, element, or power from which a being may grow. There are germs of Elementals, Minerals, Plants, Animals, Human Beings, and Gods.

SILVER.—(Alch) An emblem of Intelligence. symbolized by the Moon. Amalgamated with *Mercury* (the Mind) and penetrated by the Fire of divine *Love,* it becomes transformed into the *Gold* of Wisdom.

SOL.—(Alch.) See *Sun.*

SOL-OM-ON.—The name of the Sun of Wisdom expressed in three languages.

SOLUTIO.—(Alch.) Solution. The act of bringing a thing into a fluid condition.

SON OF GOD.—One of the three powers constituting the Trinity. The Light, or Christ. The regenerated spiritual man. The celestial Adam. The *Logos.* Only the inner spiritual and divine man is a direct Son of God; the unregenerated man is his indirect descendant. The *Spirit* is the Son of God; the *Soul* is the son of the Sun (astral influence); the *Body* the son of the Earth.

SOPHIA.—Wisdom.

SOPHIST.—Originally this term meant a "wise man;" but now it means a false reasoner, a skeptical speculator, a person who is cunning but possesses no wisdom; one who judges things not by what they are, but by what he imagines them to be; one who dogmatizes about things which he cannot grasp spiritually; a material scientist, a would-be-wise, an intellectual person without love; one who lives, so to say, in his brain and receives no light from his heart.

SOUL.—The semi-material principle connecting matter with spirit. It leads, so to say, an amphibious existence between these two poles of substance, and may ultimately become amalgamated either with one or the other. The Body is the mask of the Soul; the Soul, the body of the Spirit.

SPES.—Hope.

SPIRITUS.—Spirit. God in his aspect as an eternal, universal, and invisible principle or power in a state of the greatest purity and perfection. The divine element in Nature. The antithesis of Matter, yet "material" in a transcendental sense. Spiritual substance. A conscious, organized, invisible principle. The Substance or Body of Christ. The term "Spirit" is also used to signify the essence or character of a thing, the sum of the highest attributes or powers.

SPIRITS.—Powers.

Note:—The modern usage to apply the term "spirits" to disembodied astral forms and souls of men and animals has originated in the modern misconception of the true nature of man.

SUBLIMATIO.—(Alch.) Sublimation. The rising of a lower state into a higher one. Vices may become sublimated into virtues.

SUBSTANCE.—That unknown and invisible something which may manifest itself either as matter or force; in other words, that substratum of all things, which is *energy* in one of its aspects, and *matter* in another.

The Three Substances: Salt, Sulphur, and Mercury represent the trinity of all things. They are the basis of all existence, and in each of these three substances the other two are contained. They form an inseparable Unity in a Trinity, differing, however, in its aspects and manifestations. Consequently, in some things the Salt, in others the Sulphur, and in still others the Mercury is preeminently manifest. They represent *Thought, Word,* and *Form; Body, Soul,* and *Spirit; Earth, Water,* and *Fire; Fire, Light,* and *Heat,* etc. See *Trinity.*

SULPHUR.—(Alch.) One of the three substances. The principle of Love. The invisible fire.

SUN.—(Alch.) The symbol of Wisdom. The Centre of Power or *Heart* of things. The Sun is a centre of energy and a storehouse of power. Each living being contains within itself a centre of life, which may grow to be a sun. In the heart of the regenerated, the divine power, stimulated by the Light of the *Logos,* grows into a Sun which illuminates his mind.

The spiritual Sun of Grace. The *Logos* or Christ.

The Natural Sun. The centre of all powers contained in our solar system.

Note:—The terrestrial sun is the image or reflection of the invisible celestial sun; the former is in the realm of Spirit what the latter is in the realm of Matter; but the latter receives its power from the former. See *Logos.*

SUPERIUS & INFERIUS.—(Alch.) The *Above* and *Below,* the Internal and External, the Celestial and Terrestrial. Everything *below* has it ethereal counterpart above, and the two act and react upon other; in fact, they are *one* and merely *appear to be* two.

TARTARUS.—(Alch.) Matter. Residuum. A substance which has been deposited by a fluid, or crystallized out of the latter. The gross elements of the soul.

TERRA.—Earth.

TERRESTRIAL.—An earthly or imperfect state.

THEOLOGY.—A system which teaches the nature and action of divine powers and their relation to Man. Some ancient theologies are the products of certain spiritually developed persons who were capable to perceive and understand spiritual truths, and who laid down the results of their experience in certain systems, and described what they knew, usually in some allegorical forms. Modern Theology is a system of speculation based upon the knowledge of external symbols and allegories without any understanding of the true meaning of the latter.

THEOSOPHY.—Supreme Wisdom. The knowledge of divine powers obtained by him who possesses such powers. *"Theosophy"* is therefore identical with *self-knowledge.*

THEOSOPHIST.—A person whose mind is illuminated by the spirit of Divine Wisdom. One who is able to mentally grasp the spirit of a thing, and to understand it. One who has attained a self-knowledge of the divine powers existing in his own organization.

TINCTURA.—(Alch.) Tincture. An ethereal or spiritual substance which, by impregnating another substance, endows (tinctures) the latter with its own properties. If a gross principle is penetrated by a higher one, the former is said to be *tinctured* (colored) by the latter one.

TRINITY.—The All. The whole of the Universe. Everything is a trinity, and Three is the number of *Form.* Every conceivable thing consists of *Matter* and *Motion* in *Space,* and the three are forever one and inseparable. "God" is a trinity, and the Universe being a manifestation of God, every part of the Universe must necessarily be a trinity. Everything is a product of *thought. will,* and *substance* (form); i. e. *Mercury, Sulphur,* and *Salt.*

UNIFICATION.—*At-one-ment.* The art of uniting into one. Unification with the eternal One is the only aim and object of all true religion. All things are originally one; they are all states of one universal divine consciousness; they merely *appear to be* different from each other on account of the illusion of *Form.* Differentiation and separation exist merely at the surface of the periphery of the All; the *Centre* is one. To become reunited with the Centre is to enter the *Real,* and to become divine and immortal. After a man has become united with his own higher self, he may become united with *Christ.*

Note:—This process of regeneration and unification is taught in all the religions of the East, but—although the whole Christian religion is based upon this truth—it is nevertheless universally misunderstood by modern Christians, who expect to obtain salvation rather through the merit of another than by their own exertion. To understand the process of regeneration and unification requires an understanding of the real nature of man and of his relations to nature; a science which in our modern times is nowhere in Europe taught in schools, because our theologians and scientists are themselves ignorant of the true nature of man, and because mankind finds it easier to accept a belief than to acquire knowledge.

UNIVERSE.—The All. The Cosmos. The All; beyond which nothing can exist, because there is no "beyond." The whole of the visible universe is a manifestation of the internal invisible divine power called the Spirit of God. It is the substance of God, shaped by his thought into images and thrown into objectivity by an exercise of his Will. Whatever God *thinks,* that he expresses in the *Word,* and what he speaks becomes an *Act.* All this takes place according to *Law,* because God is himself the Law, and does not act against himself.

VENUS.—(Alch.) The principle of Love.

VERBUM.—The *Word,* the Alpha and Omega. The Christ or *Logos.* The expression of a divine thought. The power emanated in the beginning from the Eternal Centre. The origin of all life.

VIR.—Man. A human being in whom the male elements are preponderating.

VIRGIN, CELESTIAL.—See *Eve.*

VISIBLE & INVISIBLE.—Relative terms; refering to things which are usually beyond the powers of perception of ordinary man in his normal state. What may be invisible to one may be visible to another.

WATER.—See *Elementa.*

WILL.—The one universal and fundamental power in the universe, from which all other powers take their origin. Fundamentally it is identical with Life. It manifests itself in the lower planes of existence as Attraction, Gravitation, Cohesion; on the higher planes as Life, Will, Spiritual Power, etc., according to the conditions in which it acts. The Will is a function of the universal Spirit of God, and there is no other power in the Universe but the Will of God, acting consciously or unconsciously, natural or unnatural, if perverted by man. Man can have no will of his own; he is merely enabled to employ the universal will acting in his organization during his earthly existence, and to pervert and misuse it on account of his ignorance with the eternal laws of nature.

WISDOM.—The highest conceivable attribute of the Spirit; conceivable—like all other powers—only by him in whom wisdom has become manifest, and who is thereby rendered wise. Wisdom is not of man's making; he cannot invent, but he can acquire it. The same may be said of all other spiritual powers; they exist in the universe, and are to be attained by Man.

WOMAN.—A human being in whose organization the female elements are preponderating over the male ones.

WORD.—See *Verbum. Alpha* and *Omega.*

ZODIAC.—The twelve signs of the Zodiac represent the twelve universal principles which form the basis of the construction of the material universe.

Editorial

(Continued from Page 170)

While the plants may be all that he believes them to be, still he is being cramped into one tiny viewpoint that never gives expression to that bigger part of himself which is only truly happy when it senses the universality of ideals and activity. To such a type of mind, vacation is to leave the study or nursery filled with flowers and go out into the great world with its mountains, its clouds, its animals, its precious stones, its shining metals, and, most of all, its varied and endlessly interesting human population. To such a reclusive soul we say, "Give the subject of botany a rest and learn to see the beauty in other creatures and things. In this way the mind may be preserved in sanity and man accomplish the *magnum opus* which he came here to do."

John Doe No. 2 is a great artist and John Doe No. 3 a great musician. These two men apparently have nothing in common. Yet, if they but realized it, they have everything in common, for one really *paints* with the harmony of sound and the other *composes* with the harmony of color. What a wonderful vacation it would be if these two men could change places with each other! Each would step into a new world, a beautiful world, for just around the corner in each one's life is a sphere of unrecognized beauty from which each divides himself by confining his life and activity within the confines of a single thought-room.

Development of the mental faculties can be verified by the application of the law of interest and indifference. Those faculties which are awake respond readily to external stimuli harmonious to themselves, whereas those faculties which are asleep give no response. Thus, if the faculty of art is active, the individual exhibits a love and appreciation of the beautiful. He is drawn irresistibly to beautiful objects, making note of them and commenting thereon. If, however, the faculty of art be asleep, the individual shows no inclination to interest himself in the artistic or the beautiful. In fact, he may be totally devoid, as it were, of the æsthetic, as in the case of a person we once knew who hung his hat on one of the leading art objects of a well-known European museum.

With few exceptions, a single mental faculty thus overshadows and dominates the entire mental nature. It may be a religious tendency or a commercial urge; it may be an altruistic inclination or one absolutely selfish. These mental "ruts" are plainly visible in the personalities of the world's so-called great men and women. The weird melancholia of Poe, the pessimism of Nietzsche, the sarcasm of Voltaire, and the asceticism of Dante are examples of dangerous mental bias, which in the case of Nietzsche ended in violent insanity. Even the philosopher is not immune, for more often than otherwise his philosophy is a solace for the thwarted hopes of life and therefore tinctured with the venom of cynicism.

In our daily life we encounter people with the most peculiar mental attitudes toward their environments. We know one individual who firmly believes that children should be tied up in the back yard and animals given the freedom of the streets. This is an instance where interest in the welfare of the animal kingdom has been carried to such an extreme that mental unbalance on this particular subject has been the inevitable result. In the realms of religion and philosophy extremists are very common—so common, in fact, that it is seldom a well-balanced type of intellectualist can be found.

When the mind thus becomes crystallized and "set," it is incapable of further development. It is no longer plastic, no longer responsive to the influences of its environment upon which it is wholly dependent for its evolutionary progress. And all things when they stop growing or become incapable of further growth we know are marked for death. Thus the economy of Nature asserts its prerogative and the physical brain and constitution are resolved once more into their primary elements in order that the mind may be released from its prison-house of clay and at some future date re-embark upon the divine adventure of human life. Manifestation of the spiritual nature of man is directly dependent—from one point of view —upon refinement of its vehicles of expression. Growth of the spiritual nature is the product of neither "affirmation" nor "denial." It is achieved only by lofty idealism, right-thinking, self-less service, and divine love. Philosophy offers no substitute for this program of labor and achievement, no "short cut" to the goal of self-completion. Philosophy represents only that method—both safe and sane—by which individual effort is wisely directionalized. No sublimer expression of this ideal of self-completion exists in literature than that given by one of our own well-known poets:

> Build thee more stately mansions, O my soul,
> As the swift seasons roll!
> Leave thy low-vaulted past!
> Let each new temple, nobler than the last,
> Shut thee from heaven with a dome more vast,
> Till thou at length are free,
> Leaving thine outgrown shell by life's unresting sea!

Q. Is the Lord's Prayer as we have it correct? I have read in a certain book that it should be, "Lead us *in* temptation." Anon.

A. The interpretation which you give is not familiar to the writer. We do know, however, that the Lord's Prayer is capable of many interpretations, especially because of the peculiar use of tenses found in early languages. The Lord's Prayer is a Qabbalistic epitome of the powers of the universe and is an invocation of the Universal Spirit of Light. As time goes on and we become more familiar with the subtle shades of meaning existing in ancient languages, we shall undoubtedly discover new and deeper meanings to nearly all scriptural documents and works of a similar nature.

Questions & answers·

Q. Is suffering necessary to spiritual growth? If not, what qualifications permit of growth without suffering? L. J.

A. Suffering is not necessary to spiritual growth any more than disease
is necessary to human life. Yet both are present and equally difficult to
combat. Suffering has two causes: ignorance and egotism. By ignorance
we lay ourselves open to painful reactions as the result of ill-considered
action. By egotism—a false emphasis of self—we lay ourselves open to
injury by others and magnify the seriousness of our troubles. We can successfully combat suffering by learning natural processes and obeying them;
we can become so impersonal that we cannot be offended or caused to suffer
by the actions of others. Suffering is the whip which Nature uses to keep
man in line. If he stays in line, he will not feel its blows, but refusing to
recognize the value of the experience of others, he is forced to suffer in order
to learn that which, fundamentally, he already knows. By developing dis-
crimination, observation, and self-control, the average individual can eliminate
the greater portion of the suffering which he is now forced to undergo. A
most dangerous form of egotism is selfishness, which may be defined as the
desire to possess. This is one of the primary causes of sorrow, for we grieve
over the loss of something which was never ours and fear lest we shall
receive something which has always been ours. It was the Brahmin who said,
"Steadfast in pain and pleasure, man is fitted for immortality."

Q. How did Sunday come to be kept as the Sabbath in place of
Saturday? When and by what authority did the change take place? F. L.

A. From all information available, it would seem that the first Christians preserved with great strictness the Jewish feast days and Sabbath. The
break which resulted in the Christians choosing other days for their ceremonials seems to have been made by St. Paul, who has long been regarded
as the real cause of misunderstanding existing between the Jews and the
Christians. During the lifetime of Justin Martyr, who lived about 150
years after the birth of Christ, the Christians worshipped on Sunday. In
the 89th section of his *Apology*, Justin describes the reason for this as follows:
"Upon Sunday we all assembled, that being the first day in which God
set Himself to work upon the dark void, in order to make the world, and
in which Jesus Christ our Saviour rose again from the dead: for the day
before Saturday, He was crucified; and the day after, which is Sunday, He
appeared to His Apostles and disciples, and taught them what I have now
proposed to your consideration." Constantine the Great was the first to
ordain by law the sacredness of Sunday. His edict reads as follows: "Let
all judges and towns-people, and the occupations of all trades, rest on the
venerable day of the sun. But let those who are situated in the country,
freely and at full liberty, attend to the business of agriculture; because it
often happens, that no other day is so fit for sowing corn, or planting vines,
lest the critical moment being let slip, men should lose the commodities
granted them by the providence of Heaven." It is further significant that
the worship of all deities related to the sun or considered as aspects or attri-

butes of the solar power, were revered upon the day of the sun. Here again we undoubtedly find the influence of the Mithraic Mysteries showing itself in Christianity.

Q. Would you recommend that I read the books written by Mr.——?· Do you think he is reliable and a safe person to study under? Anon.

A. We have had a great many letters asking us to pass judgment upon the character and teachings of various persons. We make it a practice to keep as far from personalities as possible. Our work is concerned with principles, and when we attack principles it is with conviction. We believe that the promulgation of certain doctrines is dangerous to the good of the community but it is impossible for us to attack personalities without bringing down upon ourselves just criticism. Therefore we recommend none, pass judgment upon none, and criticise none. If we recommend a certain person, we become responsible for what that person does and also for having deflected the natural course of human life into some possibly unnatural channel. It is absolutely necessary for each person to make up his own mind concerning what is good, what is bad, and what is indifferent so far as he is concerned, and anyone who attempts to make up another man's mind for him is undertaking a thankless job and doing the other person an actual injury. We are in this world to think and the only way that some of us can be made to think is by being placed in a position where the effects of our thoughts will have a powerful influence upon our happiness and health. If under such conditions another person by assisting us over this hard point makes it entirely unnecessary for us to think, we are robbed of our divine right to make up our own minds. When choosing such an important element in our lives as a book to read or a teacher to follow, we can, however, apply a certain acid test, and if the doctrine or the doctor does not live up to a reasonable standard it is better we search elsewhere. When about to affiliate with an organization or accept its doctrine, ask yourself these questions, and if you can answer them in the affirmative the doctrine is reasonably safe: Is the teaching free from unnecessary involvements and elaborate ritualism, whose only purpose is to attract and fascinate the foolish? Is it free from commercialism, emphasizing the depth of the understanding and not the depth of the pocketbook? Is it practical, assisting man to solve the problems of his daily life and not leaving him stranded somewhere in the clouds? Is it free from the cheating Nature element; or, in other words, does it demand that man shall work for everything he gets and that his reward will be according to his labor? Is it progressive, nonsectarian, interreligious, philosophical, reasonable, rational, and permanent? Is it free from hero-worship, free from the over-emphasis of personality, and free from that idealizing of some poor human sinner? Is it free from dangerous metaphysical practices, free from affirmations and denials, free from pernicious sex doctrines and dangerous exercises and practices? Does it appeal only to the highest, noblest, truest, most unselfish and impersonal part of the nature, offering no other reward for attainment than labor and self-sacrifice? If it be all these things, then—and then only—is it worthy to receive a moment's consideration from a sane person who values his life, health or integrity.

Q. What is meant by the "impersonal" attitude in occultism? In cultivating it is there not danger of losing the qualities of sympathy and compassion? Does it contemplate the extinction of the different forms of personal or individual love—romantic, parental, filial, platonic, etc.? F. R. C.

A. Two of the least understood attitudes are *impersonality* and *non-*

resistance. An intellectual concept alone of either of these is extremely dangerous. In the last analysis, impersonality is the highest expression of feeling and non-resistance is the highest expression of thought. Impersonality is not the annihilation of emotion; it is the universal distribution of the affections and feelings and the recognition of universal relationship in contra-distinction to the recognition of clan, tribal or family relationship. The impersonal attitude is dependent upon the recognition of the fundamental *unity of life.* The emotions are then expended in the service of the entire, whereas previously they were limited to that which is physically or mentally close to the individual himself. In the same way, the law of non-resistance is based upon the recognition of *fundamental and universal good.* The mind which realizes that all things work together for the good of each and that each thing works for the good of all, no longer attempts to resist life's experiences and occurrences but, accepting each as necessary for its own growth, substitutes assimilation for resistance.

Q. What is the "subconscious" mind? Is control over the "subcon-scious" mind acquired through auto-suggestion, and if so, is it the key to the ultimate conscious control of all the present involuntary functions of the body? A. L. R.

A. Prof. William James describes the subconscious mind as "the great-est discovery in 100 years." The subconscious mind holds in the problem of thought the same relative position that ether occupies as a scientific postulate. From observation of mental phenomena certain scientists have induced the hypothesis of a mental reservoir not subject to the limitations of conscious thought or memory. Like electricity, the subconscious mind has never been defined and it is known only through the manifestations attributed to it. Popular psychology makes considerable of the subconscious mind, but actually knows nothing concerning it or its function. It will yet be discovered that the thing which we call *thought* is the product of the combined activities of several intellectual mechanisms. For example, each organ of the body has its own faculty of memory. The physical structure, as a whole, has its own mind, functioning as a unit separate from the mental equipment of the spiritual individual dwelling within that body. In brief, it may be said that the spiritual nature of man has a separate and distinct form of thinking appa-ratus upon each of its various levels of manifestation. Even emotion is supplied with certain recollective qualities. The physical body has no less than four brains, while each nerve plexus and ganglion is a potential center of mental expression. The greatest plexus in the body—the solar plexus— may prove to be the seat of the subconscious mind. It is certainly the area most subject to instinctual reflexes. Science now realizes that man actually thinks throughout the entire length of the spinal cord. The heart also is an organ of thought but its intellectual activities as yet have received little con-sideration. Whether the subconscious mind is a physical faculty or a super-physical one has been the subject of much controversy. Each faculty or function is triangular in essence and expression, and the triangle of the mind is created by dividing the mental equipment into a superconscious, a conscious, and a subconscious mind. By philosophical analogy, the super-conscious mind should be the spiritual activity or phase of thought, the conscious mind the human activity of thought, and the subconscious the subhuman, or elementary, activity of thought. The fact that the subconscious mind is considered as a reservoir which is a receptacle would indicate that it is recognized as a negative or receptive mental attribute with the superconscious mind as its opposite pole. Between these two is the conscious mind —the normal thinking equipment of the human being. It is extremely unlikely that the subconscious mind will ever control the involuntary functions of the body because all these functions are now demonstrating symptoms of voluntary expression. For example, involuntary muscles are beginning to show signs of the voluntary cross fibres, and the heart which has been long considered the chief involuntary muscle will in the future be under the direct control of the human intellect. Like the tonsils which show traces of being a survival of the gills of primitive man, the subconscious mind may prove to be a survival of the intellectual equipment of the irrational human creature, for it produces phenomena which, to a certain degree at least, resemble the mental activity of the animal kingdom. The so-called science of auto-suggestion is based upon the natural phenomena of environment affecting whatever creature is placed within its sphere of influence. Being very susceptible to extraneous influences, man may be very easily diverted from his natural course. Auto-suggestion is an effort to engraft upon intellect a certain attitude which will cause the person to perform a labor or accomplish an end to which previously he had been indifferent. This auto-suggestion is a mild form of hypnosis, its danger lying in the fact that the labor which the individual accomplishes is the result of neither an innate desire nor a direct realization of its import. We grow only by rational decision. When the natural trend of the mind therefore is interfered with it often results disastrously. The influences exerted by auto-suggestion are apparently stored in the subconscious mind. In reality, auto-suggestions exist as patterns of various geometric forms in the substance of a mysterious etheric vesicle surrounding the brain and serving as the subtle substance in which thought-images are produced. Once a suggested thought-form is imprinted upon this ether, it will reflect this image into the brain at any time, when the brain, becoming negative, no longer creates pictures of its own making. The "suggested" thought depends upon repetition for its vividness.

Q. Do we go from this planet to another? If so, which? Anon.

A. Several schools of philosophy teach that after man's life upon the physical planet earth he is transported to one of the other planetary bodies. We can find, however, no justification for this in the deeper teachings of the ancient Mysteries, for the planet earth itself, being septenary in its constitution, contains within its own body planes or spheres corresponding with each of the planets of this solar system. The next step of solar consciousness above the earth is that of Jupiter, but the Jupiterian environment is to be found within the sevenfold body of the earth itself. At the end of this day of manifestation consisting of uncounted millions of years, the planets will be reabsorbed into the body of the sun. When they are brought forth again into being, it is quite probable that those creatures who have finished their work upon the earth will begin their new day of labor upon the body of Jupiter, but the prevalent idea that we flutter indiscriminately from star to star or pick out one for our next life is totally out of accord with the slow and consistent workings of natural law.

Q. How can one safeguard himself against the inroads of vampirism or the sapping of one's vitality by those with whom we come in contact? J. D.

A. Life itself is a continuous process of vampirism. All through

Nature life subsists by stealing life and we lengthen our own days by shortening the days of other creatures. Generally speaking, the weak vampirize the strong through the aura. There are certain esoteric methods whereby this can be prevented but it is impossible to discuss them in print. Suffice it to say, that a positive mental attitude is of great assistance in this matter. The human body is an open circuit, the greatest amount of leakage being through the hands and feet, from which a clairoyant can see streams of force continually pouring. When in the presence of an individual or a group of individuals whom you believe are likely to sap your vitality, one reasonably sure preventive is to cross the hands and feet. This can be done without attracting attention by simply crossing one ankle over the other and clasping the hands together. In this position only a minimum of energy can escape. Conscious vampirism—which is very rare—must be handled in a scientific manner.

Index to Volume IV

CPSIA information can be obtained
at www.ICGtesting.com
Printed in the USA
BVHW042347030222
627738BV00008B/229

9 781162 732176